Nigel Davies

play the
Catalan

EVERYMAN CHESS

Gloucester Publishers plc www.everymanchess.com

First published in 2009 by Gloucester Publishers plc (formerly Everyman Publishers plc), Northburgh House, 10 Northburgh Street, London EC1V 0AT

British Library Cataloguing-in-Publication Data
A catalogue record for this book is available from the British Library.

ISBN: 978 1 85744 591 6

Distributed in North America by The Globe Pequot Press, P.O Box 480, 246 Goose Lane, Guilford, CT 06437-0480.

All other sales enquiries should be directed to Everyman Chess, Northburgh House, 10 Northburgh Street, London EC1V 0AT
tel: 020 7253 7887 fax: 020 7490 3708
email: info@everymanchess.com; website: www.everymanchess.com

Dedicated to the brilliant and humorous inventor of the Catalan Opening,
Savielly Tartakower

EVERYMAN CHESS SERIES
Chief advisor: Byron Jacobs
Commissioning editor: John Emms
Assistant editor: Richard Palliser

Typeset and edited by First Rank Publishing, Brighton.
Cover design by Horatio Monteverde.
Printed and bound in the US by Versa Press.

Contents

Bibliography

Books

Zoom 001: Zero Hour to the Operation of Opening Models, Bent Larsen & Steffen Zeuthen (Dansk Skakforlag 1979)
The Catalan, Alexander Raetsky & Maxim Chetverik (Everyman Chess 2004)
Play the Catalan I: Open Variation by Yakov Neishtadt (Pergamon 1987)
Play the Catalan II: Closed Variation by Yakov Neishtadt (Pergamon 1988)

Chess Databases

The Week in Chess
Megabase 2008
Chess Informator

Chess Engines

Extensive use has been made of *Fritz 11*

Introduction

The Catalan Opening was introduced into tournament practice by Savielly Tartakower at the Barcelona tournament of 1929. The subtle development of White's bishop on g2 was not fully appreciated at the time, but it was gradually realized that the placement of this piece could make it difficult for Black to successfully develop his queenside, in particular his light-squared bishop.

To explain exactly what I mean by this, in the standard Queen's Gambit Declined (1 d4 d5 2 c4 e6 3 ♘c3 ♘f6 4 ♗g5 ♗e7 5 e3 ♘bd7 6 ♘f3 0-0) Black usually captures on c4 and then equalizes in the centre with one of two pawn levers, either ...c7-c5 or ...e6-e5. In the Catalan this plan is complicated by the fact that this procedure runs the risk of making the bishop on g2 very strong, and Black often fails to equalize even after getting in the thrust ...c7-c5. It's worth looking at a game to illustrate this point:

G.Kasparov-V.Korchnoi
London (7th matchgame) 1983

1 d4 ♘f6 2 c4 e6 3 g3 d5 4 ♗g2 dxc4 5 ♘f3 ♗d7 6 ♕c2 c5 7 0-0 ♗c6 8 ♕xc4 ♘bd7 9 ♗g5 ♖c8 10 ♗xf6 ♘xf6 11 dxc5 ♗xf3 12 ♗xf3 ♗xc5 13 ♕b5+ ♕d7 14 ♘c3 ♕xb5 15 ♘xb5 ♔e7 16 b4 ♗xb4 17 ♘xa7 ♖c7 18 ♖fc1

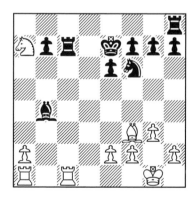

Despite the innocuous appearance of this position, Black is now losing his b7-pawn. The rest, as they say, is history.

18...♖d7 19 ♖ab1 ♗d2 20 ♖c2 ♖hd8 21 ♗xb7 ♔f8 22 ♘c6 ♖c7 23 ♖bb2 ♖d6 24 a4 ♗e1 25 ♖b1 ♘d5 26 ♗a8 ♖c8 27 ♗b7 ♖c7 28 ♖c4 ♘e7 29 ♘e5 ♗a5 30 ♖b5 ♘g6 31 ♘c6 ♖d1+ 32 ♔g2 ♗e1 33 a5 ♘e7 34 a6 ♘xc6 35 ♖xc6 ♖xc6 36 ♗xc6 ♖a1 37 ♖b8+ ♔e7 38 ♖b7+ ♔d6 39 ♗b5 ♗c3 40 ♖xf7 ♗f6 41 ♖d7+ ♔c5 42 ♗d3 h6 43 ♖b7 ♖a3 44 a7 ♔d5 45 f3 ♔d6 46 ♖b6+ 1-0

Another plan for Black is when he takes on c4 and then tries to hold the pawn, which seems feasible with the white bishop on g2. In this case White usually builds up a mighty pawn centre with e2-e4, often just letting the pawn go and relying on dynamic compensation. This kind of play usually occurs after 4...dxc4; it can become quite sharp and there's quite a bit of theory involved. Fortunately White can avoid this if he wants to by adopting an English or Réti type move order. This is a great boon to players who like the Catalan but don't want to burn much midnight oil.

There is a third scenario in which Black simply tries to strongpoint the d5-pawn and develop his queenside pieces via ...c7-c6, ...♘bd7, ...b7-b6 and ...♗c8-b7. This is actually very common amongst club players who are facing the Catalan for the first time and decide that being sensible will keep them out of trouble. These lines are known as *Closed Variations* (as opposed to

...d5xc4 lines which are *Open Variations*) and are covered in Chapters 6-8. Whilst being playable, Black certainly has to know what he's doing here, and in my experience he often doesn't – unless his name happens to be Smbat Lputian or Rafael Vaganian.

At club level people usually answer White's plan of e2-e4 with ...d5xe4, which can land them in a rather cramped and horrid position. I will take the liberty of showing you one of my own games at this point which I played while preparing this book. It's a good example of what you're likely to face in your own games:

N.Davies-M.Brown
Liverpool League 2009

1 d4 d5 2 c4 e6 3 ♘f3 ♘f6 4 g3 ♗e7 5 ♗g2 0-0 6 ♕c2 ♘bd7 7 0-0 c6 8 ♘bd2 b6 9 e4 dxe4

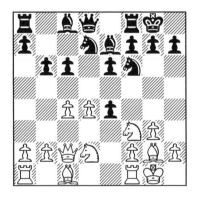

As I mentioned above, Black should probably not do this. But at club level I wager that this will be played almost exclusively.

10 ♘xe4 ♘xe4 11 ♕xe4 ♗b7 12 ♖d1
♕c7 13 ♗f4 ♗d6 14 ♗xd6 ♕xd6 15 c5
♕c7 16 ♖ac1 ♖fd8 17 a3 h6 18 ♕e3 ♖e8
19 b4 a5 20 ♘d2

The knight is headed for d6.

20...axb4 21 axb4 bxc5 22 bxc5 ♘f6 23
♘c4 ♗a6 24 ♕e5 ♖e7 25 ♖a1 ♘d5 26
♖a3 ♗b7 27 ♖xa8+ ♗xa8 28 ♖a1 ♕d8
29 ♕d6 ♖d7 30 ♕e5 ♗b7 31 ♗xd5 exd5
32 ♘b6 ♖b8 33 ♕xb8 1-0

Who has played the Catalan (besides Garry Kasparov and myself, that is)? Over the years a vast array of the World's top players have understood the potential of this opening and used it to deadly effect. Amongst World Champions you can find Catalan games by Mikhail Botvinnik, Vassily Smyslov, Tigran Petrosian, Anatoly Karpov and Vladimir Kramnik. And the leading exponents include such notables as Victor Korchnoi, Leonid Stein, Bent Larsen, Alexander Beliavsky, Vladimir Tukmakov, Boris Gulko, Lev Alburt, Jonathan Speelman, Oleg Romanishin, Zoltan Ribli, Boris Gelfand, Grigory Kaidanov, Yuri Razuvaev and others. This is quite a pedigree by any standards.

My own relationship with the Catalan blossomed in the 1990s when it became one of my main weapons as White, and indeed the touchstone to my gaining the Grandmaster title. I was inspired to play it by the book *Zoom 001: Zero Hour to the Operation of Opening Models* by Bent Larsen and Steffen Zeuthen, the authors offering Catalan-type positions as a means of playing both Black and White. The Catalan suited my then dynamic style as I liked the initiative and wasn't worried about sacrificing the pawn on c4. Even when I became less interested in opening theory in the late 1990s, the Catalan remained one of the mainstays of my repertoire, though at this time I started to avoid the sharpest lines based on 4...dxc4 and instead aimed to reach a Catalan via Flank Openings or 1 d4 ♘f6 2 ♘f3 e6 3 g3.

My approach to writing this book has been to try and give the reader a good overview of the Catalan, whilst recommending specific ways to play it. In this way I hope to give the reader a decent understanding while getting him or her up and running with it as quickly as possible. Whilst many of the games are very recent, I have not tried to produce a definitive snapshot of current theory; indeed, such a book would be outdated by the time it was published. Instead I have presented games and variations that I personally have found interesting, in the hope that my views and ideas will get the reader's own creative juices flowing.

There are various ways in which you might use this book, either as reading material or a reference source. The way I'd recommend studying it is to go through the text and main games fairly quickly, without getting bogged down in each and every sub-variation. Then, as you start to get a feel for Catalan positions (i.e. recognize the patterns at a subconscious level), you might want

Move Orders

The Catalan is a highly transpositional opening which can be reached via a large number of different move orders, and depending on the move order he adopts White can avoid some of Black's defensive options. This struck me as being such an important topic that it merits its own section.

The Catalan's 'official' move orders are 1 d4 ♘f6 2 c4 e6 3 g3

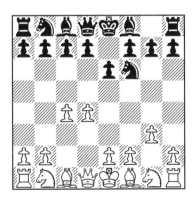

3...d5 4 ♗g2 (or 3 ♘f3 d5 4 g3), and 1 d4 d5 2 c4 e6 3 ♘f3 ♘f6 4 g3, but it

can also be reached via Flank Openings (1 c4, 1 ♘f3 or 1 g3) or even 1 d4 ♘f6 2 ♘f3 e6 3 g3.

With the official move orders White has to know how to deal with the various lines based on 4...dxc4, which form a substantial part of this book. With the unofficial move orders he can avoid these lines, though he does lay himself open to other possibilities. I'll summarize these below.

Standard Catalan

This occurs after 1 d4 ♘f6 2 c4 e6 3 g3 (or 3 ♘f3 d5 4 g3) 3...d5 4 ♗g2 or 1 d4 d5 2 c4 e6 3 ♘f3 ♘f6 4 g3. White needs to study every line in the book, as in addition to 4...♗e7, Black can play 4...dxc4.

Note that 1 d4 d5 2 c4 e6 3 g3?! is not a good idea because of 3...dxc4! 4 ♘f3 c5 5 ♗g2 ♘c6 when Black would equalize quite comfortably. White should play 3 ♘f3 (intending 3...♘f6 4 g3) after which 3...dxc4 would lead to a form of Queen's Gambit Accepted.

Flank Catalan

In this scenario White only adopts a Catalan once Black has shown that he intends to develop with ...♘f6, ...e7-e6 and ...d7-d5, and in this way he can avoid the 4...dxc4 lines. For example 1 ♘f3 d5 2 g3 ♘f6 3 ♗g2 e6 4 0-0 ♗e7 5 c4 0-0 6 d4 brings about a Catalan, but with Black's only options being to take on c4 (6...dxc4) or play a Closed Catalan with 6...♘bd7.

Should White play c2-c4 before Black has played ...♗f8-e7, he still has to reckon with the possibility of 4...dxc4. For example, 1 c4 ♘f6 2 ♘f3 e6 3 g3 d5 4 d4 can be met by 4...dxc4, when White can continue with 5 ♕c2, getting the pawn back, but Black is close to equality.

The 4...dxc4 option is not available in the move order 1 ♘f3 d5 2 g3 ♘f6 3 ♗g2 e6 4 0-0, but here White needs to reckon with possibilities such as 3...c6 instead of 3...e6.

Queen's Pawn Catalan

The move order 1 d4 ♘f6 2 ♘f3 e6 3 g3 is one that has been used extensively by World Championship candidates Jonathan Speelman and Oleg Romanishin.

After 3...d5 4 ♗g2, followed by 5 0-0 and 6 c4, White will get a main line Catalan, while avoiding sharp 4...dxc4 lines.

Admittedly, White also has to reckon with 4...c5 5 0-0 ♘c6 6 c4 dxc4 (Chapter 10), 3...b6 4 ♗g2 ♗b7 5 c4 (a Queen's Indian, though one in which Black doesn't have the popular ...♗a6 option), and 3...b5!?, but once again he manages to sidestep the sharp 4...dxc4 lines.

My Own Approach

During the rare moments of my chess career in which I've had an appetite to study sharp variations, I've been prepared for 4...dxc4. But for the most part I've preferred to avoid such lines with either the Flank Openings or Queen's Pawn move order, thus cutting out many of Black's defensive options.

By doing it this way you can get by very economically, say by having an approach against the 6...dxc4 main line (I've been pre-empting this with 6 ♕c2 of late, as in Chapter 5), and looking at the ♕c2, ♘bd2 and e2-e4 lines against the Closed (see Games 27 and 28 in Chapter 6). It's probably worth getting my book on the Réti for details on how to deal with an early ...d5xc4 against that move order, but basically that's all you need besides gaining experience with these openings.

Chapter One

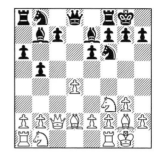

Main Line with 10 ♗d2

1 d4 ♘f6 2 c4 e6 3 g3 d5 4 ♗g2 ♗e7 5 ♘f3 0-0 6 0-0 dxc4 7 ♕c2 a6 8 ♕xc4 b5 9 ♕c2 ♗b7 10 ♗d2

From a club player's point of view this chapter should probably be seen as nothing more than fodder for building pattern recognition and as a point of reference from which to follow top-level Catalan games. The 10 ♗d2 variation is currently being discussed by the world's top players, with Vladimir Kramnik leading the champions of the white pieces and Viswanathan Anand heading up the black cause. With this chapter likely to be out of date before I've even finished writing it, this is clearly a high maintenance line.

The main idea behind 10 ♗d2 is that after Black's apparently natural reply, 10...♘bd7, White can create a most unpleasant pin on Black's c-pawn with 11 ♗a5. This has prompted a variety of waiting moves by Black instead, such as the 10...♖a7 of Kramnik-Anand

(Game 1) in which the heads of the White and Black schools had a memorable clash.

In Kramnik's game against Magnus Carlsen (Game 2), the young Norwegian star played 10...♘c6 and was probably okay until he overlooked 17 ♘b3!. The plan of 10...♗e4 and 11...♕c8 was adopted in Kramnik-Leko (Game 3), but here we see an interesting new twist with 13 ♕f4!?. Finally, we see 10...♗d6 adopted in Landa-Melkumyan (Game 4), which might be a good line for Black if he follows up with 11...♗e4. Look out for some more games on Mount Olympus!

Game 1
V.Kramnik-V.Anand
Wijk aan Zee 2007

---

1 d4 ♘f6 2 c4 e6 3 g3 d5 4 ♗g2 ♗e7 5 ♘f3 0-0 6 0-0 dxc4 7 ♕c2 a6 8 ♕xc4 b5

9 ♕c2 ♗b7 10 ♗d2

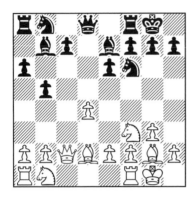

10...♖a7

This strange-looking idea essentially plays a waiting game with a move that can be useful in many lines. Black's problem is that the natural 10...♘bd7 is met by 11 ♗a5 quite strongly, for example 11...♖a7 (11...♖c8 12 ♘bd2 ♘b8?! 13 a3! ♘c6 14 ♗c3 b4?! 15 axb4 ♘xb4 16 ♕b3 ♗d5 17 ♕a4 was good for White in I.Almasi-A.Lauber, Gyula 1997) 12 ♘bd2 ♕a8 13 b4 ♘b8 (trying to embarrass the bishop on a5 by coming to c6; White can meet 13...e5 with 14 ♗h3 exd4 15 ♘xd4 intending ♘d4-f5) 14 a3 ♘c6 15 ♘b3 (15 ♗xc7?! ♖c8 16 ♗b6 ♘xb4 is messy) 15...♘xa5 (15...e5 should probably be answered by 16 ♘h4, trying to come to f5) 16 ♘xa5 ♗e4 17 ♘e1! ♗xc2 18 ♗xa8 ♖axa8 19 ♘xc2 ♗d6! 20 f4 gave White the better endgame in M.Chetverik-B.Furman, Karvina 1998.

So the idea behind 10...♖a7 is to be able to meet ♗d2-a5 with ...♘b8-c6.

11 ♖c1

This looks logical, applying pressure down the c-file while getting

ready to tuck the queen out of the way on d1.

Yet in a subsequent game (V.Kramnik-J.Werle, clock simul, Enschede 2008) Kramnik varied with the experimental 11 a3!?, after which 11...♗e4 12 ♕c1 ♘c6 13 e3 ♕a8 14 ♕d1 ♘d5 15 ♕e2 e5 16 ♖e1 (16 ♖c1 ♗d6 17 ♗e1 exd4 18 ♘bd2 ♗g6 19 ♘h4 dxe3 20 ♘xg6 hxg6 21 ♘f1 ♘ce7 22 ♘xe3 c6 23 ♘xd5 ♘xd5 24 ♖c2 gave White just about enough for the pawn in A.Shirov-D.Jakovenko, European Club Cup, Kemer 2007) 16...exd4 17 exd4 f5 18 ♘c3 ♘xc3 19 ♗xc3 ♗f6 20 d5 ♗xc3 21 bxc3 ♘d8 22 ♖ad1 ♗xd5 23 ♘g5! gave White a strong attack, the point being that 23...♗xg2? is answered by 24 ♕h5 h6 25 ♖e7 with a winning attack.

At the time of writing there are very few games with 11 a3, but on the evidence thus far it seems quite promising.

11...♗e4 12 ♕b3 ♘c6 13 e3 ♕a8

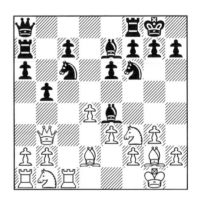

14 ♕d1

14 ♘c3 is an interesting possibility pointed out by *Fritz 11*, but then 14...♘xd4 (14...♘a5 15 ♕d1 ♗c6 16 b3

looks better for White because of the poor position of the knight on a5) 15 exd4 ♗xf3 16 ♗xf3 ♕xf3 17 ♘xb5 leads to nothing more than a drawn end-game: 17...♕xb3 18 axb3 ♖b7 19 ♖xc7 ♖xb5 20 ♖xe7 ♖xb3 21 ♗c3 ♘d5 22 ♖d7 ♘xc3 23 bxc3 ♖xc3 24 ♖xa6 g5 etc.

14...♘b8

In subsequent games Anand pre-ferred 14...b4, preventing White from bringing his knight to c3. White seems to have a tiny pull, but it is difficult to make much of it, for example 15 ♕f1 (15 ♗e1 ♗d5 16 ♘bd2 ♘b8 17 ♘h4 ♗xg2 18 ♘xg2 c5 19 dxc5 ♖c8 20 ♕f3 ♖xc5 21 ♕xa8 ♖xa8 22 ♘b3 ♖xc1 23 ♖xc1 ♘bd7 was equal in M.Suba-R.Vaganian, Bazna 2007; while R.Ponomariov-V.Anand, Leon rapid 2007, was agreed drawn af-ter 15 a3 ♖b8 16 ♗e1 a5 17 ♘bd2 ♗d5 18 ♗f1 bxa3 19 bxa3 a4 20 ♘c4 ♘a5 21 ♗xa5 ♗xf3 22 ♕e1 ♘d7 23 ♖ab1 ♖xb1 24 ♖xb1 ♗xa3 25 ♖a1 ♗f8 26 ♖xa4 ♘b6 ½-½) 15...♖d8 (15...♘b8 16 ♘e1 c5 17 dxc5 ♘c6 18 ♘f3 ♖d8 19 a3 bxa3 20 ♖xa3 ♕b7 21 ♗c3 ♘d5 22 ♘bd2 ♗xf3 23 ♘xf3 ♗xc5 24 ♖aa1 gave White a nag-ging two-bishop edge in A.Grischuk-D.Jakovenko, FIDE Grand Prix, Sochi 2008; while 15...♗d5 16 ♗e1 ♖c8 17 ♘bd2 ♘a5 18 ♘e5 c5 19 dxc5 ♗xc5 20 ♘d3 ♗f8 21 ♗xd5 ♘xd5 22 e4 gave White a slight space advantage in V.Kramnik-P.Leko, Moscow 2007) 16 ♗e1 a5 17 a3 ♗d6 18 ♘fd2 ♗xg2 19 ♕xg2 ♖a6 20 ♘c4 ♘d5 21 ♘bd2 bxa3 22 bxa3 ♗e7 23 ♖ab1 a4 24 ♕f1 ♘b8 25 ♘e4 ♘d7 26 ♘c3 c5 27 dxc5 ♘xc3 28 ♗xc3 ♘xc5 29 ♗b4 ♗f8 30 ♖d1 and White still had a tiny edge in L.Aronian-

V.Anand, Mainz (rapid) 2007, though he subsequently managed to lose.

15 ♗a5 ♖c8

Black later tried other moves here:

a) 15...♗d6 16 a3 ♘bd7 17 ♘bd2 ♗d5 18 ♕f1 c5 19 dxc5 ♗xc5 20 ♖c2 ♕b7 21 ♖ac1 ♗b6 22 ♗xb6 ♕xb6 23 ♘d4 ♘e5 24 ♗xd5 ♘xd5 25 ♘4f3 saw White main-tain some pressure in L.Aronian-S.Karjakin, Wijk aan Zee 2007. Black successfully achieved the thematic ...c7-c5 break, only to find himself facing strong pressure on the c-file.

b) 15...♘c6 16 ♗e1 ♘b8 was seen in B.Avrukh-C.Sandipan, Turin Olymp-iad 2006, but driving White's bishop back to e1 enables him to develop his queen's knight on d2. The game con-tinued 17 b4 ♘bd7 18 a4 ♘d5 19 ♘bd2 ♗g6 20 ♘b3 ♗e4 (20...♗xb4 21 ♗xb4 ♘xb4 22 ♘e5 ♕c8 23 ♘xg6 hxg6 24 axb5 would be very good for White) 21 axb5 ♗xb4 (or if 21...axb5 22 ♘e5! ♗xg2 23 ♖xa7 ♕xa7 24 ♘xd7 ♖d8 25 ♖a1 ♕b7 26 ♘dc5 ♗xc5 27 ♘xc5 ♕c6 28 e4, winning material) 22 ♗xb4 ♘xb4 23 ♘bd2 with a clear advantage.

16 a3

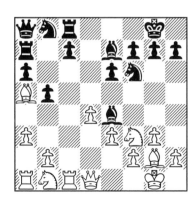

A familiar concept in a new setting; White prepares the possibility of b2-b4 without actually committing himself to it, thus inviting Black to injure himself in his attempts to avoid a bind.

Of the alternatives 16 ♗b6 looks a bit early as the bishop still has its uses on a5. R.Ponomariov-V.Anand, Wijk aan Zee 2007, went on 16...♖b7 17 ♗c5 ♗xc5 18 dxc5 (18 ♖xc5 ♘bd7 19 ♖c1 c5 would free Black's game) 18...♖a7 19 ♘bd2 ♗d5 20 ♕c2 a5 21 a3 a4 22 ♕d3 ½-½.

Another possibility is 16 ♘bd2, but then B.Gelfand-S.Karjakin, Wijk aan Zee 2006, saw Black equalize after 16...♗d5 17 ♘b3 ♘bd7 18 ♖c2 ♗e4 19 ♖c3 ♘d5 20 ♖cc1 ♘5f6 21 ♖c3 ♘d5 22 ♖cc1 ♘5f6 ½-½.

16...♗d6

Unfortunately for Black his thematic 16...c5 is answered by 17 ♘bd2 ♗d5 18 ♗b6, winning the pawn on c5.

17 ♘bd2 ♗d5 18 ♕f1 ♘bd7 19 b4

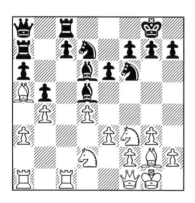

With Black finally ready to play ...c7-c5, White fixes control of this square with a second pawn advance. The drawback to this move is that the

bishop on a5 is temporarily stranded, but it does do an effective job from where it is.

19...e5

If Black doesn't get some counterplay White will simply increase the pressure by doubling rooks on the c-file.

20 dxe5 ♗xe5!?

After 20...♘xe5 White maintains an edge with 21 ♘xe5 ♗xe5 22 ♖a2 intending ♖ac2.

21 ♘xe5 ♘xe5

After 21...♗xg2 22 ♕xg2 ♕xg2+ (22...♘xe5 23 ♕xa8 ♖axa8 24 ♖xc7 wins a pawn) 23 ♔xg2 ♘xe5 White maintains an edge with 24 ♗b6! ♖b7 25 ♗d4.

22 f3!

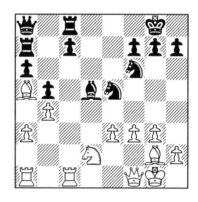

An ugly move containing a deep idea. By avoiding the exchange of bishops White leaves his opponent with too few squares for his minor pieces.

22...♘c4 23 ♘xc4 ♗xc4 24 ♕f2 ♖e8 25 e4 c6 26 ♖d1 ♖d7 27 ♖xd7 ♘xd7 28 ♖d1 ♕b7 29 ♖d6 f6 30 f4

Emerging from his self-inflicted cramp. White's two bishops and greater control of terrain now give him a clear advantage.

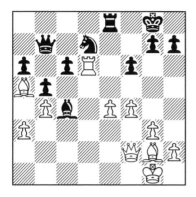

30...♖e6 31 ♖d2 ♖e7 32 ♕d4 ♘f8 33 ♕d8 ♖d7 34 ♖xd7 ♕xd7 35 ♕xd7 ♘xd7 36 e5?!

Unnecessarily complicated. 36 ♗h3! ♘f8 37 ♗c8 would have been simpler.

36...fxe5 37 ♗xc6 ♘f6 38 ♗b7 exf4 39 gxf4 ♘d5 40 ♔f2 ♘xf4 41 ♔e3 g5

Another possibility was 41...♘e2, though then White maintains his advantage with 42 ♗c7 (42 ♗xa6 ♔f7 43 ♗b6 ♔e6 is less clear, for example 44 a4 ♘c3 45 a5 ♘d5+ 46 ♔d4 ♘xb4 etc) 42...♔f7 43 ♗e5 g6 44 ♔e4, finally intending to take on a6 after having boxed in Black's knight.

42 ♗xa6 ♔f7 43 a4 ♔e7 44 ♗xb5 ♗xb5 45 axb5 ♔d7 46 ♔e4 ♘e2 47 ♗b6 g4 48 ♗f2 ♘c3+ 49 ♔f5 ♘xb5 50 ♔xg4 ♔e6 51 ♔g5 ♔f7 52 ♔f5 ♔e7 53 ♗c5+ 1-0

Game 2
V.Kramnik-M.Carlsen
Dortmund 2007

---

1 ♘f3

Many Catalan players start out with this move in order to avoid certain defensive systems. For example, Black can meet the 'main' Catalan move order of 1 d4 ♘f6 2 c4 e6 3 g3 with 3...c5, when 4 d5 exd5 5 cxd5 d6 6 ♘c3 g6 leads into a Modern Benoni.

1...♘f6 2 c4 e6 3 g3 d5 4 d4 ♗e7 5 ♗g2 0-0 6 0-0 dxc4 7 ♕c2 a6 8 ♕xc4 b5 9 ♕c2 ♗b7 10 ♗d2 ♘c6 11 e3 ♘b4 12 ♗xb4 ♗xb4 13 a3

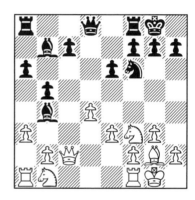

13...♗e7

Black can also play 13...♗d6, for example 14 ♘bd2 ♖c8 (14...♕e7 15 e4 e5 16 ♘h4 g6 17 f4 exd4 18 e5 d3 19 ♕xd3 ♗c5+ 20 ♔h1 ♖fd8 21 ♕c2 ♘d5 22 ♖ae1! gave White a nice space advantage in E.Pigusov-E.Rozentalis, Sevastopol 1986; and 14...♕b8 15 ♖ac1 ♖c8 16 ♘g5! h6 17 ♘ge4 ♘xe4 18 ♘xe4 a5 19 f4!? ♖a6 20 f5 set in motion dangerous threats on the kingside in G.Orlov-R.Vaganian, New York Open 1990) 15 b4 (another possibility is 15 e4!? ♗e7 16 e5 ♘d7 17 b4 a5 18 ♘b3!? axb4 19 ♘g5 ♗xg5 20 ♗xb7 ♖b8 21 ♘a5, threatening ♘a5-c6, as in A.Budnikov-Z.Almasi, Budapest 1991) 15...a5!? 16 e4 (16 bxa5 c5! would be quite good for Black) 16...♗e7 17 ♖ab1 axb4 18 axb4 ♖a8 19 ♖fe1 (19 ♖fc1 is also worth considering) 19...♖a4 20 ♕c3 ♕a8 21 ♘e5 ♖d8 led to complex play in A.Beliavsky-A.Karpov, Brussels 1988.

14 ♘bd2 ♖c8 15 b4

Hereabouts there is an intense struggle for the c5-square, White's last move preventing ...c7-c5 and Black's next attempting to force it through.

15...a5 16 ♘e5

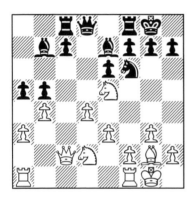

This excellent move secures a small advantage. But it seems that White is also slightly better after 16 ♕b2, for example 16...axb4 17 axb4 ♕d6 18 ♖fb1 ♖a8 (18...♘d5? 19 ♘e4! ♕xb4? is refuted by 20 ♕c1! ♕c4 21 ♕xc4 bxc4 22 ♖xb7) 19 ♖a5 ♘d5 (19...♖xa5 20 bxa5 b4 21 ♘e5 also looks better for White) 20 ♘e4 ♕xb4 21 ♖xb5 ♕xb2 22 ♖5xb2 ♘b6 23 ♘e5 as in L.Bruzon Batista-U.Capo Vidal, Morelia 2007.

16...♘d5?

Carlsen probably came up with this dubious move over the board, overlooking White's powerful reply. Black should prefer 16...♗xg2 17 ♔xg2 c6

(17...axb4 18 ♘c6 ♕d7 19 axb4 was unpleasant for Black in J.Speelman-J.Cox, British Ch., Southport 1983) 18 ♘d3 axb4 19 axb4 ♘d5 20 ♕b3 ♖a8 21 ♖fc1, when White's greater control of terrain gave him the edge in M.Marin-D.Marciano, Bucharest 1993.

17 ♘b3!

With the b4-pawn attacked three times it's easy to miss this idea. Black's reply is forced.

17...axb4 18 ♘a5 ♗a8 19 ♘ac6 ♗xc6 20 ♘xc6 ♕d7 21 ♗xd5! exd5 22 axb4

White has retrieved the sacrificed pawn while maintaining a huge positional plus. Black's position is almost completely paralysed and he can't defend the pawn on b5.

22...♖fe8

White can meet 22...♖a8 with 23 ♖a5!?, for example 23...♖xa5 24 bxa5 ♖a8 25 a6! ♖xa6? 26 ♘b8 etc.

23 ♖a5 ♗f8 24 ♘e5

It doesn't look like Black has enough after 24 ♖xb5 ♖e6 25 ♖c1 ♖h6 26 h4, but Kramnik prefers not to have his knight pinned.

24...♕e6

Sacrificing the exchange with 24...♖xe5 25 dxe5 ♗xb4 doesn't help because White can win the c7-pawn with 26 ♖a7 followed by ♖c1.

25 ♖xb5 ♖b8?!

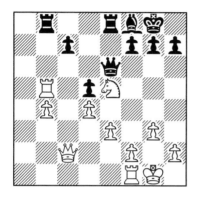

Going meekly to his doom. The surprising 25...♗xb4!? 26 ♖xb4 c5 would have been a better try, though it's unlikely to have changed the course of the game after 27 dxc5 ♕xe5 28 ♖d1 etc.

26 ♖xb8 ♖xb8 27 ♕xc7 ♗d6

After 27...♖xb4 28 ♖a1, White's rook would be ready to penetrate.

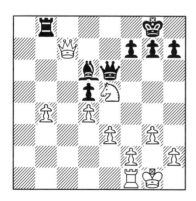

28 ♕a5 ♗xb4

And here 28...♗xe5 29 dxe5 ♕xe5

would have obliged White to find 30 ♖d1 ♕e4 31 ♖xd5, after which he escapes the checks via 31...♕b1+ 32 ♔g2 ♕e4+ 33 ♔f1 ♕b1+ 34 ♔e2 ♕b2+ (or 34...♕c2+ 35 ♔f3) 35 ♔f3 ♕f6+ 36 ♔g2 etc.

29 ♖b1 ♕d6 30 ♕a4 1-0

Further resistance is futile as, with rooks coming off, Black will lose his d5-pawn.

Game 3
V.Kramnik-P.Leko
World Championship,
Mexico City 2007

---

1 d4 ♘f6 2 c4 e6 3 g3 d5 4 ♗g2 ♗e7 5 ♘f3 0-0 6 0-0 dxc4 7 ♕c2 a6 8 ♕xc4 b5 9 ♕c2 ♗b7 10 ♗d2 ♗e4 11 ♕c1

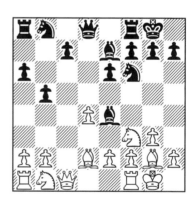

11...♕c8

A logical move: Black prepares ...c7-c5 while delaying the development of his queen's knight. This means that 12 ♗a5 can be answered by 12...♘c6.

There are a number of alternatives, none of which promise full equality for Black:

a) 11...♘bd7 is natural, but the early commitment of the knight to this square once again allows White to play 12 ♗a5, for example:

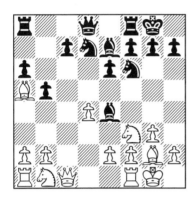

a1) 12...♖c8 13 ♘bd2 ♗a8 14 a3! ♘b8! (14...♕e8 15 b4 ♗d6 16 ♖e1! ♘e4 17 ♖a2! f5 18 ♖c2 ♘b6 19 ♕a1! ♗d5 20 ♖ec1 was better for White in A.Beliavsky-G.Kovacs, Hungarian Team Ch. 2003) 15 ♖d1 ♕e8 16 ♘b3 ♗d5 17 ♘c5 ♗xc5 18 ♕xc5 ♘bd7 19 ♕c3 c5 20 ♕e1 and White had a slight initiative in V.Ivanchuk-B.Gelfand, Monte Carlo (blindfold rapid) 2004.

a2) 12...♖a7!? is interesting, but this still looks better for White after 13 ♘bd2 ♗d5 14 ♖e1 ♘e4 (14...♕a8? is bad because of 15 e4!, when 15...♘xe4 16 ♘xe4 ♗xe4 17 ♖xe4 ♕xe4 18 ♘e5 ♕xd4 19 ♘c6 ♕c5 20 b4 wins material) 15 ♘xe4 ♗xe4 16 ♕f4!? ♘f6 17 ♘e5 ♗xg2 18 ♔xg2 ♗d6 and now 19 ♕f3 ♗xe5 20 dxe5 ♘d7 21 ♖ed1 with ongoing pressure.

b) 11...♘c6 seems to be well met by 12 ♗e3 ♘b4 13 ♘c3 ♗b7 14 ♖d1, for example 14...♕c8 15 a3 ♘bd5 16 ♘xd5 ♘xd5 17 ♗g5 f6 18 ♗d2 a5 19 ♕c2 ♘b6

20 ♖ac1 ♘c4 21 a4 ♘xd2 22 ♘xd2 ♗xg2 23 ♔xg2 bxa4 24 ♕xa4 gave White an edge in A.Grischuk-K.Solomon, FIDE World Ch., Tripoli 2004.

c) 11...c6 is a speciality of the Lithuanian GM Rozentalis,

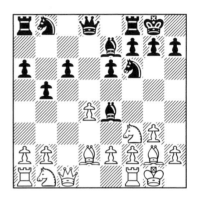

but he recently ran into trouble in this line after 12 ♖d1!? ♗xf3 13 ♗xf3 ♕xd4 14 a4 bxa4 15 ♘a3 ♘bd7 16 ♘c4 ♘e5 17 ♘xe5 ♕xe5 18 ♗f4 ♕c5 19 ♕xc5 ♗xc5 20 ♗xc6 ♖ad8 21 ♖xd8 ♖xd8 22 ♖xa4 ♘d5 23 ♗xd5 ♖xd5 24 ♖xa6 and White was a good pawn up and went on to win in T.Nyback-E.Rozentalis, German League 2007.

d) 11...b4!? has been played by Karpov and makes a lot of sense. Black takes c3 away from White's knight and prevents ♗d2-a5. On the other hand it does lose time. Z.Rahman-S.Irwanto, Kuala Lumpur 2007, continued 12 ♗g5 ♘bd7 13 ♘bd2 ♗d5 14 ♖e1 c5 15 e4 ♗b7 16 e5 ♘e8 and now 17 ♗xe7 ♕xe7 18 dxc5 seems to keep an edge.

e) 11...♗b7 12 ♗f4 (12 ♖d1!? ♕c8 13 a4 c5 14 axb5 axb5 15 ♖xa8 ♗xa8 16 dxc5 ♗xc5 17 ♘c3 ♗c6 18 ♗e3 ♗xe3 19 ♕xe3 b4 20 ♘a2 ♕b7 21 ♘c1 was a tiny bit better for White in E.Bareev-A.Shirov, Monte Carlo rapid 2004) 12...♘d5 13 ♘c3 ♘xf4 14 ♕xf4 c5 15 dxc5 ♗xc5 16 ♘g5 ♕b6 17 ♗xb7 ♕xb7 18 ♖fd1 with slightly the more comfortable game for White, E.Ubilava-A.Karpov, Canada de Calatrava (rapid) 2007.

12 ♗g5

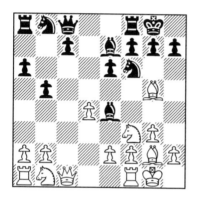

White's most important move; it seems that Black doesn't have too much trouble after the alternatives:

a) 12 b4 ♘d5 13 ♘c3 ♘xc3 14 ♕xc3 ♕b7 15 ♖fc1 was A.Fauland-H.Benda, Austrian Team Ch. 2003, and now 15...♘c6 would have given Black excellent counterplay.

b) 12 ♗e3 ♘bd7 13 ♘bd2 ♗d5 14 ♘b3 ♕b7 15 ♖d1 a5 16 ♘c5 ♘xc5 17 dxc5 ♖fd8 gave Black an excellent game in B.Thorfinnsson-J.Thomassen, Copenhagen 2007.

c) 12 ♘c3 ♗b7 13 ♕c2 ♘bd7 14 ♖ac1 c5 left Black with no further problems in D.Cori Tello-U.Andersson, Benidorm 2008.

d) 12 a4 is interesting and deserves more tests, for example 12...♘bd7 13

♘c3 ♗c6 14 ♗g5 ♕b7 15 e4 b4 16 d5 initiated wild complications but was agreed drawn at this point in J.Gonzales-E.Ghaem Maghami, Calvia 2006.

12...♘bd7

With White's bishop having gone to g5 there's no further reason to delay this move, though Black has tried a couple of alternatives:

a) 12...h6 13 ♗xf6 ♗xf6 14 ♘bd2 ♗b7 15 ♘b3 ♘d7 16 ♕c2 a5 17 ♖fc1 a4 18 ♘c5 ♘xc5 19 ♕xc5 gave White a typical Catalan plus in R.Markus-S.Cvetkovic, Serbian Team Ch. 2004. Black is under strong pressure down the c-file.

b) 12...c5 is a very reasonable attempt to equalize immediately, but it seems that White can maintain a slight edge. For example 13 dxc5 ♕xc5 14 ♘bd2 (14 ♕f4 ♘bd7 15 ♘bd2 ♗b7 16 ♖ac1 ♕b6 17 ♕c7 ♖fc8 gave Black equality in W.Arencibia-L.Bruzon, Santa Clara 2007) 14...♗b7 15 ♕xc5 (15 ♘b3!? ♕b6 16 ♖d1 ♗d5 17 ♗e3 ♕d8 18 ♘fd4 ♘bd7 19 ♘c6 ♕e8 20 ♘xe7+ ♕xe7 gave White a slight but enduring edge in L.Aronian-K.Asrian, Stepanakert 2005) 15...♗xc5 16 ♗xf6 (16 ♖fc1 ♗d6 17 ♗xf6 gxf6 18 ♘e1 ♗xg2 19 ♔xg2 ♗b4 20 ♘e4 ♗xe1 21 ♖xe1 was also slightly better for White in B.Avrukh-F.Jenni, Biel 2006) 16...gxf6 17 ♖fc1 ♗b6 18 ♘e1 ♗xg2 19 ♔xg2 ♘d7 20 ♘d3 ♖fc8 21 a4 (21 ♘e4 ♔f8 22 g4 ♗e7 23 ♔f3 ♗d4 24 ♖xc8 ♖xc8 25 a4 ♖c2 26 axb5 axb5 27 ♖a5 ♘e5+ 28 ♘xe5 ♗xe5 29 b4 ♗xh2 30 ♖xb5 was slightly better for White in B.Gelfand-A.Grischuk, Bastia rapid 2003) 21...♖xc1 22 ♖xc1 bxa4 23 ♖a1 ♘c5 24 ♘xc5 ♗xc5 25 ♖xa4 a5 26 ♘c4 gave White a nagging edge in A.Beliavsky-A.Grischuk, FIDE World Ch, Tripoli 2004. There wasn't enough to win but evidently Black is suffering in this line.

13 ♕f4!?

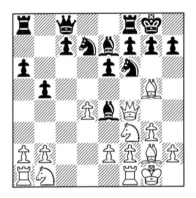

An interesting new move by Kramnik, which spices up a rather welltrodden variation.

The usual and rather obvious move is 13 ♘bd2, for example 13...♗b7 14 ♘b3 (14 ♘e5 ♗xg2 15 ♔xg2 c5 16 ♘xd7 ♕xd7 17 dxc5 ♕d5+ 18 ♘f3 ♕xc5 19 ♕xc5 ♗xc5 20 ♗xf6 gxf6 21 ♖fd1 ♖fc8 was more or less equal in E.Bareev-A.Onischuk, Russian Team Ch. 2007) 14...c5 (Black has tried alternatives here, for example 14...♖e8 15 ♖d1 ♗d5 16 ♗xf6 ♗xf6 17 ♕c2 a5 18 e4 ♗xb3 19 ♕xb3 c6 was a bit better for White in A.Lastin-A.Korotylev, Moscow 2004; and 14...a5 15 ♗xf6 ♗xf6 16 ♘c5 ♘xc5 17 ♕xc5 ♖d8 18 ♖ac1 ♗xf3 19 ♗xf3 ♗xd4 20 ♕xb5 ♕b8 21 ♕c4 ♖a7 22 b3 ♕b4 23 ♖fd1 ♕xc4 24 bxc4 became very drawish in Y.Pelletier-A.Onischuk, Biel 2007) 15 ♗xf6 ♗xf6 (15...gxf6 is risky,

and 16 ♕f4 ♕b8 17 ♕h4 cxd4 18 ♖ad1 ♖a7 19 ♖xd4 gave White quite a dangerous-looking initiative in A.Grischuk-V.Bologan, Poikovsky 2005) 16 ♘xc5 ♘xc5 17 dxc5 ♗e7 18 b4 ♗f6 19 ♖b1 ♗e4 20 ♖b3 a5 21 a3 ♗d5 22 ♘d2 ♗xb3 23 ♗xa8 ♕xa8 24 ♘xb3 axb4 25 axb4 ♕a4 recovered the pawn with equality in B.Gelfand-A.Onischuk, World Team Ch., Beersheba 2005.

13...♗b7

Leko thought long and hard about this, finally refraining from the natural 13...c5 which was played in a later game: T.Nyback-M.Agopov, Jyvaskyla 2008, continued 14 ♖c1 c4 15 b3 cxb3! 16 axb3 (and not 16 ♖xc8? b2!) 16...♕b8 17 ♕xb8 ♖fxb8 18 ♘bd2 ♗b7 19 ♘e5 ♘xe5 20 ♗xb7 ♖xb7 21 dxe5 ♘d5 22 ♗xe7 ♘xe7 23 ♘e4 with ongoing pressure for White.

Another possibility is 13...♕b7, but then 14 ♘c3 ♗c6 15 e4 b4 16 d5 exd5 17 exd5 ♘xd5 18 ♘xd5 ♗xg5 19 ♕xb4 ♗xd5 20 ♕xb7 ♗xb7 21 ♘xg5 ♗xg2 22 ♔xg2 would give White an endgame with the better pawn structure. This kind of position would be especially dangerous against an endgame wizard like Kramnik.

14 ♖c1

Inhibiting the advance of the c7-pawn.

14...♗d6 15 ♕h4 h6

In the game S.Brunello-G.Kovacs, European Club Cup, Kallithea 2008, Black tried to improve with 15...♘e4, but after 16 ♘bd2 ♘xd2 17 ♗xd2 ♘f6 he would have found himself in a highly unpleasant position had White chosen 18 ♗g5 (rather than 18 ♗f4) 18...♕d8 19 ♗xf6 ♕xf6 20 ♘g5 h6 21 ♗xb7 hxg5 22 ♕e4 ♖a7 23 ♗c6 etc.

16 ♗xf6 ♘xf6 17 ♘bd2

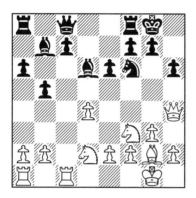

White has now managed to prevent ...c7-c5 and will have pressure down the c-file. The only negative aspect of his position is the slightly awkward position of his queen.

17...♖e8 18 e4

18 ♖c2 is worth considering, trying to build pressure on the c-file at once.

18...♘d7

The immediate 18...e5 leaves White with an edge after 19 dxe5 ♗xe5 20 ♘xe5 ♖xe5 21 ♕f4.

19 ♘b3 a5

Preventing 20 ♘a5, which would have been the answer to 19...e5.

20 ♘c5

There were other moves worth considering, for example 20 ♖c2 makes sense, but Black might have answered with 20...e5. Another possibility is 20 a4 after which 20...bxa4 (if 20...b4 21 ♘fd2) 21 ♖xa4 ♗b4 is met by 22 ♕f4 with ongoing pressure.

20...♗e7

Normally Black would like to capture on c5 in such positions, but White would then have the unpleasant threat of c5-c6. For example 20...♗xc5?! 21 dxc5 ♗c6 is answered by 22 ♘d4.

A better way is 20...♘xc5 21 dxc5 ♗e7, for example 22 ♕h5 (22 ♕f4 e5 23 ♘xe5 ♗f6 would give Black excellent counterplay) 22...♗xe4 23 ♘e5! g6 24 ♕xh6 ♗xg2 25 ♔xg2 ♗f6 26 ♕f4 ♗xe5 27 ♕xe5 ♖d8 when Black is only slightly worse.

21 ♕f4 e5

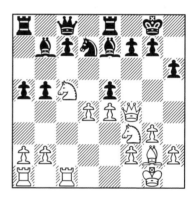

This wins material, but White gets excellent compensation. A safer line would have been 21...♘xc5 22 dxc5 e5!, transposing into the note with 20...♘xc5 while also avoiding 22 ♕h5.

22 ♘xe5 ♘xe5 23 dxe5

23 ♕xe5? ♗g5 24 ♕f5 is bad because of 24...♕xf5 25 exf5 ♗xc1 26 ♗xb7 ♗xb2 etc.

23...♗g5 24 ♕f3 ♗xc1 25 ♖xc1 ♖xe5 26 ♕c3

Black has won the exchange but finds himself under terrible pressure. All White's pieces are ideally placed, while Black will have difficulty getting his queenside pieces into play.

26...f6?!

In retrospect it might have been better to return the exchange with 26...♖e7 27 ♘xb7 ♕xb7 28 e5 ♕a7 29 ♗xa8 ♕xa8. White would be better here too, but the reduction of material makes it difficult for White to win.

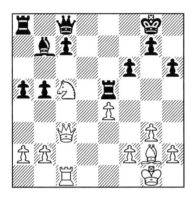

27 ♕b3+ ♔h8?!

This turns out to be the wrong square for the king. Black should have played 27...♔h7, when 28 ♕f7 (28 ♕xb5 looks better with strong pressure for the sacrificed exchange) 28...♗c6 29 ♘d3 ♗e8 30 ♕f8 is no longer check. This makes a critical difference compared to the game.

28 ♕f7!

Threatening both ♘xb7 or ♘d3 followed by ♖xc7.

28...♗c6 29 ♘d3 ♖e6

In this position 29...♗e8? 30 ♕f8+ would win on the spot.

30 ♘f4!

Playing for the attack rather than simply winning back the exchange with 30 ♗h3. Black is in terrible trouble now.

30...♖d6 31 ♘g6+ ♔h7 32 e5!

This move wins material for White.

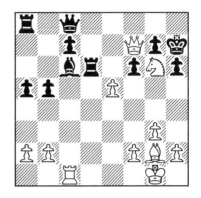

32...fxe5 33 ♗xc6 ♖f6 34 ♕d5 ♕f5 35 ♗xa8 ♕xf2+ 36 ♔h1 ♕xb2 37 ♕c5 ♔xg6 38 ♗e4+ ♔h5 39 ♖b1 1-0

Game 4
K.Landa-H.Melkumyan
European Club Cup,
Kallithea 2008

---

1 ♘f3 ♘f6 2 c4 e6 3 g3 d5 4 ♗g2 ♗e7 5 0-0 0-0 6 d4 dxc4 7 ♕c2 a6 8 ♕xc4 b5 9 ♕c2 ♗b7 10 ♗d2 ♗d6

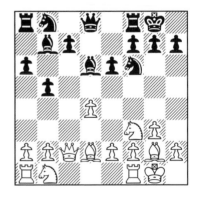

A high-class waiting move that has

become popular of late. Black prepares the possibilities of ...e6-e5 (after further preparation) or ...♕d8-e7 and defends the pawn on c7. Meanwhile White must find another useful move, 11 ♗a5 being simply met by 11...♘c6.

11 ♖e1

White finds a classy waiting move in turn, keeping the option of ♗d2-a5 while preparing a possible e2-e4. Other moves don't seem to promise much:

a) 11 ♗g5 ♘bd7

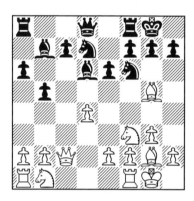

12 ♘bd2 (12 ♖d1 ♕b8 13 ♗xf6 ♘xf6 14 ♘bd2 ♖c8 15 ♘g5 ♗xg2 16 ♔xg2 ♕b7+ didn't leave White with much in J.Speelman-W.Browne, Wijk aan Zee 1983) 12...♖c8 13 ♘b3 c5 14 ♗xf6 ♘xf6 15 ♘xc5 ♗e4 16 ♕c3 e5 17 e3 ♗xc5 18 dxc5 ♕d5 19 ♖ad1 ♕a8 20 ♘h4 ♗xg2 21 ♘xg2 ♘e4 22 ♕xe5 ♖xc5 23 ♕d4 ♖c4 24 ♕d3 ♘g5 gave Black compensation for his sacrificed pawn in V.Kramnik-M.Carlsen, Moscow 2007.

b) 11 ♖d1 ♘bd7 12 ♗a5 ♕b8 13 b4 e5 14 ♘bd2 exd4 15 ♘xd4 ♗xg2 16 ♔xg2 c5 17 bxc5 ♗xc5 18 ♘2b3 ♗a3 was fine for Black in B.Gelfand-V.Anand, FIDE World Ch., Mexico City 2007.

c) 11 ♗e3 ♘bd7 12 ♘bd2 ♕e7 13 ♘b3 ♗e4 14 ♕c1 e5 15 dxe5 ♘xe5 16 ♘xe5 ♗xg2 17 ♘c6 ♗xc6 18 ♕xc6 ♘g4 19 ♗d4 ♕xe2 20 ♖fe1 ♕d3 21 h3 ♘h6 22 ♗e5 ♗xe5 23 ♖xe5 ♘f5 24 ♖ae1 g6 25 ♖d5 ♕c4 26 ♖c5 ♕d3 was soon drawn by repetition in M.Carlsen-A.Onischuk, Foros 2008.

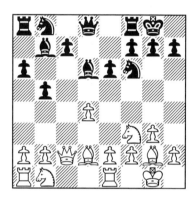

11...♘bd7

This suffers from the old problem of allowing White to get ♗d2-a5 in. For this reason Black's best may be 11...♗e4 12 ♕c1 ♗b7 (here too 12...♘bd7 is met by 13 ♗a5!, for example 13...♕e7 14 ♘bd2 ♗xf3 15 ♘xf3 ♖ac8 16 e4 e5 17 ♘h4 g6 18 f4 exf4 19 e5 won a piece for inadequate compensation in A.Volokitin-A.Onischuk, Foros 2008) 13 ♗g5 ♘bd7 14 e4 ♗e7 15 ♘bd2 c5 16 e5 (16 ♗xf6 ♗xf6 17 dxc5 ♖c8 18 b4 ♗xa1 19 ♕xa1 gave White some compensation for the sacrificed exchange in P.Harikrishna-A.Pashikian, European Club Cup, Kallithea 2008, though it's probably only barely adequate at this stage) 16...♘d5 17 ♘e4 cxd4 18 ♕d2 (18 ♗xe7 ♕xe7 19 ♕d2 ♘e3 20 fxe3 ♗xe4 21 exd4 ♗d5 was also fine for Black in

A.Delchev-E.Ubilava, Benasque 2008) 18...♗xg5 19 ♘exg5 h6 20 ♘e4 ♘e3 21 fxe3 (and not 21 ♕xd4? ♘c2) 21...♗xe4 22 exd4 ♗d5 23 ♘h4 ♘b6 24 ♗e4 ♖c8 25 ♘g2 ♗xe4 was fine for Black in B.Gelfand-V.Anand, Wijk aan Zee 2008. The onus seems to be on White to find something here.

12 ♗a5 ♕e8?!

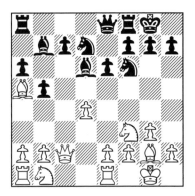

Well, that's one way to unpin the c-pawn, though it does look rather artificial. Black might have rejected 12...♕e7 because in some lines he saw a white knight coming to f5. But this could be a case of the cure being worse than the disease.

13 e4 e5 14 ♘bd2 c5 15 dxe5 ♘xe5 16 ♘xe5 ♗xe5 17 ♘f3 ♖c8 18 ♖ad1 b4

This stops the a5-bishop from returning to c3, but loses yet more time and additionally creates further weaknesses.

19 ♗h3 ♖c6 20 a3 ♗c7 21 e5!

This leads to the break-up of Black's kingside and subsequently a strong attack. Black has some tricks but they don't really work.

21...♗xa5 22 exf6 b3 23 ♕xb3 ♗xe1?!

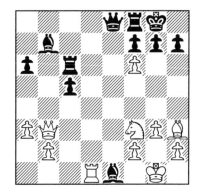

23...♖b6 was probably a better try, but then 24 ♖xe8 ♖xb3 25 ♖xf8+ ♔xf8 26 ♘e5 gxf6 27 ♘c4 ♗c7 28 ♗f5 is just one good line.

24 fxg7 ♔xg7 25 ♖xe1 ♕a8 26 ♘h4

Threatening to come to f5. Another good move was 26 ♖e7!, when 26...♗c8 27 ♗g2 ♖e6 28 ♕c3+ ♔g8 29 ♘h4 is very unpleasant.

26...♖f6 27 ♘f5+ ♔h8??

27...♔g8 had to be tried, though this is still very good for White after 28 ♕e3 ♕d8 29 ♕g5+ ♖g6 30 ♘e7+ ♔g7 31 ♕e5+ f6 32 ♕e3 etc.

28 ♕c3 ♕d8 29 ♖e7 ♕d1+ 30 ♗f1 1-0

Summary

As I mentioned in the introduction, 10 ♗d2 is not really suitable for club players with a life outside of chess, as there are subtle new developments coming through all the time. Yet the patterns and strategic themes we've seen in this section are applicable to other variations of the Catalan, in particular the thematic contest for the c5-square and play on the d- and c-files.

Chapter Two

Main Line with 10 ♗f4 and Others

1 d4 ♘f6 2 c4 e6 3 g3 d5 4 ♗g2 ♗e7 5 ♘f3 0-0 6 0-0 dxc4 7 ♕c2 a6 8 ♕xc4 b5 9 ♕c2 ♗b7

The variation with 10 ♗f4 is much more suitable for busy mortals than 10 ♗d2 because it is comparatively less popular at the top level. It is also a very natural developing move, aiming at c7.

The obvious response is 10...♘d5 (see Game 5), attacking the bishop whilst simultaneously defending c7. White in turn is quite happy to let Black capture on f4, arguing that the loss of time with the knight is more important than the two bishops or apparent weakening of White's kingside.

Less obvious but probably stronger is 10...♘c6 of Damljanovic-Sanikidze (Game 6), which paradoxically plays for ...c7-c5 despite the initial blockade of the c7-pawn. This seems to be quite a good line for Black and he doesn't appear to have particular problems after the anti-intuitive 14...♗xd5 (in-

stead of 14...♘xd5 in the game).

In Kramnik-Shirov (Game 7) Black reaches the 10...♗d6 variation by transposition, which probably isn't the most comfortable line. Besides Kramnik's 11 ♘bd2, White could also play 11 ♗g5, which transposes into Landa-Melkumyan from Chapter 1 (Game 4).

The move 11 ♗g5 used to be White's most popular 11th move alternative, but these days it is quite a rare bird. I've played it a few times myself as can be seen in the notes to Kaidanov-Onischuk (Game 8). Black shouldn't have too many problems here, though he has to know what he's doing. Onischuk evidently did, but will your opponents?

Game 5
V.Kramnik-P.Svidler
Linares 1998

---

1 ♘f3 ♘f6 2 c4 e6 3 g3 d5 4 d4 ♗e7 5

♗g2 0-0 6 0-0 dxc4 7 ♕c2 a6 8 ♕xc4 b5 9 ♕c2 ♗b7 10 ♗f4 ♘d5

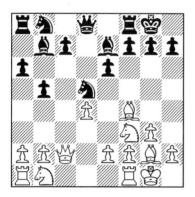

The most obvious attempt to exploit the position of the bishop on f4, but it turns out that the doubling of White's f-pawns may not particularly hinder his cause.

11 ♘c3 ♘xf4 12 gxf4 ♘d7 13 ♖fd1 ♗xf3?!

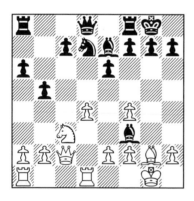

This exchange is probably a bad idea. Black hopes that the opposite-coloured bishops will help him to defend, but the weakness of the c6-square makes his life a misery. There are several better moves, for example:

a) 13...♕c8 14 ♘e4 (this sharp move

is probably best; 14 a4 bxa4 15 ♘xa4 ♖b8 16 ♖ac1 ♗d6 17 e3 ♘f6 18 ♘c5 ♗xc5 19 ♕xc5 ♗d5 20 ♕xc7 was agreed drawn in G.Sosonko-I.Rausis, Aaland-Stockholm 1997; and 14 ♖ac1 c5 15 dxc5 ♘xc5 16 ♕b1 ♖d8 17 b4 ♘a4 18 ♖xd8+ ♕xd8 19 ♘xa4 bxa4 20 ♘e5 ♗xg2 21 ♔xg2 was okay for Black at this stage in B.Kurajica-M.Gavric, Banja Luka 1985) 14...c5 (14...f5 gains time but is a bit weakening, for example 15 ♘ed2 ♗d6 16 ♘e5 ♗xg2 17 ♔xg2 ♕b7+ 18 ♘df3 ♘f6 19 e3 g5 20 fxg5 ♗xe5 21 dxe5 ♘e4 was P.H.Nielsen-S.B.Hansen, Copenhagen 1995, and now 22 h4 would have made life unpleasant for Black) 15 dxc5 ♘xc5 16 ♘xc5 ♕xc5 17 ♕xc5 ♗xc5 18 ♖ac1 ♖fc8 19 ♘e5 ♗xg2 20 ♔xg2 f6 21 ♘f3 ♗f8 22 e3 g6 23 b3 ♗b4 24 h3 ♔f8 25 ♘d4 ♔f7 26 a4 gave White a tiny edge in Z.Ribli-A.Karpov, Amsterdam 1980.

b) 13...♘f6 14 ♘e5 ♗xg2 15 ♔xg2 ♗d6 16 e3 ♕c8 17 ♘e4 ♘d5 18 ♖ac1 f6 19 ♘c6 left Black under pressure in H.Bohm-A.Luczak, Polanica Zdroj 1980.

14 ♗xf3 ♖b8 15 e3

Another possibility is 15 ♘e4, for example 15...♗d6 16 e3 ♕h4 17 ♔h1 ♘f6 18 ♘xf6+ ♕xf6 19 ♖g1 ♕e7 20 ♗c6 left Black unable to free himself in V.Smyslov-L.Barczay, European Team Ch., Kapfenberg 1970.

15...♘f6

And not 15...c5? 16 dxc5 ♗xc5, which just loses material after 17 ♗c6.

16 ♖ac1 ♕d6 17 ♘e2 ♖fc8 18 e4!?

Exploiting the vulnerable position of the black queen. Black should now have moved the lady to b6, as by leaving her on the d-file he allows a breakthrough.

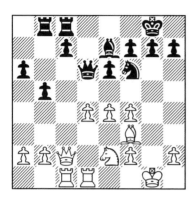

18...♕d7? 19 d5! exd5

Another possibility was 19...♗f8, but then 20 dxe6 ♕xe6 21 e5 ♘e8 22 ♘d4 ♕h6 23 ♘c6 ♕xf4 24 ♕e4! would win the exchange for inadequate compensation.

20 e5 ♘e8

20...♘g4 21 ♖xd5 ♕e6 22 ♘d4 would win a piece.

21 ♖xd5 ♕h3 22 ♗g2 ♕h4

Or if 22...♕g4 there follows 23 h3 ♕h4 24 ♘d4! threatening ♘f5 or ♘c6.

23 ♘d4!

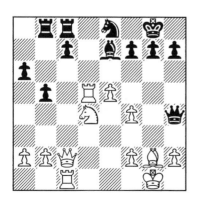

This powerful manoeuvre is a key idea in many variations.

23...♕xf4 24 ♘c6 ♗h4 25 ♖cd1!

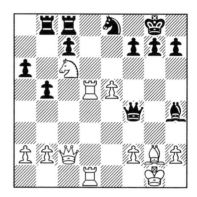

And not 25 ♖d4?? because of 25...♗xf2+ 26 ♕xf2 ♕xc1+ etc.

25...♖b6

After 25...♖a8 there could follow 26 ♖5d4 ♕h6 27 ♕e4 ♗g5 28 h4 ♗c1 29 ♕c2 when Black's bishop runs out of squares.

26 ♖5d4 ♖xc6

Giving up the exchange in the hope of freeing himself from White's pythonesque bind. Both 26...♕g5 27 ♕e4 and 26...♕h6 27 ♕f5 would be forlorn prospects.

27 ♗xc6 ♕xe5 28 ♗d7 ♖d8 29 ♖xh4 1-0

Game 6
B.Damljanovic-T.Sanikidze
European Championship,
Dresden 2007

1 ♘f3 ♘f6 2 d4 d5 3 c4 e6 4 g3 ♗e7 5 ♗g2 0-0 6 0-0 dxc4 7 ♕c2 a6 8 ♕xc4 b5 9 ♕c2 ♗b7 10 ♗f4 ♘c6

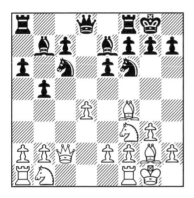

11 ⌶d1

Defending the d4-pawn while shadowing Black's queen on the d-file, though this is not the only move. White can also ignore the attack on d4 with 11 ♘bd2, for example 11...♘xd4 12 ♘xd4 ♗xg2 13 ♘xe6 fxe6 14 ♔xg2 was played in R.Bates-S.Gordon, British League 2008, with about even chances after 14...c5 15 ♘f3 ♕b6 16 e4 ⌶ad8 17 b3.

11...♘b4 12 ♕c1

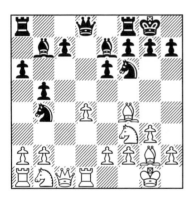

12...⌶c8

Logically supporting ...c7-c5. Another way to try and do this is by 12...♕c8, but then 13 ♗g5 is awkward.

After 13...c5 14 ♗xf6 Black would have to weaken his kingside with 14...gxf6 because 14...♗xf6 15 a3 ♘d5 16 dxc5 leaves him a pawn down.

13 ♘c3 ♘bd5

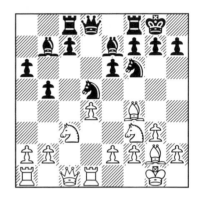

14 ♘xd5

White has tried other moves here:

a) 14 ♘e5?! ♘xc3 15 bxc3 ♗xg2 16 ♔xg2 c5 17 dxc5 ♕c7 was already quite nice for Black in H.Lieb-A.Simon, Berlin 1987.

b) 14 ♗e3 c6 15 ♘e5 ♕b6 16 ♘xd5 cxd5 17 ♕d2 b4 18 ♗g5 ⌶c7 19 ⌶ac1 ⌶fc8 20 ⌶xc7 ⌶xc7 21 ⌶c1 a5 was equal in U.Andersson-A.Beliavsky, Reggio Emilia 1989/90.

c) 14 ♗e5 c5 (14...♘xc3 15 ♕xc3 b4 16 ♕b3 was unpleasant for Black in A.Delchev-S.Rezan, Zadar 2002) 15 dxc5 ♗xc5 16 ♗xf6 ♕xf6 17 ♘e4 ♕e7 18 ♘xc5 ⌶xc5 19 ♕d2 ♘f6 20 ♕d6 (20 ⌶ac1 h6 21 ⌶xc5 ♕xc5 22 ⌶c1 ♕b6 23 ♘e5 ♗xg2 24 ♔xg2 was rather equal in U.Andersson-A.Beliavsky, European Team Ch., Debrecen 1992) 20...♕xd6 21 ⌶xd6 ⌶fc8 22 ♘e1 ♗xg2 23 ♔xg2 a5 24 ⌶a6 a4 25 b3 axb3 26 axb3 g5 27 ♘d3 ⌶c2 28 ⌶a8 ⌶xa8 29 ⌶xa8+ ♔g7 30 ♔f1 and Black's weak pawn on b5 left him slightly worse in Jo.Horvath-P.Wells, Odorheiu Secuiesc 1993.

14...♘xd5

Despite its natural appearance this may not be the best. Black is better advised to play 14...♗xd5, for example 15 ♗e3 ♘g4 (another way to play it is with 15...c6, for example 16 ♘e1 ♘g4 17 ♗f3! ♘xe3 18 ♕xe3 ♗f6 19 ♕a3 ♗xf3 20 ♘xf3 ♕b6 as in S.Atalik-R.Vaganian, Manila Olympiad 1992) 16 ♘e1 ♗xg2 (16...c5 17 dxc5 ♘xe3 18 ♕xe3 ♗xc5 19 ♕f4 g5 20 ♕g4 ♕f6 21 ♘d3 ♗xg2 22 ♔xg2 ♖fd8 23 ♖ac1 ♗b6 24 ♖xc8 was slightly better for White in U.Andersson-M.Tal, Brussels 1988) 17 ♘xg2 ♕d5 18 h3 ♘xe3 19 ♕xe3 c5 20 ♘f4 ♕f5 21 dxc5 ♗xc5 22 ♕d3?! (22 ♕f3 is better, with equality) 22...♕f6! 23 ♕d2 ♖fd8 24 ♕a5 e5 and Black had a strong initiative in M.Carlsen-V.Anand, Mainz (rapid) 2008.

15 ♗g5

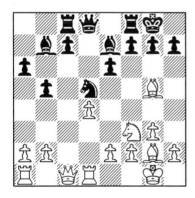

15...f6

Creating a weakness on e6, not that this is anywhere close to fatal. Nevertheless, Black does better with 15...c5 16

dxc5 ♕e8 (or 16...h6 17 ♗xe7 ♕xe7 18 ♕d2 ♖xc5 19 ♖ac1 ♖fc8 with equality as in L.Galego-P.Dias, Portuguese Ch., Almada 2008; but not 16...♖xc5?? because of 17 ♕xc5!) 17 ♗xe7 ♕xe7 18 ♕d2 (or 18 ♕g5 ♕xc5 19 ♖ac1 ♕b6 20 ♕d2 ♖fd8 21 ♕d4 ♖xc1 22 ♖xc1 ♖c8 as in A.Kochyev-R.Tischbierek, Leningrad 1984) 18...♖xc5 19 ♖ac1 ♖fc8 20 ♘e5 h6 21 ♘d3 ♖c4 and White had very little to show in I.Stohl-Kir.Georgiev, European Cup, Chalkidiki 2002.

16 ♗e3 ♕e8 17 ♘e1 c5 18 dxc5 ♘xe3 19 ♗xb7 ♘xd1 20 ♗xc8 ♕xc8 21 ♕xd1 ♕xc5 22 ♖c1 ♕b6 23 ♘d3

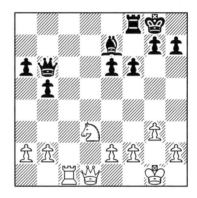

White has a slight edge here because of the weakness of the e6-pawn and effective cooperation between his queen and knight. This isn't easy to play for Black but he manages to hold a draw.

23...♖d8 24 ♕b3 ♔f7 25 ♖c3 ♗d6 26 ♕c2 ♖d7 27 ♖c6 ♕b7 28 b3 g6 29 a4

Trying to create a second target on the queenside.

29...bxa4 30 bxa4 ♔e7 31 ♕c4 ♖c7 32 ♖xc7+ ♗xc7 33 ♕h4 h5 34 ♕c4 ♗d6 35 h4 ♔d7 36 g4

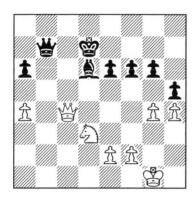

It looks like this might have been an attempt to exploit Black's time trouble, but the defender proves to be more than up to the task. Objectively speaking White is slightly better in the queen endgames following, say, 36 ♘f4 ♗xf4 37 ♕xf4 ♔e7 38 a5, but these are nonetheless rather drawish.

36...♕c6! 37 ♕d4 e5 38 ♕a7+ ♔e6

38...♕c7 39 ♕xa6 hxg4 would not be worse for Black, but it is double edged.

39 gxh5 gxh5 40 ♕h7 ♕xa4 41 ♕xh5?!

41 ♕g8+ ♔f5 42 ♕h7+ ♔e6 would have been a repetition, so presumably White was still pushing his luck at this stage.

41...a5 42 f4 exf4 43 ♕g4+ ♔f7 44 ♕h5+ ♔e6 ½-½

Black could well have continued here, say with 44...♔g7. Presumably the clock was still a factor.

Game 7
V.Kramnik-A.Shirov
Moscow 2007

---

1 ♘f3 d5 2 d4 ♘f6 3 c4 e6 4 g3 ♗e7 5

♗g2 0-0 6 ♕c2

We'll be seeing more of this 6 ♕c2 move order later; in this game there is a transposition into the 10 ♗f4 line. Here 6 0-0 dxc4 7 ♕c2 a6 8 ♕xc4 b5 9 ♕c2 ♗b7 10 ♗f4 ♗d6 would be a standard route to the position at move 10.

6...dxc4 7 ♕xc4 a6 8 ♗f4 ♗d6 9 0-0 b5 10 ♕c2 ♗b7

As previously noted White can now transpose into the 10 ♗d2 ♗d6 11 ♗g5 line with 11 ♗g5, but Kramnik gives the game a different twist.

11 ♘bd2

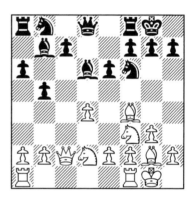

This seems like the most testing line for Black, aiming to bring the knight to b3 from where it inhibits ...c7-c5.

Black seems to be doing fine after the alternatives, for example:

a) 11 ♗xd6?! cxd6 immediately solves Black's problem of the weakness on c5.

b) 11 ♘e5 is well met by 11...♗xg2 12 ♔xg2 c5, the point being that 13 dxc5 is answered by 13...♗xe5 14 ♗xe5 ♕d5+ etc.

c) 11 ♗g5 ♘bd7 12 ♘bd2 ♖c8 (12...h6 13 ♗xf6 ♘xf6 14 e4 ♗e7 is unclear) 13 ♗xf6 ♘xf6 14 ♘b3 ♗e4 15 ♕c3 ♕e7 16 ♖ac1 ♘d7! 17 ♕e3 f5!? (17...♗d5! 18 ♘c5 ♗xc5 19 dxc5 c6 would have equalized, but Bologan wants more) 18 ♘e5 (the critical line was 18 ♘c5 when 18...♗d5 19 ♘xa6 f4 20 ♕c3 b4 21 ♕d3 c5 would give Black play for his pawn) 18...♗xg2 19 ♔xg2 ♗xe5 20 dxe5 c5 gave Black active counterplay in C.Bauer-V.Bologan, Belfort 2002.

11...♘bd7

Black can also try doubling the white pawns, though here too White is for preference: 11...♗xf4 12 gxf4 ♘bd7 (after 12...♕d6 White can consider 13 ♖ac1!?, for example 13...♕xf4 14 ♕xc7 ♕xc7 15 ♖xc7 gives Black serious problems, and 13...♘c6 would make it difficult for him to ever move his c-pawn) 13 e3 ♖c8 14 b4 ♘b6 15 a3 g6 16 ♖fc1 ♗d5 17 ♘e5 ♗xg2 18 ♔xg2 ♘fd5 19 ♕e4 gave White the better game in Y.Seirawan-A.Karpov, London 1984.

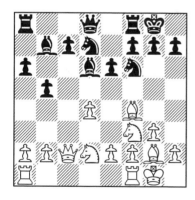

12 ♘b3

White has an interesting alternative in 12 a4!?, for example 12...♕b8 (12...♗xf4 13 gxf4 ♕b8 14 ♘e5 ♗xg2 15 ♔xg2 c5 16 dxc5 ♘xe5 17 fxe5 ♕xe5 18 ♘f3 ♕f4 was agreed drawn at this point in E.Bukic-M.Diesen, Stip 1977, though White might have continued thanks to his strong passed c-pawn; another possibility was 14 e3, just securely defending the f4-pawn) 13 ♘e5! ♗xg2 14 ♔xg2 c5 15 ♘df3! ♗xe5 (15...cxd4? is bad because of 16 ♘c6! ♕c7 17 ♘e7+ ♔h8 18 ♕xc7; while 15...c4? is answered by 16 axb5 axb5? 17 ♖xa8 ♕xa8 18 ♘xd7) 16 ♗xe5 ♘xe5 17 dxe5 ♘d7 18 axb5 axb5 19 ♖xa8 ♕xa8 20 ♖d1 ♘xe5 21 ♕xc5 ♘xf3 22 exf3 ♕b7 23 ♖d6! and White soon won the b5-pawn and then the game in I.Csom-J.Plachetka, Berlin 1979.

Another natural-looking move is 12 ♖ac1, but it doesn't look as testing. According to Parma Black can equalize with 12...♖c8! 13 ♘e5 ♗xg2 14 ♔xg2 ♘d5 15 ♘e4 ♘xe5 16 ♗xe5 f6!.

12...♗e4

12...♕e7 leaves Black under serious pressure after 13 ♖ac1, when V.Smyslov-M.Filip, Munich Olympiad 1958, continued 13...♗e4 14 ♗xd6 cxd6 15 ♕c7 ♘e8 16 ♕a5 with similar problems for Black to our main game.

13 ♕d2 ♕e7 14 ♖fc1 ♖fc8 15 ♗xd6

A simple move which leads to a nagging edge in a highly unpleasant position for Black. In R.Buhmann-P.Braun, Deizisau 2003, White played 15 ♘e5, but this led to a drawish endgame after 15...♗xg2 16 ♘xd7 ♘xd7 17 ♔xg2 ♗xf4 18 ♕xf4 c5 19 ♘xc5 ♘xc5 20 dxc5 ♖xc5 21 ♖xc5 ♕xc5 22 ♖c1 ♕d5+ 23 ♕f3 ♕xf3+ 24 ♔xf3 ♔f8.

15...cxd6 16 ♕a5!

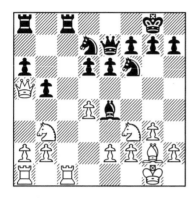

A very unpleasant move, simply tickling the a-pawn. Shirov sees nothing better than to abandon the c-file.

16...♖cb8 17 ♘bd2 ♗d5 18 ♖c2 ♕d8 19 ♕xd8+ ♖xd8 20 ♖ac1 ♘b6

And not 20...♗xa2? because of 21 b3.

21 ♘e1 ♖ac8 22 ♘d3 ♖xc2 23 ♖xc2 ♖c8 24 ♖xc8+ ♘xc8 25 ♘b4!

Just when it looked as if Black was escaping his troubles by exchanges, there comes this unpleasant move. Black's queenside pawns prove to be very weak.

25...♗xg2 26 ♔xg2 a5 27 ♘c6 a4 28 e4 ♘e8 29 ♔f3 ♔f8 30 ♔e3 ♘c7 31 ♔d3 ♔e8 32 ♔c3 ♘a6 33 ♘b4 ♘c7 34 ♘f1 ♔d7 35 ♘e3 ♘e7 36 g4

The squeeze is on, with Kramnik gaining space on the kingside in order to engineer a breakthrough there.

36...g5 37 ♘d3 f6 38 f4 gxf4 39 ♘xf4 e5 40 dxe5 fxe5

This presents White with the possibility of creating an outside passed pawn, but 40...dxe5 41 ♘h5 followed by ♔b4 is also strong for White.

41 ♘fd5 ♘cxd5+ 42 exd5 ♔c7 43 g5

♔b6 44 b4 axb3

After 44...♘g6 there would have followed 45 ♔d3! ♘f4+ 46 ♔e4, penetrating with the king.

45 axb3 ♔a5 46 h4 ♘g6 47 h5 ♘f4 48 g6 hxg6 49 h6 g5 50 h7 ♘g6 51 ♔d3 1-0

Phenomenal endgame play by the master torturer.

Game 8
G.Kaidanov-A.Onischuk
Lubbock 2008

1 d4 ♘f6 2 c4 e6 3 g3 d5 4 ♘f3 ♗e7 5 ♗g2 0-0 6 0-0 dxc4 7 ♕c2 a6 8 ♕xc4 b5 9 ♕c2 ♗b7 10 ♗g5

At one time this was one of the most popular moves; now it is considered innocuous and rarely gets played. Even so Black must know what he's doing.

10...♘bd7

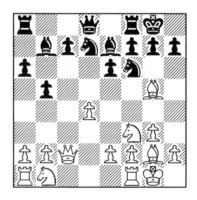

In one of my own games, N.Davies-T.Luther, European Ch., Liverpool 2008, my opponent played 10...♗e4 11 ♕c1 ♘bd7, with the continuation proving quite exciting: 12 ♘bd2 ♗d5 13 ♗xf6 ♗xf6 (after 13...♘xf6 14 ♕c2 ♖c8 15 e4 ♗b7 16 e5 ♘d5 17 ♘b3 White has slightly the better game) 14 ♕c2 (14 b4 a5 15 a3 e5 gives Black counterplay and was agreed drawn at this point in I.Stohl-D.King, German League 1999) 14...♖c8 15 ♘e4 ♗xe4 16 ♕xe4 c5 17 ♖ad1 ♕a5 18 d5 exd5 19 ♖xd5 ♘b6 20 ♖d6 ♘c4 (20...♗xb2 21 ♘g5 g6 22 ♕h4 would be very dangerous for Black) 21 ♖xf6 gxf6 22 ♕g4+ ♔h8 23 ♕h4 ♔g7 24 ♕g4+ ♔h8 25 ♕h4 ♔g7 ½-½. Of course from a theoretical point of view a draw with Black is a decent result, so this represents quite a good alternative.

11 ♗xf6 ♘xf6

After 11...♗xf6 White has 12 ♘g5 ♗xg5 13 ♗xb7 ♖b8 14 ♗c6, when the blockade of the black c-pawn gave him an edge in V.Topalov-P.Leko, Nice (blindfold rapid) 2008.

12 ♘bd2 ♖c8 13 ♘b3

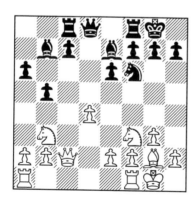

13...♗e4

Black can equalize here with 13...c5, for example 14 dxc5 ♘e4 (14...♗e4 15 ♕c3 ♗d5 16 ♖ac1 ♗xb3 17 ♕xb3 ♗xc5 18 ♖c2 ♕b6 was also fine for Black in

L.Aronian-V.Kramnik, Nice blindfold rapid 2008) 15 ♖fd1 ♕c7 16 c6 ♕xc6 17 ♕xc6 ♗xc6 18 ♘e5 ♗d5 19 ♘d7 ♖fe8 20 ♘b6 ♖c2 21 ♘xd5 exd5 22 ♖xd5 ♗f6 with equality in V.Topalov-V.Anand, Nice (blindfold rapid) 2008.

14 ♕c3 ♕d5 15 ♖fc1 ♖fd8 16 ♕a5

Putting pressure on the a-pawn in the style of Kramnik-Shirov. But here Black can defend it far more economically.

16...♕b7 17 ♘c5 ♗xc5 18 ♖xc5 ♘d7

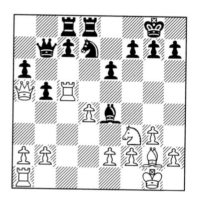

19 ♖cc1

An earlier Onischuk game had gone 19 ♖c3 ♘b6 20 b3 ♘d5 21 ♖c5 b4 22 a3 ♘c3 23 ♔f1 ♘b1 24 ♕xb4 ½-½ P.Schlosser-A.Onischuk, German League 1998. Presumably Kaidanov had prepared the text, but he doesn't get much with it. And in the later stages it is Onischuk who is playing for the full point.

19...e5 20 ♖d1 exd4 21 ♖xd4 ♘f8 22 ♖ad1 ♖xd4 23 ♖xd4 ♘e6 24 ♖d7 ♖d8 25 ♕d2 ♖xd7 26 ♕xd7 c5 27 ♕xb7 ♗xb7 28 ♘e5 ♗xg2 29 ♔xg2 ♔f8 30 f4 ♔e7 31 e4 f6 32 ♘f3 g5 33 fxg5 ♘xg5 34 ♘d2

White must be careful here, as 34 ♘xg5? fxg5 would lead to a king and pawn endgame in which Black could create an outside passed pawn on the queenside.

34...♔d6 35 ♔f2 ♘e6 36 ♔e3 ♘d4 37 ♔d3 ♘c6 38 ♔e3 ♘d4 39 ♔d3 ♔e5 40 b3 ♘c6 41 a4 ♔d6 42 axb5 axb5 43 h3 ♘d4 44 ♔e3 h5?!

After this White equalizes. 44...♔e5 still leaves him with some work to do to make a draw.

45 ♔f4 ♔e6 46 h4 ♘e2+ 47 ♔f3 ♘d4+ 48 ♔f4 ½-½

Summary

Although the lines in this section may not have as much bite as 10 ♗d2 at super-GM level, White should carefully consider the advantages offered by their relative rarity. Players at every level forget what to do against unfashionable lines, and as there are fewer games played, they require less maintenance.

Chapter Three

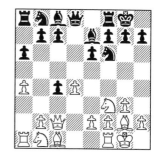

Main Line with 8 a4

1 d4 ♘f6 2 c4 e6 3 g3 d5 4 ♗g2 ♗e7 5 ♘f3 0-0 6 0-0 dxc4 7 ♕c2 a6 8 a4

The 8 a4 variation is the workhorse of many players who play the Catalan for a living. White keeps his opponent cramped by preventing him from gaining space on the queenside with ...b7-b5. The drawback is that it creates a weakness on b4. White's usual plan in this line is to build a broad pawn centre with e2-e4, with the goal of either breaking through in the centre or alternatively gradually advancing on the kingside.

In Romanishin-Papp (Game 9) we see a leading exponent of 8 a4 plying his trade. Black plays the theoretically approved 8...♗d7 and the game follows theoretical lines for some time. Then on move 17 Romanishin improves on previous play to keep some pressure on his opponent, and the game turns in his favour with surprising rapidity.

Besides Romanishin's choice of 10 ♗g5 White can also play 10 ♗f4. Inarkiev-Jakovenko (Game 10) is an interesting example of this, with White finding an interesting positional exchange sacrifice that led to a tough and interesting struggle. Certainly this provides food for thought.

In Banas-Kujala (Game 11) Black plays the less common 8...♘c6, but in the endgame that soon arose Black was somewhat cramped. He certainly doesn't need to lose as rapidly as he did, but it's fair to say that the position isn't easy for Black.

The move 8...c5 has enjoyed a pretty good theoretical reputation, but Granda Zuniga-Rowson (Game 12) poses quite serious questions for Black. Granda's 10 ♗e3 is actually the first thing that *Fritz 11* thinks of, which may provide a clue about its origins. I don't really see how Black can equalize after this move.

1 d4 ♘f6 2 ♘f3 e6 3 g3 d5 4 ♗g2 ♗e7 5 c4 0-0 6 0-0 dxc4 7 ♕c2 a6 8 a4 ♗d7

This is thought to be the best move, though Black does have major alternatives in 8...♘c6 and 8...c5 (see Games 11 and 12).

9 ♕xc4 ♗c6 10 ♗g5

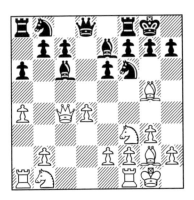

10 ♗f4 and 10 ♘c3 are featured in the next game.

10...♗d5

Probably the best, but not the only move.

a) 10...♘bd7 11 ♘c3 ♘d5 12 ♗xe7 ♕xe7 13 ♘xd5 ♗xd5 is an interesting pawn sacrifice, but it seems inadequate for equality after 14 ♕xc7 ♖ac8 15 ♕f4 ♕b4 16 e4 ♗c4 17 ♖fc1 ♕xb2 18 ♖ab1! (18 ♕d2 ♕xd2 19 ♘xd2 ♗d3 saw Black equalize in N.Davies-O.Korneev, Hamburg 1993) 18...♕a3 19 ♖xb7 ♕xa4 20 h4 ♗b5 21 ♖xc8 ♖xc8 22 ♘e5 ♘xe5 23 ♕xe5, which left Black in a difficult

position in Av.Grigorian-G.Kjartansson, World Junior Ch., Yerevan 2006. The exposure of his king and White's potentially strong d-pawn outweighs the passed a-pawn.

b) 10...a5 11 ♘c3 ♘a6 leaves Black with a solid but cramped position after 12 ♗xf6 ♗xf6 13 e4, for example 13...♘b4 14 ♖fd1 b6 (14...g6 15 ♖ac1 ♗g7 16 d5 exd5 17 exd5 ♗d7 18 ♘d4 ♕c8 19 b3 c6 20 d6 was better for White in B.Gelfand-P.Svidler, FIDE World Ch., Moscow 2001) 15 ♖d2 (other moves have been tried here, for instance 15 ♖ac1 ♗b7 16 ♕e2 g6 17 ♕e3 ♗g7 18 ♘b5 c6 19 ♘a3 ♕b8 20 ♘c4 ♗a6 21 b3 was interesting in O.Romanishin-C.Wilhelmi, Bled 1999) 15...♗b7 16 ♕e2 g6 (16...♗a6 17 ♕e3 c6 18 h4 ♕c7 19 ♖c1 ♖ad8 20 e5! ♗e7 21 ♘g5 was promising for White in A.Karpov-G.Milos, Bali 2000) 17 ♕e3 ♕e7 18 h4 ♖ad8 19 ♖ad1 c5 20 e5 ♗g7 21 dxc5 ♗xf3 22 ♖xd8 ♖xd8 23 ♖xd8+ ♕xd8 24 ♗xf3 bxc5 25 ♕xc5 ♘d3 26 ♕d6 ♗f6! saw Black hold equality in O.Romanishin-Kir.Georgiev, European Ch., Ohrid 2001.

11 ♕d3

11 ♕c2 inhibits Black's ...c7-c5 but then 11...♗e4 leaves White with only passive queen moves: 12 ♕c1 (12 ♕d1 doesn't offer much either, for example 12...c5 13 dxc5 ♗xc5 14 ♕xd8 ♖xd8 15 ♘bd2 ♗c6 16 ♘b3 ♘bd7! was fine for Black at this stage in V.Kramnik-B.Gelfand, Astana 2001) 12...h6 13 ♗xf6 (13 ♗f4 ♘c6 14 ♖d1 ♘d5 15 ♘c3 ♘xc3 16 bxc3 ♘a5 gave Black good counterplay in E.Gleizerov-G.Tunik, St Peters-

burg 2003) 13...♗xf6 14 ♘c3 ♗xf3 15 ♗xf3 c6 16 e3 a5 17 ♘e4 ♘a6 gave Black a very solid position in Z.Ilincic-B.Abramovic, Serbian Team Ch. 2003.

11...c5

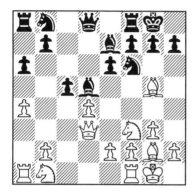

Eliminating White's central pawn majority makes him reliant on piece play alone to demonstrate an initiative.

After 11...♗e4 White has an interesting possibility in 12 ♕e3!? (rather than 12 ♕d1 as in the previous note), for example 12...♗c6 13 ♘c3 ♘bd7 14 ♕d3 ♗b4 (14...♖b8 15 ♕c2 b5 16 axb5 axb5 17 ♘e5 ♗xg2 18 ♔xg2 ♘xe5 19 dxe5 ♘d5 20 ♗xe7 ♕xe7 21 ♘e4 gave White an edge in V.Akopian-E.Ghaem Maghami, World Team Ch., Yerevan 2001; 14...h6 15 ♗xf6 ♘xf6 16 e4 b6 17 ♖fd1 ♗b7 18 ♕e2 ♖e8 19 ♘e1 c6 20 ♖ac1 ♖c8 21 h4 gave White the better game because of his space in O.Romanishin-A.Moiseenko, Ukrainian Team Ch. 2004) 15 ♖fe1 h6 (15...♗xf3 16 ♕xf3 c6 17 ♖ed1 ♕a5 18 h4! h6 19 ♗d2 e5 20 ♗e1 ♖fe8 21 e3 ♖ad8 22 ♕f5 exd4 23 ♕xa5 ♗xa5 24 ♖xd4 was marginally more promising for White because of his bishop pair in

A.Beliavsky-Z.Almasi, Ubeda 1997) 16 ♗f4 ♖c8 17 ♕c2 b6 18 e4 ♗b7 19 ♖ad1 ♖e8 20 ♘e5 ♘xe5 21 ♗xe5 ♘d7 22 ♗f4 ♕e7 23 ♖e2 c5 24 d5!? (after 24 ♖ed2 cxd4 25 ♖xd4 ♘f6 26 ♗d6 ♗xd6 27 ♖xd6 b5 equalized for Black in A.Yusupov-L.Portisch, Linares 1989) 24...e5 25 ♗e3 ♕d6 26 ♗h3 ♖c7 was A.Khalifman-J.Lautier, Biel Interzonal 1993, and now besides the 27 ♘b1 that was played, White might well have considered 27 f4!?.

12 ♘c3

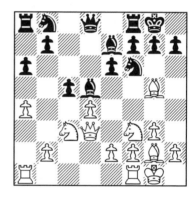

12...♗c6

Giving up the light-squared bishop with 12...cxd4 seems less good. For example, A.Karpov-A.Beliavsky, Linares 1994, continued 13 ♘xd5 ♕xd5 (13...♘xd5 14 ♗xe7 ♕xe7 15 ♘xd4 ♘c6 was R.Hübner-A.Karpov, Tilburg 1979; evidently Karpov felt he preferred White in this line, and indeed White has an edge after either 16 ♖ac1 or 16 ♗xd5; Hübner's choice of 16 ♘xc6 looks less good because it gave Black the possibility of counterplay along the b-file) 14 h4! ♘bd7 (14...♘c6 is strongly met by 15 ♗xf6 ♗xf6 16 ♘g5 ♕f5 17

♗e4 ♕a5 18 ♗xc6 ♗xg5 19 ♗xb7 ♖a7 20 ♗e4, winning a pawn) 15 ♘xd4 ♕d6 16 ♖fd1 ♘c5 17 ♕c4 ♖fd8 18 b4! ♘xa4 (or 18...♘ce4 19 ♗xf6 ♘xf6 20 ♗xb7 ♖ab8 21 ♕xa6 ♕xb4 22 ♘b5) 19 ♕b3! ♕b6 (if 19...♕xb4 20 ♕xb4 ♗xb4 21 ♖xa4 ♗c3 22 ♖c4 ♗b2 23 ♖d2 leaves White a piece up) 20 e3 1-0, as the knight on a4 is lost.

13 ♖fd1 cxd4 14 ♘xd4 ♗xg2 15 ♔xg2

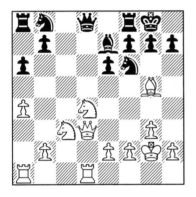

15...♘bd7

This natural move may not be the best. Another and perhaps superior possibility is 15...♕a5, for example 16 ♗xf6 (16 ♘e4 ♘bd7 17 ♕b3 ♘c5 18 ♘xc5 ♕xc5 19 h4 ♖fd8 20 ♖ac1 ♕d5+ 21 ♕xd5 ♖xd5 22 e4 ♖dd8 23 ♔f3 ♖ac8 24 ♖xc8 ½-½ was O.Romanishin-S.Melia, Athens 2008) 16...♗xf6 17 ♘e4 ♗xd4 18 ♕xd4 ♘c6 19 ♕c5 ♖ac8 20 ♕xa5 ♘xa5 21 ♘d6 (21 ♖ac1 also gave White very little in L.Aronian-R.Kasimdzhanov, Turin Olympiad 2006) 21...♖c2 22 b4 was V.Tukmakov-A.Beliavsky, Portoroz 1996, and now according to Tukmakov Black can equalize with 22...♘c6! (22...♘c4? 23 ♘xb7 ♖xe2 24 ♘c5! was good for White in the game)

23 b5 ♘a5 24 ♘xb7!? ♘xb7 25 bxa6 ♘a5! 26 ♖ab1 ♖c6 27 a7 ♖a6 28 ♖b8 ♘c6! 29 ♖d6 ♖xa7 with a drawn endgame.

Instead, 15...h6 loses time, for example 16 ♗xf6 ♗xf6 17 ♘e4 ♗xd4 18 ♕xd4 ♕xd4 19 ♖xd4 ♘c6 20 ♖d7 ♖ab8 21 ♘c5 left Black under pressure in Z.Kozul-P.Nikolic, Sarajevo 1998.

16 ♕f3

This is probably the best here, simply hitting the b7-pawn. Of the other moves to have been tried for White, 16 e4 ♕a5 17 ♗d2 ♘e5 18 ♕e2 ♕c5 19 ♗f4 ♖fd8 20 ♘f3 ♘c6 left Black very comfortably placed in V.Bogdanovski-C.Bauer, European Team Ch., Batumi 1999; while 16 f4?! is a bit loose, and after 16...♖c8 17 e4 h6 18 ♗h4 ♕b6 Black was already doing well in Z.Kozul-A.Beliavsky, Portoroz 1999.

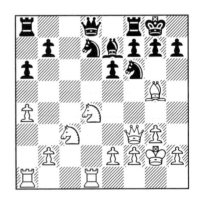

16...♕b8

16...♕b6 can be answered by 17 a5! because 17...♕xb2 18 ♖db1 wins the queen.

17 ♗f4!

Improving on G.Kaidanov-A.Onischuk, US Ch., Stillwater 2007, which went 17 ♘b3 ♘e5 18 ♕f4 h6 19 ♗xf6 ♗xf6 20 ♘e4 ♗e7 21 a5 ♖c8 22 ♖ac1 ♖xc1 23 ♖xc1 ♘c6 24 ♖d1 ♕xf4 25 gxf4 ♖d8 with equality.

17...♕a7 18 e4 g6?!

This isn't good, but White has the initiative in any case. For example 18...♗b4 is good for White after the simple 19 ♘de2, and he might also consider 19 e5!?.

19 e5 ♘h5 20 ♘f5! ♘xf4+ 21 gxf4 gxf5?!

21...exf5 would have been better, though White is still in command after 22 ♖xd7.

22 ♖xd7 ♕c5 23 ♖xb7 ♗h4 24 ♘e2

24 ♖f1 intending 25 ♔h3 looks even stronger, as then White might get to mobilize down the g-file.

24...♖ab8?

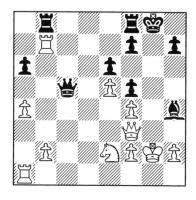

The losing move. 24...♖a7 would have been much more tenacious, though White is still a good pawn up.

25 ♖c1 ♕a5 26 ♔h3 ♖xb7 27 ♕xb7 ♔h8

The horrible truth dawns on Black: he is unable to save his bishop, as 27...♗xf2 28 ♕g2+ picks it up, or if 27...♕d8 28 ♕g2+ ♔h8 29 ♖g1 ♖g8 30

♕xg8+ ♕xg8 31 ♖xg8+ ♔xg8 32 ♔xh4 etc; while 27...♗d8 28 ♕g2+ ♔h8 29 ♖g1 forces mate.

28 ♔xh4 ♕d8+ 29 ♔h3 ♖g8 30 ♘g3 ♕d2 31 ♖c8 ♕xf2 32 ♕xf7! 1-0

If 32...♖xc8 33 ♕f6+ ♔g8 34 ♕xe6+ wins back the rook with interest.

Game 10
E.Inarkiev-D.Jakovenko
World Rapid Cup, Odessa 2008

---

1 d4 d5 2 ♘f3 ♘f6 3 c4 e6 4 g3 ♗e7 5 ♗g2 0-0 6 0-0 dxc4 7 ♕c2 a6 8 a4 ♗d7 9 ♕xc4 ♗c6 10 ♗f4

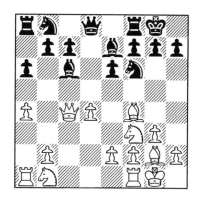

Compared with 10 ♗g5, putting the bishop on f4 is more likely to keep pieces on, but it doesn't threaten the idea of ♗xf6 followed by a later e2-e4.

One other possibility is the natural 10 ♘c3, though this has the drawback of allowing 10...b5!?, for example 11 ♕d3 (11 axb5?? axb5 threatens both the queen and the rook on a1) 11...b4 12 ♘b1 ♗e4 13 ♕d1 c5 14 ♘bd2 ♗d5 15 dxc5 (15 ♘e5 ♗xg2 16 ♔xg2 ♕xd4 17 ♘dc4 ♕e4+ 18 f3 ♕b7 19 ♗g5 gave

White compensation for the pawn because of his hold on the light squares, but this was barely enough in G.Gajewski-M.Mchedlishvili, Polanica Zdroj 2008) 15...♘bd7 16 ♘b3 (16 c6 ♗xc6 17 ♘c4 ♗d5 18 ♘e3 ♗e4 19 ♘d4 ♖c8 20 ♗xe4 ♘xe4 21 f3 ♘ef6 was fine for Black in E.Mochalov-E.Ubilava, Krasnodar 1980) 16...♖c8 17 ♗e3 ♘xc5 18 ♗xc5 ♗xc5 19 ♘e5 ♕d6 20 ♘xc5 ♕xe5 21 ♘d3 ½-½ A.Beliavsky-J.Polgar, Madrid 1997.

10...a5 11 ♘c3 ♘a6 12 ♖ae1

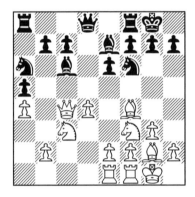

Black's powerful grip on b4 virtually rules out any gains by White on the queenside, so he'll need to operate in the centre and on the kingside. This last move intends to gain space with e2-e4, and by playing the queen's rook to this square (rather than 12 ♖fe1) a possible ...♘a6-b4 won't threaten ...♘b4-c2.

12...♗d5

12...♗d6 13 ♗g5 h6 14 ♗xf6 ♕xf6 15 e4 e5 was T.Vasilevich-Hou Yifan, Beijing (rapid) 2008, and now 16 ♘d5 (rather than 16 ♘b5) 16...♕e6 17 dxe5 ♗xe5 18 ♘xe5 ♕xe5 19 f4 would have

been interesting, keeping a slight pull.

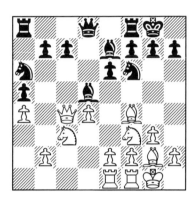

13 ♘xd5!?

A new idea from Inarkiev which involves the sacrifice of the exchange. Certainly it enlivens a position which had previously seemed rather dull, but would he have played this way in a game with a longer time limit? Instead:

a) 13 ♕d3 ♘b4 14 ♕b1 c5 15 dxc5 ♗xc5 16 ♘xd5 ♘bxd5 17 ♘e5 ♘xf4 18 gxf4 ♕b6 was very comfortable for Black in V.Tkachiev-B.Gelfand, Cap d'Agde (rapid) 2002.

b) 13 ♕b5 is probably best met by 13...♗c6 (13...♗b4 14 ♗g5 ♗c6 15 ♕c4 h6 16 ♗xf6 ♕xf6 17 e4 ♖fd8 18 ♔h1 ♗e8 19 ♖d1 ♖ac8 20 h3 ♕e7 21 ♖fe1 ♘b8 22 ♘e5 ♘c6 23 ♘xc6 ♗xc6 24 ♔h2 ♕d7 25 b3 b6 26 ♖e3 ♗xc3 27 ♕xc3 ♗b7 28 h4 c5 29 d5 exd5 30 exd5 was good for White E.Bareev-N.Short, Geneva rapid 1996), when 14 ♕b3 (14 ♕xa5!? is interesting, despite the fact that White's queen is precariously placed, but Black seems to be able to at least equalize with 14...♘c5 15 ♕xc7 ♘xa4, for example 16 ♕xd8 ♖fxd8 17 ♖a1 ♘xc3 18 bxc3 ♘d5 19 ♗d2 ♗b5 etc)

14...♞b4 15 ♖c1 ½-½ represented a moral victory for Black in V.Tkachiev-A.Delchev, European Ch., Istanbul 2003.

13...exd5 14 ♕b5 ♖b8 15 ♕xa5 ♝b4

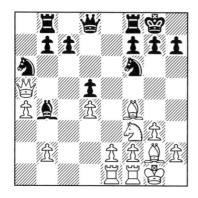

This 'wins' the exchange, but White has long-term compensation because of his two bishops and space.

16 ♕b5 c6 17 ♕d3 ♝xe1 18 ♞xe1 ♖a8 19 ♕b3 b5 20 axb5 ♕b6 21 ♞d3 ♕xb5 22 ♕xb5 cxb5 23 ♝e5 ♖fd8 24 ♖c1 ♞e4 25 ♝h3 ♞g5 26 ♝g4 ♞e6 27 ♖c6 ♞b8 28 ♖b6 ♞d7 29 ♖b7?!

Inarkiev is chancing his arm a bit here. 29 ♖xb5 ♞xe5 30 dxe5 ♖ab8 31 ♖a5 ♖a8 could have produced a draw by repetition.

29...♞xe5 30 ♞xe5 ♞xd4 31 ♞xf7 ♖f8 32 ♞d6 ♖ab8 33 ♖e7 ♖b6 34 ♞e8 ♖f7 35 ♖e5 ♖f8 36 ♞c7 ♖d6?!

Instead 36...♖g6 first was probably better.

37 ♞xd5 ♞c6 38 ♖e3 h5 39 ♝e6+ ♔h7 40 ♞f4 ♞d4 41 ♝a2 b4 42 h4 ♞f5 43 ♖e5 g6 44 ♝d5 ♞xh4 45 ♝e4 ♞f5 46 ♞xh5 ♖d2 47 ♞f4 ♖xb2 48 g4 ♞h4

It might have been better just to sacrifice the g6-pawn with 48...♞d4, for example 49 ♞xg6 ♖f7 50 ♞f4+ ♔g7.

49 e3 b3?!

Instead of this Black should have played 49...♔h6, after which 50 g5+ ♔h7 gives him a retreat square for his knight on f5.

50 g5?

50 ♔h2!, threatening 51 ♔g3, seems to leave Black with no good way to save the knight on h4.

50...♖xf4

Probably not necessary, but Black has seen a way to ease the pressure and make a draw.

51 exf4 ♖d2 52 ♖e7+ ♔h8 53 ♖b7 b2 54 ♔h2 ♖xf2+ 55 ♔g3 ♖e2 56 ♖b8+ ♔g7 57 ♖b7+ ♔h8 58 ♝d3 ♖e3+ 59 ♔xh4 ♖xd3 60 ♖xb2 ♖d4 61 ♔g4 ♔g7 62 ♖b7+ ♔g8 63 ♔f3 ♖a4 64 ♖d7 ♖b4 65 ♔e3 ♖a4 66 ♖d4 ♖a1 67 ♖d7 ♖a4

This endgame is now a standard book draw.

68 ♖c7 ♖b4 69 ♖a7 ♖c4 70 ♖d7 ♖a4 71 ♖d4 ♖a1 72 ♖d8+ ♔f7 73 ♖d7+ ♔e6 74 ♖g7 ♔f5 75 ♖f7+ ♔g4 76 ♖f6 ♖a4 77 ♖f7 ♖b4 78 ♖f8 ♖a4 79 ♖f6 ♖b4 80 ♖xg6 ♖xf4 81 ♖g8 ♖a4 82 g6 ♔g5 83 g7 ♔g6 84 ♖b8 ♔xg7 85 ♖b7+ ½-½

1 c4 e6 2 ♘f3 d5 3 g3 ♘f6 4 ♗g2 ♗e7 5 0-0 0-0 6 d4 dxc4 7 ♕c2 a6 8 a4 ♘c6

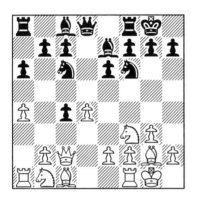

This is one of two less fashionable ways of playing it for Black, the other one being 8...c5 (see the next game). Black gets active piece play but suffers from a lack of space.

9 ♕xc4 ♕d5

Black has an alternative in 9...♘b4, though this seems better for White after 10 ♘c3 (10 a5? b5! 11 axb6 cxb6 12 ♗d2 a5 13 ♗xb4 ♗xb4 14 ♘e5 ♗a6 was good for Black in R.Cifuentes Parada-A.Rivera, Cienfuegos 1996) 10...b5 11 ♕b3 bxa4 12 ♘xa4 ♗b7 13 ♘c5! (13 ♗g5 ♖b8 14 ♗xf6 ♗xf6 15 ♖fd1 ♗e4 was fine for Black in R.Hübner-M.Chandler, German League 1994) 13...♗xf3 (13...♗xc5 14 dxc5 ♖b8 15 ♕xb4 ♗xf3 16 ♕c4 ♗xg2 17 ♔xg2 is also better for White because of the weakness of Black's a-pawn) 14 ♗xf3

♖b8 15 ♕c4 and White has an edge because of his bishop pair and the weaknesses in Black's pawn structure.

10 ♘bd2!

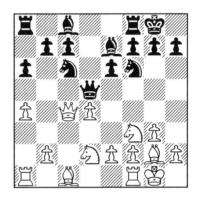

Black is invited to exchange queens but in doing so he will bring White's knight to a better square.

10...♖d8 11 e3 ♕xc4

The attempt to keep queens on the board with 11...♕h5 is risky, for example 12 e4! ♗d7 13 b3 b5 14 ♕c3 ♗e8 15 axb5 axb5 16 ♖xa8 ♖xa8 17 ♗b2 left the queen doing nothing on the kingside in V.Kramnik-J.Piket, Dortmund 1995.

12 ♘xc4 ♗d7

In Z.Doda-E.Geller, European Team Ch., Bath 1973, Black played the superior 12...a5, but was still slightly worse after 13 b3 ♘b4 14 ♖d1 c6 15 ♗b2 ♗d7 16 ♘b6 ♖a6 17 ♘xd7 ♘xd7. Admittedly this isn't easy for White to win, but Black would be under long-term pressure because of the danger of the position opening up for the white bishops.

13 ♘fe5!

In O.Panno-J.Gomez Baillo, Santiago 1987, White played 13 ♗d2 and after 13...♘b4 14 ♘fe5 ♘fd5 could have

kept a clear edge with 15 ♘xd7 followed by a4-a5. But the text is simple
and very strong.

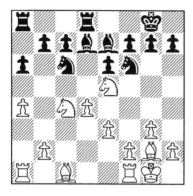

13...♘xe5 14 ♘xe5 ♗c8?!

14...♖ab8 is better, as after 15
♘xd7?! ♖xd7 16 ♗d2 Black can free
himself with 16...c5, but 15 ♗d2 ♗e8 16
b4 leaves White with a clear advantage.

15 ♗d2 a5?

The a5-pawn is just a target now.
Here 15...♘d7 was better, though
White has all the play after 16 ♘c4 c5?!
17 ♗a5 ♖f8 18 ♖fc1 with a huge lead in
development and likely penetration of
a rook to the seventh.

16 ♖fc1 c6 17 ♘c4!

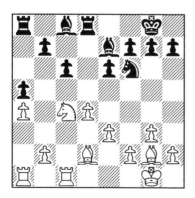

**17...♗b4 18 ♗xb4 axb4 19 ♘b6 ♖a6 20
♘xc8 ♖xc8 21 ♖c4 ♖b6**

The b-pawn is doomed, for example
21...b3 22 ♖c3 b5 23 a5 ♘d5 24 ♖xb3
♖ca8 25 ♗xd5 exd5 26 ♖c3 etc.

22 a5 ♖b5

Or 22...♖a8 23 ♖a4 etc.

**23 ♖a4 ♖a8 24 ♖cxb4 ♖xb4 25 ♖xb4
♖xa5 26 ♗xc6! 1-0**

The sting in the tail, winning not
one pawn but two.

Game 12
J.Granda Zuniga-J.Rowson
Turin Olympiad 2006

**1 ♘f3 d5 2 c4 e6 3 g3 ♘f6 4 ♗g2 ♗e7 5
0-0 0-0 6 d4 dxc4 7 ♕c2 a6 8 a4 c5**

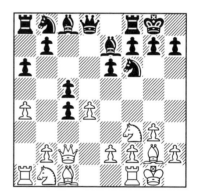

A simple and direct attempt to
equalize in the centre. By exchanging
the pawns on d4 and c5, Black hopes to
free himself from the sort of problems
he often gets along the c-file.

9 dxc5 ♘c6 10 ♗e3!?

A very interesting new move from
Granda. At first sight it looks as if it
makes it easier for Black to gain active

piece play, but closer examination shows that this is not the case.

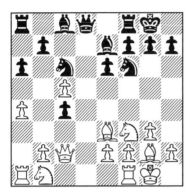

Other moves offer White little, for example 10 ♗f4 ♗xc5 11 ♘bd2 c3 12 ♕xc3 ♕e7 13 ♘c4 ♘d5 14 ♕b3 ♘xf4 15 gxf4 ♗d7 16 ♖fd1 ♖fd8 17 e3 ♖ab8 was fine for Black in O.Cvitan-D.Ippolito, Groningen 1997; as was 10 ♕xc4 e5 11 ♗e3 ♗e6 12 ♕c1 ♖c8 13 ♖d1 ♕a5 14 ♘g5 ♗g4 15 ♘c3 ♗xc5 16 ♗xc5 ♕xc5 in P.Nikolic-S.Gligoric, Yugoslav Team Ch. 1988.

10...♘d5 11 ♗d2 ♘a5 12 ♘a3 ♘b3

After 12...♗xc5 13 ♘xc4 ♘xc4 14 ♕xc4 b6 White gains time with 15 e4, which proves to be one of the advantages of luring Black's knight to d5.

13 ♖ad1 ♗d7

The critical move, but one which looks good for White. After 13...♗xc5 there is 14 ♗g5 f6 15 ♘xc4 fxg5 16 ♕xb3, while 13...♘xd2 is also better for White after 14 ♘xd2 ♗xc5 15 ♘axc4. This second option may be Black's best chance, but in that case 10 ♗e3 looks like it offers a nice edge.

14 e4 ♗xa4

14...♘xc5 15 exd5 exd5 16 ♖de1

♗xa4 17 ♕b1 leaves Black with three pawns for the piece, but White would be better because of the activity of his forces.

15 exd5 exd5 16 ♘g5!?

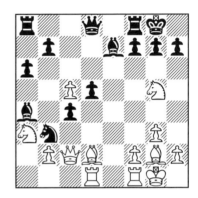

White decides that it's better to keep the initiative in this sharp position. 16 ♖de1 ♘xc5 17 ♕b1 ♗f6 gives Black a lot of play.

16...g6

After 16...♗xg5? 17 ♗xg5 ♕xg5 18 ♖xd5 Black would have trouble rescuing his bishop and knight.

17 ♗b4 ♘xc5 18 ♕e2 ♗xd1

18...♗xg5 19 ♖xd5 ♘d7 20 ♗xf8 ♔xf8 21 ♕xc4 leaves White the exchange up.

19 ♖xd1 ♕c7

19...♗xg5 also leaves Black struggling to save the game after 20 ♖xd5 ♕e8 21 ♕xe8 ♖fxe8 22 ♗xc5 ♗f6 23 ♘xc4 etc.

20 ♖xd5 ♖ad8 21 ♕xc4 ♖xd5 22 ♕xd5

The endgame arising after 22 ♗xd5 ♗xg5 23 ♕xc5 ♕xc5 24 ♗xc5 ♖c8 25 ♗b6 would be difficult for Black.

22...b5 23 ♘c2 ♘a4 24 ♗xe7 ♕xe7 25 h4 ♘xb2

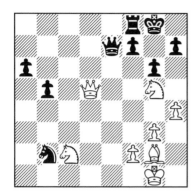 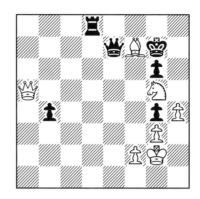

In such a complex position it's very hard to find the best moves. Another possibility was 25...♖d8 26 ♕f3 h6 27 ♘e4 ♘xb2, but then 28 ♕c3 ♘c4 29 ♘f6+ ♔f8 30 ♘g4 keeps the pressure up.

26 ♘e3 ♖d8 27 ♕b3 ♘d3 28 ♗d5 ♘e5 29 ♕c3

After 29 f4 Black hangs on with 29...h6.

29...h6 30 ♘e4 h5 31 ♔g2 b4 32 ♕a1 a5 33 ♕xa5 ♘g4?

This one is definitely wrong, though you can understand Black's eagerness to get rid of one of the knights. 33...♔g7 was better, when there's still everything to play for.

34 ♘xg4 hxg4 35 ♘g5 ♔g7 36 ♗xf7

The fall of the f7-pawn is the beginning of the end.

36...♖d1 37 ♕a8 ♕e1 38 ♕g8+ ♔f6 39 ♕xg6+ ♔e7 40 ♕e6+ ♕xe6 41 ♗xe6 ♖d6 42 ♗xg4 b3 43 ♗f5 ♖d5 44 ♗e4 b2 45 ♘f3 ♖d1 46 g4 ♔d6 47 h5 ♔e6 48 ♔g3 b1♕ 49 ♗xb1 ♖xb1 50 ♘g5+ ♔f6 51 ♔f4 ♖b4+ 52 ♘e4+ ♔g7 53 g5 ♖a4 54 f3 ♖b4 55 ♔g3 ♖b5 56 f4 ♖a5 57 ♔g4 ♖d5 58 f5 ♖d1 59 f6+ ♔f7 60 g6+ ♔e6 61 ♔g5 ♖g1+ 62 ♔h6 ♖g4 63 ♔g7 1-0

A great fighting game of theoretical interest.

Summary

White has reasonable chances of keeping a little something with 8 a4, and the fact that these lines are dependent more on understanding than specific moves makes them suitable for time-challenged competitors.

Chapter Four

Main Line with 7 ♘e5 and Others

1 d4 ♘f6 2 c4 e6 3 g3 d5 4 ♗g2 ♗e7 5 ♘f3 0-0 6 0-0 dxc4

Besides 7 ♕c2, White has a bevy of sharp but little played alternatives. If nothing else these should discourage Black from playing the main line as he really needs to know what he's doing.

7 ♘e5 used to be one of the main lines of the Catalan before Black discovered 7...♘c6. He certainly gets free play for his pieces after this, though there is still some discussion about whether it compensates him for his weaknesses and/or the sacrifice of a pawn.

White's initial choice is between 8 ♘xc6 (Andreikin-Karthikeyan, Game 13) and 8 ♗xc6 (Meier-Zhigalko, Game 14), the former going for a structural advantage and the latter a material one. Black seems to be okay in both cases, but there is a requirement to know quite a bit of theory. And this may be seen as a generic challenge in-

herent in playing 6...dxc4.

Moving onto 7 ♘a3, the critical line arises if Black just holds onto his extra pawn with 7...♗xa3 8 bxa3 b5 (Krasenkow-Arbakov, Game 15), though he certainly has to defend against a powerful initiative. The more solid option is 8...♗d7, which isn't at all easy to break down. In (Mikhalevski-Huzman, Game 16) White made it interesting with a positional exchange sacrifice (15 ♖xc6), which reminded me a bit of Inarkiev-Jakovenko (Game 10) from the previous chapter.

The 7 ♘c3 line can be reached via several different move orders, such as 1 d4 d5 2 c4 e6 3 ♘c3 ♗e7 4 ♘f3 ♘f6 5 g3 0-0 6 ♗g2 dxc4 7 0-0. Games in which the Catalan has been introduced in this way are in fact scattered throughout the book; for example, the Closed Variation with 6...♘bd7 can transpose into 6...dxc4 7 ♘c3 ♘bd7 after 7 ♘c3 dxc4. Unfortunately, there was no reasonable way to bring them into the same chapter without creating even more confusion, but hopefully I've provided enough guidance on the matter.

Here we will deal mainly with 7 ♘c3 ♘c6, and now White playing either 8 e3 (Wojtaszek-Peterson, Game 17) or 8 e4 (Antic-Van Riemsdijk, Game 18). As with so many of the 6...dxc4 lines Black should be fine with accurate play, but the problem he faces is in just knowing all these variations.

Game 13
D.Andreikin-P.Karthikeyan
World Junior Championship,
Gaziantep 2008

1 ♘f3 ♘f6 2 c4 e6 3 g3 d5 4 ♗g2 ♗e7 5 0-0 0-0 6 d4 dxc4 7 ♘e5 ♘c6!

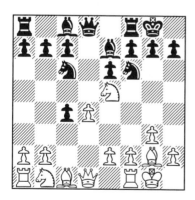

This excellent move turned 7 ♘e5 into a relative backwater. Black allows his pawn structure to be wrecked, but gains a lot of time for development. Prior to the discovery of this move it

was thought that Black should play 7...c5, but that gives White a nice endgame after 8 dxc5 ♗xc5 9 ♕xd8 ♖xd8 10 ♘c3, for example 10...♗e7 11 ♗f4 ♘d5 12 ♖fd1 g5 13 ♗d2 ♘b6 14 a4 ♘8d7 15 ♘xd7 ♘xd7 16 ♗e3 ♘f8 17 a5 a6 18 ♘e4 ♖xd1+ 19 ♖xd1 h6 20 ♘d6 ♗xd6 21 ♖xd6 saw Black in serious trouble in R.Buhmann-I.Vasilevich, Zvenigorod 2008.

8 ♘xc6

For 8 ♗xc6 see the next game.

8...bxc6 9 ♘a3 ♗xa3 10 bxa3 ♘d5 11 ♕a4 ♘b6 12 ♕a5

The best attempt. After 12 ♕xc6 ♖b8 13 ♗f4 ♗b7 14 ♕xc7 ♗xg2 15 ♔xg2 ♕xd4 16 ♕xa7 (16 ♕xb8 ♖xb8 17 ♗xb8 ♘d5 18 e3 ♕e4+ 19 ♔g1 a6 left Black's queen and knight very active in O.Ruest-C.Thibaud, French Team Ch. 2004) 16...e5 17 ♗e3 ♕e4+ 18 ♔g1 ♘d5 19 ♖fd1 ♖fc8 20 ♖ac1 h5 21 ♗g5 f6 22 ♕a5 ♘e7 23 ♗e3 ♘f5 24 ♕d5+ ♕xd5 25 ♖xd5 ♘xe3 26 fxe3 ♖b2 led to a draw in J.Sunye Neto-R.Vaganian, Yerevan 1980.

12...♗b7?!

Defending c6 but going very passive. The main line is 12...♖b8, which also looks okay for Black, for example 13 ♖d1 ♘d5 14 a4 ♕d6 15 e4 ♕b4 16 ♗d2 c3 17 ♕xb4 ♖xb4 18 ♗e1 ♘b6 19 ♗xc3 ♖xa4 20 a3 ♖d8 21 ♗b4 ♗a6 and Black had equalized in A.Iljushin-P.Kiriakov, Maikop 1998.

13 ♖d1 ♕c8 14 e4 f5 15 f3!

Correctly depriving Black of the d5-square. Now White is clearly better.

15...♗a6 16 a4 ♗b7 17 ♗f4 ♖f7 18 ♖ab1 h6 19 ♗e5 ♔h7 20 ♖e1 g6?!

Creating further weaknesses. 20...♕f8 is preferable, though this position is still very nice for White.

21 ♖e3 ♕d7 22 f4 ♕c8 23 g4!?

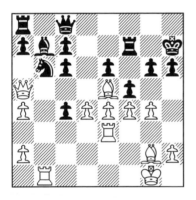

23...fxe4?

Letting White's pieces into the attack. 23...fxg4 was a better move, though it still looks very unpleasant for Black. A sample line is 24 h3 gxh3 25 ♖xh3 ♘d7 26 ♔f2 ♘xe5? 27 ♖xh6+! ♔xh6 28 ♕xe5 with a winning attack.

24 ♖h3 ♕f8?

But if 24...c5 25 ♕e1 ♕f8 26 ♗xe4 ♗xe4 27 ♕xe4 threatening 28 g5 h5 29 ♖xh5+ etc.

25 ♗xe4 ♖xf4

Desperation.

26 ♗xf4 ♕xf4 27 ♕h5! 1-0

Game 14
G.Meier-S.Zhigalko
Martuni 2008

---

1 d4 ♘f6 2 c4 e6 3 g3 d5 4 ♘f3 ♗e7 5 ♗g2 0-0 6 0-0 dxc4 7 ♘e5 ♘c6 8 ♗xc6

White's Catalan bishop is not to be given up lightly. In the present situation White gains time and eliminates Black's dark-squared bishop.

8...bxc6 9 ♘xc6 ♕e8 10 ♘xe7+ ♕xe7 11 ♕a4

11 ♘a3 e5 12 dxe5 ♕xe5 13 ♘xc4 ♕h5 gives Black dangerous attacking chances on the kingside, while 11 b3 is well met by 11...cxb3 12 ♗a3 ♕d7.

11...c5

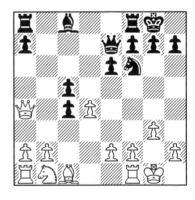

This looks like the soundest move, trying to eliminate his weak c7-pawn. But perhaps Black should consider the alternatives:

a) Geller preferred 11...e5!? and maybe he was right, for example 12 dxe5 (12 ♕xc4 exd4 gave Black a tremendous game in E.Garcia Gonzales-E.Geller, Bogota 1978) 12...♕xe5 13 ♕xc4 ♗e6

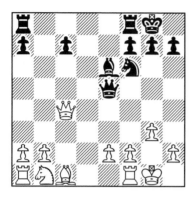

14 ♕d3 (14 ♕c2 ♗f5 15 ♕c4 ♗e6 16 ♕c2 resulted in a draw in N.Kirov-E.Geller, Sochi 1976; while 14 ♕a6 ♗h3 15 ♖e1 ♕d5 16 f3 ♘g4 17 ♘c3 ♕c5+ 18 e3 ♘e5 19 ♕e2 ♖ad8 was good for Black in N.Spiridonov-E.Geller, Novi Sad 1978) 14...♖ad8 15 ♕e3 ♕h5 (15...♕a5 16 ♘c3 ♗h3 17 ♖e1 ♖fe8 18 ♕f3 ♗g4 19 ♕c6 ♖e6 20 ♕b5 ♕xb5 21 ♘xb5 ♖xe2 equalized in P.Maletin-P.Kiriakov, Tomsk 2004) 16 f3 ♗c4! (instead 16...♗h3 17 ♖e1 ♖fe8 18 ♕f2 ♘d5 19 ♗d2 ♕e5 20 ♘c3 ♘b4 21 ♖ed1 ♗f5 22 ♗f4 ♕a5 23 a3 ♘c6 24 ♖ac1 saw White consolidate his extra pawn in J.Ehlvest-D.Sharavdorj, Agoura Hills 2004; and 16...♖fe8 17 ♕g5 ♗c4 18 ♕xh5 ♘xh5 19 ♘c3 ♗xe2 20 ♖f2 ♗a6 21 ♗g5 f6 22 ♗d2 f5 23 ♖c1 h6 24 ♘a4 ♗b5 25 ♘c5 ♖d6 26 ♗a5 left White with a nagging endgame plus in Kir.Georgiev-A.Karpov, Dubai rapid 2002) 17 ♘c3 ♖fe8 18 ♕g5 ♕h3 19 ♗e3 (19 ♖f2 ♗xe2!) 19...♘d5 20 ♗d4 f6 21 ♕c1 ♘xc3 22 ♕xc3 ♗xe2 23 ♖f2 a6 and

Black had equalized in V.Filippov-A.Grischuk, FIDE World Ch., Tripoli 2004.

b) 11...♕d6!? probably deserves more tests, for example 12 ♖d1 ♕a6 13 ♕xa6 ♗xa6 14 ♘c3 ♖ab8 15 e4 was okay for Black in B.Gelfand-A.Shneider, Uzhgorod 1987.

c) 11...a5 12 ♖d1 ♖d8 13 ♗g5 c5 14 dxc5 ♖xd1+ 15 ♕xd1 ♗b7! 16 ♘c3 ♖d8 17 ♕c2 ♕xc5 18 ♗xf6 gxf6 19 ♖d1 ♖xd1+ 20 ♕xd1 gave White an edge because his queen and knight worked well together in Kir.Georgiev-P.H.Nielsen, French Team Ch. 2004.

12 ♕a3

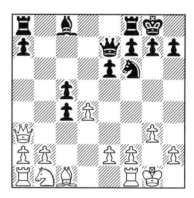

This is more testing than 12 ♕xc4 cxd4 13 ♕xd4 ♖d8 (13...e5 14 ♕h4 ♖b8 15 b3 ♕e6, sidestepping ♗a3 or ♗g5, was also okay for Black in K.Kaiszauri-H.Schussler, Malmö 1979) 14 ♕h4 ♖b8 15 b3 ♗a6 16 ♘c3 ♕c5 17 ♘e4 ♘xe4 18 ♕xe4 ♖b4 19 ♕e3 ♕c2! 20 ♗a3 ♖e4 21 ♖fc1 ♕xe2 ½-½ as in M.Krasenkow-Z.Ribli, German League 1998.

12...♗b7

Black can also unpin the c5-pawn with 12...♕b7, for example 13 ♕xc5 e5

14 罝d1 奧h3 15 d5 罝ac8 16 豐a5 ②e4 17 f3 罝c5 18 豐e1 ②d6 (18...罝xd5?! 19 罝xd5 豐xd5 20 fxe4 豐d4+ 21 e3 豐d3 was B.Gelfand-V.Anand, Monte Carlo rapid 2001, and now 22 ②d2 would have made it difficult for Black to gain compensation for the piece) 19 ②c3 f5 20 奧e3 罝c7 21 豐d2 罝e8 22 曾h1 (22 罝ac1!?) 22...豐c8 23 罝ac1 豐d7 24 b4 cxb3 25 axb3 罝ec8 was C.Bauer-C.Lutz, European Team Ch., Plovdiv 2003. Black had compensation for the pawn, though how much isn't that clear.

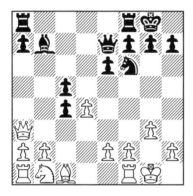

13 ②c3

A sensible new move which seems to make it hard for Black to equalize. After 13 奧g5 罝fc8 14 ②c3 Black can protect his queen with 14...曾f8, when 15 罝fd1 cxd4 16 豐xe7+ 曾xe7 17 罝xd4 e5 was more or less equal in J.Gustafsson-D.Baramidze, German Ch., Osterburg 2006.

13...罝fd8

It makes more sense to play the immediate 13...罝fc8, but then 14 罝d1 makes it difficult for Black. A sample line is 14...曾f8 15 奧e3 ②g4 16 奧f4 e5 17 奧xe5 ②xe5 18 dxe5 豐xe5 19 罝d2 with

a clear advantage for White.

14 豐xc5 豐xc5 15 dxc5 罝dc8 16 奧e3 ②g4 17 罝ad1

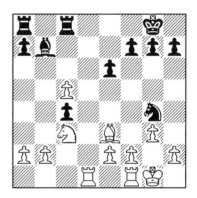

Offering the pawn back to get his rook to the seventh.

17...罝ab8 18 奧f4 e5 19 奧c1 罝xc5 20 f3 ②f6 21 e4 曾f8?!

21...罝c7 is better, though still preferable for White after 22 奧e3 奧c6 23 罝f2.

22 b4!

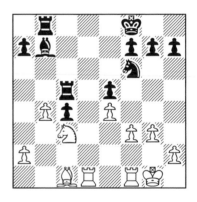

Gaining a further trump in a queenside pawn majority. Black cannot take en passant because of 23 奧a3.

22...罝c6 23 b5 罝e6 24 a4 a6 25 奧a3+ 曾e8 26 a5 ②d7 27 b6 罝c8 28 ②d5

♗xd5 29 exd5 ♖g6 30 f4 c3 31 fxe5 c2
32 ♖c1 ♘xe5 33 ♖fe1 f6 34 ♖xc2!

Using the strength of the b7-pawn to initiate a winning combination.

34...♖xc2 35 b7 ♔d7 36 ♖xe5! ♔c7 37 ♖e7+ 1-0

After 37...♔b8 there is 38 ♗d6+ etc.

Game 15
M.Krasenkow-V.Arbakov
Moscow 1989

---

1 ♘f3 d5 2 d4 ♘f6 3 c4 e6 4 g3 ♗e7 5 ♗g2 0-0 6 0-0 dxc4 7 ♘a3!?

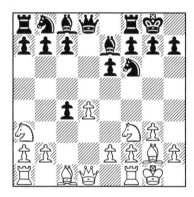

7...♗xa3

Black is really obliged to enter this critical line as quiet play allows White good chances. For example, 7...c5 8 dxc5 ♗xc5 9 ♘xc4 ♘c6 10 a3! a5 11 ♗g5!? h6 12 ♕xd8 ♖xd8 13 ♗xf6 gxf6 14 ♖fd1 ♗d7 15 ♘fd2! was good for White in Z.Kozul-B.Ivanovic, Yugoslav Ch. 1989; while 7...c3 8 bxc3 c5 9 ♘e5 ♘bd7 (9...♘d5 10 ♕b3 cxd4 11 cxd4 ♘c6 12 ♘xc6 bxc6 13 e4 ♘b6 14 ♖d1 is also good for White) 10 ♘ac4 ♘xe5 11 ♘xe5 ♕c7 12 ♕b3 ♖d8 13 ♗f4 ♘h5 14

♗e3 ♘f6 15 ♖fd1 ♘d5 16 ♗d2 left White with much the better game in S.Grabuzov-P.Vavra, Pardubice 1993.

8 bxa3 b5 9 a4 a6

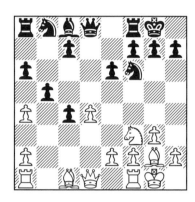

10 ♗a3

In the notes to his game against Kuzmin the future World Champion preferred 10 ♘g5!? c6 (or 10...♘d5 11 ♕c2!) 11 e4 h6 12 e5!, suggesting that White will have plenty of compensation here. Taking this a little further, play might continue 12...♘d5 (12...hxg5 13 ♗xg5 ♘bd7 14 ♗xc6 ♖a7 15 ♕f3 looks very dangerous for Black) 13 ♘e4 ♘d7 14 ♕h5 ♖a7 15 ♗xh6 gxh6 16 ♕xh6 ♖e8 17 ♘d6 with strong pressure for the sacrificed piece. I'm surprised this doesn't seem to have had practical tests.

10...♖e8 11 ♘e5 ♘d5 12 e4 ♘f6

In A.Poluljahov-S.Nikolaev, USSR 1988, Black played 12...♘b6, after which there followed 13 a5 (13 ♕h5!? is also interesting after 13...f6 14 ♘g4 or 14 a5) 13...♘6d7 14 f4 (if 14 ♕h5 ♘xe5! 15 dxe5 ♕d3 and Black can turn the tables by sacrificing his queen after either 16 ♗e7 ♖xe7 17 ♖ad1 c5! 18 ♖xd3

cxd3 or 16 ♗c5 ♘d7 17 ♖ad1 ♘xc5!)
14...♗b7 15 ♕h5 g6 and now, rather
than 16 ♕h6 (after which 16...♘xe5 17
dxe5 ♕d4+ 18 ♔h1 ♗xe4 19 ♖ad1
♗xg2+ 20 ♔xg2 ♕e4+ 21 ♔h3 ♘c6
would have won for Black), White
should have played 16 ♕h3!, when
16...♘xe5 17 dxe5 ♕d4+ 18 ♔h1 ♗xe4
19 ♖ad1 ♕e3! (19...♗xg2+ 20 ♕xg2 ♕a7
21 ♖d2 c6 22 ♖fd1 leaves Black ham-
strung) 20 ♖fe1 ♕xa3 21 ♗xe4 ♖a7 22
♕h4 would give White attacking
chances for the sacrificed pawns,
though whether this is enough remains
a moot point.

13 ♘xf7!?

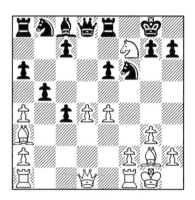

Besides this spectacular piece sacrifice White can play quietly with 13
♖b1.   E.Gleizerov-S.Zhukhovitsky,
USSR 1986, continued 13...♗b7 14 ♖e1
♘c6 15 ♘xc4 ♕xd4 16 ♕c2 (16 ♕xd4!?
♘xd4 17 ♗b2 intending 18 ♘a5 is also
worth considering) 16...♕xc4 (16...♕a7
17 ♘d2 offers White ongoing compensation) 17 ♕xc4 bxc4 18 ♖xb7 and now
18...♘d4 (in the game 18...♘e5?! 19 ♖c1
♖ec8 20 f4 ♘c6 21 ♖bb1 a5 22 ♖xc4 was
better for White) 19 e5 ♘d5 would

have been best with chances for both
sides.

**13...♔xf7 14 e5 ♘d5 15 ♕h5+ ♔g8 16
♗e4 g6 17 ♗xg6 hxg6**

Forced. In the game G.Kuzmin-
V.Anand, Frunze 1987, Black declined
the second sacrifice with 17...♖e7?! 18
♗xe7 ♕xe7, but then 19 ♗xh7+ would
have been good for White after
19...♕xh7 20 ♕e8+ ♔g7 21 ♕xc8 ♕g8 22
♕b7 ♘d7 23 axb5 etc.

18 ♕xg6+ ♔h8 19 ♖fe1

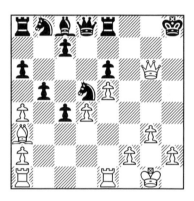

Threatening 20 ♖e4. White can also
play 19 ♖ae1, though this doesn't seem
to alter the outcome after 19...♘c3 20
♖e3 ♗b7 21 ♖xc3 ♘c6, the best being to
deliver perpetual check via 22 ♕h6+ etc.

19...♘c3 20 ♖e3

Threatening to bring the rook to f3
and then f7.

20...♗b7 21 ♖xc3 ♘d7??

This looks natural but it should
lose. The right way to defend is via
21...♘c6, when it seems that White's
best is again to give perpetual check,
starting with 22 ♕h6+.

**22 ♕h6+ ♔g8 23 ♕g6+ ♔h8 24 ♕h6+
♔g8 25 g4!**

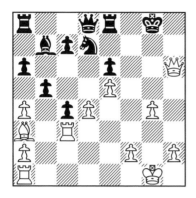

Making room for the rook to come to h3.

25...♖e7 26 ♖h3 ♘f8 27 ♕h8+ ♔f7 28 ♖h6 ♔e8 29 ♖xe6! ♖xe6 30 ♕xf8+ ♔d7 31 ♕f7+ ♖e7

31...♔c8 32 ♕xe6+ would leave White with *four*(!) connected passed pawns on the kingside.

32 e6+ ♔c6 33 ♕f6 ♕d5 34 ♗xe7 ♔b6 35 f3! ♖g8?!

35...♕xf3 was relatively best, though the endgame is lost after 36 ♗c5+ ♔a5 37 ♕xf3 ♗xf3 38 g5 etc.

36 ♗c5+ ♔a5 37 ♕f4

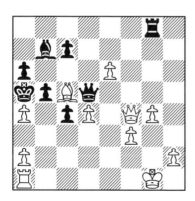

The right idea, but the execution is inaccurate. The correct way to do this is

via 37 ♔f2! ♖xg4 38 e7 ♖g8 39 ♕f4, when 39...c3 40 ♕e3! ♕c4 41 e8♕ wins Black's rook.

37...c3?

Black can still make a fight of it with 37...♕xf3 38 ♕xf3 ♗xf3 39 h3 ♔xa4 as he has his own passed pawns on the queenside.

38 axb5 axb5?

38...♕xf3 is again the best try.

39 a4 ♖c8 40 axb5+ ♔xb5 41 ♖b1+ ♔c4 42 ♕e3 1-0

The threat of ♖b4 mate is a killer.

Game 16
V.Mikhalevski-A.Huzman
Montreal 2008

---

1 d4 ♘f6 2 c4 e6 3 g3 d5 4 ♗g2 ♗e7 5 ♘f3 0-0 6 0-0 dxc4 7 ♘a3 ♗xa3 8 bxa3

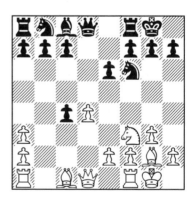

8...♗d7

Black chooses a less ambitious but less weakening approach, aiming for solid development rather than trying to keep his ill-gotten gains. There are a couple of other moves which have similar intent:

a) 8...♘bd7 was tried in N.Hryhorenko-I.Vasilevich, Beijing (blitz) 2008, and now 9 a4 ♘b6 10 ♗a3 ♖e8 11 ♖c1, intending a4-a5 and/or ♘f3-e5, would have recovered the pawn with a good game.

b) 8...♘c6 9 ♗b2 ♖b8 (9...♘d5 10 ♕c2 ♘b6 was M.Krasenkow-O.Nikolenko, USSR 1987, and now 11 e4! ♗d7 12 ♘d2 would have been the simplest, again recovering the pawn with a good game) 10 ♕c2 b5 11 ♖ad1 ♘e7 (11...♗b7?! 12 ♘g5! h6 13 d5 ♘b4 14 axb4 hxg5 15 dxe6 ♕e7 16 exf7+ ♖xf7 17 ♗xb7 ♖xb7 18 ♕g6! gave White a strong initiative in I.Glek-J.Klovans, Tashkent 1987) 12 e4 ♗b7 13 ♖fe1 ♗xe4?! (13...♘g6 is better, with complex play) 14 ♖xe4 ♘xe4 15 ♕xe4 ♘d5 16 h4 h6 17 ♘e5 and White's minor pieces were stronger than Black's rook and pawns in J.Benjamin-W.Browne, US Ch., Long Beach 1989.

9 ♕c2

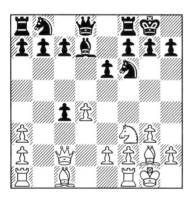

In V.Ivanchuk-A.Onischuk, Foros 2007, White played 9 ♘e5, the game resulting in a draw after 9...♗c6 10 ♘xc6 ♘xc6 11 ♖b1 (11 ♗b2 ♘d5 12 ♖b1

♘b6 13 e3 ♕d6 gave Black a solid game in A.Khalifman-L.Portisch, Reykjavik 1991) 11...♖b8 12 ♗b2 ♕d7 13 e4 ♖fd8 14 d5 exd5 15 ♗xf6 gxf6 16 exd5 ♘e5 17 ♕d4 ♕d6 18 f4 ½-½. White's two bishops and pawn centre give him compensation for the sacrificed pawn, but it's not easy to get more than that when Black's position has no weaknesses.

9...♗c6

Sticking to the plan of solid development. The weakening 9...b5 would give White a promising position after 10 a4 a6 11 ♗a3 (11 ♗g5 is also worth considering) 11...♖e8 12 ♘e5 ♘d5 13 e4.

10 ♕xc4 ♘bd7 11 ♗f4

Another possibility is 11 ♗g5, though after 11...h6 12 ♗xf6 ♘xf6 13 ♖fc1 ♕d6 14 ♘e5 ♗xg2 15 ♔xg2 ♘d5 16 ♕b3 ♖ab8 Black was solidly entrenched in K.Aseev-E.Rozentalis, USSR Ch., Leningrad 1990.

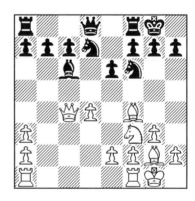

11...h6

This seems a bit odd when White's bishop is already on f4. Other moves have been tried here with solid results:

a) 11...♖c8 12 ♖ac1 ♗d5 13 ♕c2 c5 14 dxc5 ♖xc5 15 ♕b2 ♕e7 16 ♗e3 ♖a5 17 ♗d2 ♕xa3 18 ♕xa3 ♖xa3 19 ♗b4 ♖xa2 20 ♗xf8 ♔xf8 ended in a draw in R.Przedmojski-J.Zeberski, Poraj 2003.

b) 11...♘b6 12 ♕c2 ♖c8 13 ♖fc1 ♕e7 14 ♕b2 ♗e4 15 ♗d2 ♖fd8 16 ♗b4 ♕e8 17 ♘e5 ♗xg2 18 ♔xg2 ♘a4 19 ♕b3 ♖xd4 20 ♘c6 bxc6 21 ♕xa4 c5 22 ♕xe8+ ♘xe8 23 ♖xc5 soon petered out in J.Szmetan-R.Servat, Buenos Aires 1991.

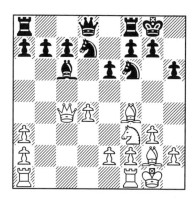

12 ♖fc1 ♘b6 13 ♕b3 ♘fd5

Clearly Black has other moves here, such as 13...♖c8.

14 ♗d2 ♘f6 15 ♖xc6!?

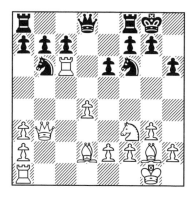

A highly imaginative and coura-

geous exchange sac from Mikhalevski, which creates long-term difficulties for Black. The main problem is his lack of play, whereas the white bishops range across the board.

15...bxc6 16 ♖c1 ♖b8 17 ♖xc6 ♘bd5

I suspect that Black underestimated the danger. He should probably have opted for 17...♕d5, when 18 ♖xc7 ♕xb3 19 axb3 ♘bd5 20 ♖xa7 ♖xb3 should be enough to draw the endgame.

18 ♕c2 ♖b6 19 ♖c4 ♕b8 20 ♗c1 ♘e7 21 ♘e5 ♖d8 22 ♗f3 ♘e8 23 e3 ♘d6 24 ♖c3

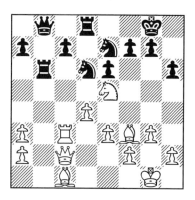

Black's last move shows quite a change of heart, as after 24 ♖xc7 ♖c8 25 ♖c5 the attempt to exchange pieces would be much more costly than earlier. In the event Mikhalevski elects to keep the pressure up.

24...f6 25 ♘d3 ♘f7 26 a4

26 ♖xc7 would still give Black a measure of freedom after 26...♖c8.

26...♘d5 27 ♖c5 ♖d7 28 ♗a3 ♘d8 29 ♔g2 ♘b7 30 ♖c6?!

Judging from the play around this point, Black was running short of time and White was attempting to exploit this. Here 30 e4 would have been quite strong, as 30...♘xc5 31 ♘xc5 leaves both the knight on d5 and the rook on d7 hanging.

30...♘a5 31 ♖c5 ♘b7 32 a5 ♘xc5 33 ♘xc5 ♖c6 34 ♕g6

34 e4 may be a stronger move, but against a man in time trouble a big queen move has shock value.

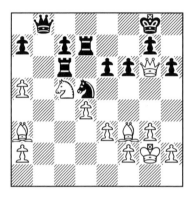

34...♖f7

34...♖dd6 was more tenacious, but the attack keeps coming after 35 ♗e4 ♘e7 36 ♕h7+ ♔f7 37 ♗f3 ♖d5 38 e4 ♖g5 39 h4 etc.

35 ♗e4 f5 36 ♗xd5 ♖f6 37 ♕xf6 1-0

Presumably Black lost on time, though the position after 37...gxf6 38 ♗xc6 is winning for White with three pieces for the queen and his opponent's many weaknesses.

> ## Game 17
> ## R.Wojtaszek-E.Peterson
> European Championship,
> Dresden 2007

1 c4 e6 2 ♘f3 d5 3 d4 ♘f6 4 g3 ♗e7 5 **♗g2 0-0 6 0-0 dxc4 7 ♘c3**

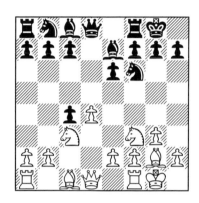

This nonchalant move just develops the knight to a strong square, while making no immediate attempt to recover the c4-pawn.

7...♘c6

The main line, preventing White from recovering the pawn with ♘e5, but blocking the c7-pawn. Alternatives are as follows:

a) 7...♗d7? is quite wrong here because of 8 ♘e5 ♗c6 9 e4! a6 10 ♘xc4 ♗b5 11 b3 ♘c6 12 ♗e3 with a clear advantage for White in R.Wojtaszek-G.Masternak, Warsaw (rapid) 2007.

b) 7...a6 8 ♘e5 c5 9 dxc5 ♗xc5 10 ♘xc4 ♘c6 11 ♗f4 ♕e7 12 ♗d6 ♗xd6 13 ♕xd6 ♕xd6 14 ♘xd6 left Black suffering in the endgame in G.Gajewski-V.Durarbeyli, European Ch., Dresden 2007.

c) 7...c5 8 dxc5 ♘c6 seems just about okay with accurate defence, for example 9 ♕a4 ♕a5 10 ♕xc4 ♕xc5 11 ♕xc5 ♗xc5 12 ♗f4 ♗d7 (12...♘d5 13 ♘xd5 exd5 14 ♖ac1 ♗b6 15 ♖fd1 ♖d8 16 ♘e5 ♘xe5 17 ♗xe5 ♗e6 18 ♗c7! ♗xc7 19 ♖xc7 b6 20 f4! was very unpleasant for

Black in A.Wojtkiewicz-S.Brynell, Aalborg 1989) 13 ♘e5 (there's a case for simply 13 ♖ac1) 13...♘xe5 14 ♗xe5 ♘g4! 15 ♗f4 e5 16 ♖ad1 ♖ad8 17 ♗g5 f6 18 ♗c1 b6 and Black had equalized in V.Tukmakov-Y.Dokhoian, Lvov 1990.

d) 7...♘bd7 transposes to 6...♘bd7 7 ♘c3 dxc4 and is covered in Games 30 and 31.

8 e3

White can also play 8 e4 as in the next game.

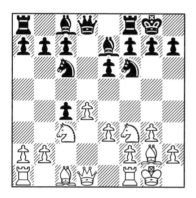

8...♘a5

Black has several other options here:

a) 8...♘d7 (or 8...♘d5 9 ♕e2 ♘b6) 9 ♕e2 ♘b6 10 ♖d1 ♗d7 11 e4 ♖e8 was A.Wojtkiewicz-L.Janjgava, Hastings 1989/90, and now 12 ♗f4 would have been pleasant for White.

b) 8...♖b8 9 ♕a4 ♗d7 (9...♘b4 10 ♕xa7 ♗d7 11 ♘e5 is good for White, for example after 11...♘fd5 he can sacrifice his queen with 12 ♘xd5 exd5 13 ♕xb8 ♕xb8 14 ♘xd7 ♕a7 15 ♘xf8 ♔xf8 16 ♗d2 with the better game) 10 ♕xc4 b5 (10...♘a5 11 ♕e2 b5 12 ♘e5 ♗e8 13

♖d1 c5 14 dxc5! ♕c7 15 ♘d3 ♗xc5 was M.Prusikin-P.Horvath, Budapest 2003, and now 16 ♘xc5! ♕xc5 17 e4 ♘c4 18 ♗f4! e5 19 ♗g5 would have been very good for White according to Prusikin) 11 ♕d3! b4 (11...♘b4 12 ♕e2 c5 13 dxc5 ♗xc5 14 e4!) 12 ♘e4 ♘xe4 13 ♕xe4 ♘a5 was V.Tukmakov-A.Beliavsky, Moscow 1990, and now Beliavsky's suggestion of 14 ♖d1!? ♗b5 15 ♕c2! ♕c8 16 e4! would have been good for White.

c) 8...♗d6 9 ♕a4 (9 ♘d2 e5 10 ♘xc4 exd4 11 exd4 ♗g4 12 ♕b3 ♘xd4 13 ♕xb7 ♗f3 was J.Lautier-A.Karpov, Dos Hermanas 1995, and now 14 ♗xf3 ♖b8 15 ♕xa7 ♘xf3+ 16 ♔g2 ♕d7 17 ♘xd6 ♘h4+ 18 gxh4 ♕g4+ leads to a draw by perpetual check) 9...e5 10 d5 ♘b4 11 ♘xe5 a6! (11...♘bxd5 12 ♘xc4 ♘xc3 13 bxc3 gave White the better game due to his powerful Catalan bishop in R.Wojtaszek-T.Kosintseva, Lausanne 2006) 12 f4!? (rather than 12 ♘f3? ♗f5 as in J.Lautier-V.Korchnoi, Moscow Olympiad 1994) 12...♘bxd5 13 ♘xd5 ♗xe5 14 fxe5 ♘xd5 15 ♕xc4 ♗e6 16 ♕c5 keeps a slight initiative for White.

9 ♕e2 c5 10 ♖d1

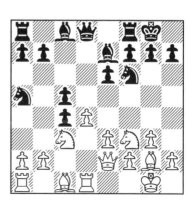

Another approach is 10 dxc5 ♕c7 11 e4 ♗xc5 12 ♗g5, as in L.Alburt-Comp Mephisto Portorose, Harvard (rapid) 1989, with White having compensation for the pawn after 12...♘g4 13 e5 f6 14 exf6 gxf6 15 ♗d2 ♗d7 16 h3 ♘e5 17 ♘xe5 ♕xe5 18 ♕xe5 fxe5 19 ♘e4 ♗b6 20 ♖ad1. It's not clear that a humanoid would have been quite as materialistic as Mephisto.

10...♕c7 11 e4 cxd4 12 ♘xd4 e5

Otherwise White plays e4-e5, though this is arguably the lesser evil.

13 ♘f5 ♗xf5 14 exf5 ♖ad8 15 ♗e3 b6 16 g4!?

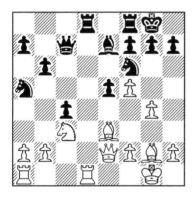

Creating problems for Black, not only because his kingside might be set alight, but also because White's minor pieces can come into e4 and/or d5. Black hurries to simplify the position but this doesn't save him.

16...♖xd1+ 17 ♖xd1 ♖d8 18 g5 ♖xd1+ 19 ♕xd1 ♘e8 20 ♕d5

20 ♗d5 is also very strong.

20...g6 21 f6 ♗f8?

Losing the extra pawn after which his position crumbles. 21...♗d6 was relatively best, though still unpleasant.

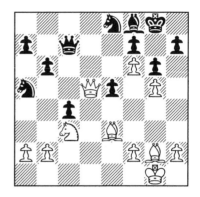

22 ♘b5 ♕c8 23 ♘xa7 ♕f5 24 h4 ♘c7 25 ♕d8 ♘e6 26 ♕e8 ♕b1+ 27 ♔h2 ♕xb2 28 ♘c8

The crushing threat of 29 ♘e7+ decides matters.

28...e4 29 ♘e7+ ♔h8 30 ♕xf7 ♕e5+ 31 ♔g1 ♕a1+ 32 ♗f1 ♗xe7 33 fxe7 1-0

Game 18
D.Antic-H.Van Riemsdijk
Australian Championship, Parramatta 2008

---

1 d4 ♘f6 2 c4 e6 3 ♘f3 d5 4 g3 ♗e7 5 ♗g2 0-0 6 0-0 dxc4 7 ♘c3 ♘c6 8 e4!?

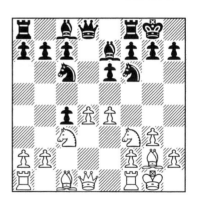

Very simple and direct: White takes the centre without worrying about the c4-pawn.

8...罝b8 9 奧f4

In L.Kavalek-E.Geller, Wijk aan Zee 1977, White played 9 奧e1, after which 9...b5 10 e5 ②d5 11 ②e4 ②cb4 12 ②fg5 h6 13 ②h3 ②d3 left him struggling to find compensation. If White wishes to play e4-e5 then it makes more sense to do it immediately with 9 e5 ②d5 10 ②e4, though personally I doubt he has enough anyway.

9...b5 10 豐e2!?

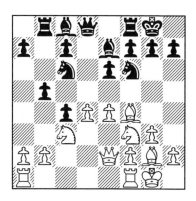

White makes room for his rook on d1, after which his compensation would become apparent, though Black can now take on d4. Other moves have also been tried:

a) 10 d5 seems well met by 10...exd5 11 exd5 ②b4 with a good game for Black.

b) 10 a3!? a6 (10...②a5 11 豐c2 ②b3 12 罝ad1 would make it difficult for Black to free his game) 11 罝e1 罝e8 12 豐d2 奧b7 13 罝ad1 奧f8 14 豐c2 and White's impressive build-up gave him compensation in R.Appel-G.Beckhuis,

German League 2006.

10...b4

10...②xd4 11 ②xd4 豐xd4 is also critical, for example 12 a4!? (12 奧xc7 罝b7 13 e5 罝xc7 14 ②xb5 豐c5 15 exf6 豐xb5 16 fxe7 罝xe7 would leave White struggling) 12...b4 (12...豐d3 13 豐xd3 cxd3 14 axb5 ②g4 15 h3 e5 16 奧c1 ②f6 17 罝d1 is another weird line unearthed by *Fritz*) 13 罝fd1 豐c5 14 ②b5 奧b7 15 罝d4! c3 16 bxc3 b3 17 罝c4 turns out to be good for White, thanks to extensive use of *Fritz 11*.

11 ②a4 奧a6

Here 11...②xd4? is quite bad, as 12 ②xd4 豐xd4 13 罝ad1 wins the queen, while if 12...奧d7 13 豐xc4 奧xa4 14 b3 and 15 奧xc7 will win the exchange.

12 罝fd1 奧b5 13 豐c2 ②xe4 14 ②e5?

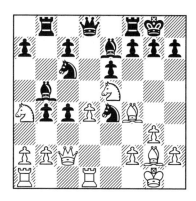

White loses his way in the complications, but this doesn't mean his opening is bad. The right way to play it is with 14 豐xe4, when 14...②xa4 15 b3 cxb3 16 axb3 奧xb3 17 豐xc6 奧xd1 18 罝xd1 is far from clear. Black has a powerful passed b-pawn but its further progress is likely to be impeded by White's very active minor pieces.

14...♘xe5

14...f5!? also looks problematic for White.

15 dxe5 ♕e8 16 ♗xe4 ♗xa4 17 b3 ♗c6 18 ♗xh7+

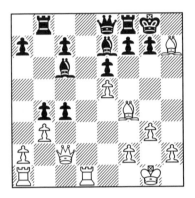

18 ♕xc4!? was probably better, though White is struggling to draw after 18...♗xe4 19 ♕xe4 ♕b5.

18...♔h8 19 ♗e4 ♗xe4 20 ♕xe4 c3 21 ♖d4 c5 22 ♖c4 ♖d8 23 h4 ♖d5 24 ♔g2 ♕d7 25 ♗e3 ♕c7 26 f4 ♕d7 27 ♔h3 ♖d8 28 a3 a5 29 axb4 cxb4 30 h5?!

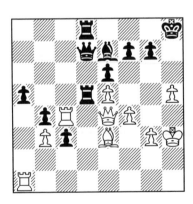

White sets too much store on his kingside chances. The grim 30 ♖a2 was his best hope.

30...♖c8?!

30...♖d1 was stronger, and if 31 ♖a2 ♖e1.

31 ♗b6?! ♗d8 32 ♗xd8 ♕xd8 33 ♖xc8 ♕xc8 34 f5 ♕d8 35 fxe6 fxe6 36 ♖f1 ♕e8 37 g4 ♖d8 38 h6 ♕d7 39 ♔h4?

This was probably time trouble. 39 hxg7+ ♔xg7 40 ♕f4 would have kept some practical chances.

39...gxh6 40 ♖f6 ♕d2 0-1

Summary

There's no doubt that 6...dxc4 is a good move from a theoretical standpoint, but there are a number of practical issues if Black plays this way. First and foremost is that White has many different possibilities and Black needs to know what he's doing against each and every one of them. The current chapter makes this very clear as all three of the White moves covered (7 ♘e5, 7 ♘a3 and 7 ♘c3) are very dangerous.

This situation gives some insights into the psychology of playing the Catalan. In order to induce the maximum pre-game stress, it makes sense for White players to have several answers to 6...dxc4 in the databases, and at least one of these should be a sharp line. Given the amount of work involved, some more anxious Black players may exhaust themselves before the first shot has been fired.

Chapter Five

Main Line with 6 ♕c2 and 6 ♘c3

1 d4 ♘f6 2 c4 e6 3 g3 d5 4 ♗g2 ♗e7 5 ♘f3 0-0

In recent years I've been playing 6 ♕c2, anticipating the possibility of Black capturing on c4. In the game Kramnik-Shirov from Chapter 2, we saw Kramnik meet 6...dxc4 with 7 ♕xc4 a6 8 ♗f4, only transposing into the 10 ♗f4 line later on. But White can also play 7 ♘bd2, as I did in my game against Bykhovsky (see Game 19 below).

One of the drawbacks of 6 ♕c2 is supposed to be 6...c5, but there are two interesting ways to meet this. In my game against Collins (Game 20) I tried 7 0-0 and managed to win in the end, though I thought Black played it pretty well up to a point and was on the verge of equalizing somewhere around move 18. Le Quang-Azmaiparashvili (Game 21) featured what may well be a more promising move, the capture 7 dxc5. Black seemed to be okay in this game

but the defence wasn't easy under the pressure of play.

Last but not least, Black can meet 6 ♕c2 with either 6...♘a6 or 6...♘c6, which will come to the same thing after 7 0-0 ♘b4. Gleizerov-Tsesarsky (Game 22) showed a nice way of dealing with this, and probably White should play 14 ♘c6 rather than 14 ♘xc4.

As I mentioned in the previous chapter, lines with ♘b1-c3 by White are scattered throughout the book and this chapter has another small enclave. After 6 ♘c3 dxc4 White can transpose into the 6 0-0 dxc4 7 ♘c3 lines by playing 7 0-0, but here we'll look at the independent 7 ♘e5. As with the 6 0-0 dxc4 7 ♘e5 line in the previous chapter, Black should probably play 7...♘c6, as in Kalinin-Zeberski (Game 23). There is an alternative in 7...c5 (see Game 24, Psakhis-Stefansson), but this seems to leave Black suffering for some time.

Game 19
N.Davies-A.Bykhovsky
Porto San Giorgio 1999

1 c4 e6 2 ♘f3 d5 3 d4 ♘f6 4 g3 ♗e7 5 ♗g2 0-0 6 ♕c2 dxc4

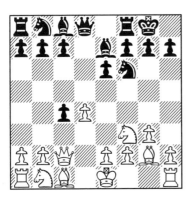

Rather than try to exploit White's last move with 6...c5 (see the next two games), Black tries to keep to normal paths with his programmed capture of the c4-pawn. But White has a couple of independent tries now.

7 ♘bd2

As we saw in the Chapter 2 game between Kramnik and Shirov (Game 7), White can transpose into the 10 ♗f4 line with 7 ♕xc4 a6 8 ♗f4 ♗d6 (8...♘d5 9 0-0 ♘xf4 10 gxf4 ♗d6 11 e3 ♗d7 12 ♕c2 ♗c6 13 ♘bd2 was better for White in H.Danielsen-S.Kristjansson, Icelandic Ch., Reykjavik 2008) 9 0-0 b5 10 ♕c2 ♗b7 11 ♘bd2. However, I think that 7 ♘bd2 is more promising than this.

7...♗d7

A couple of years earlier Bykhovsky had tried 7...a6 without notable success:

A.Wojtkiewicz-A.Bykhovsky, Agios Nikolaos 1997, proceeded 8 ♘xc4 ♘c6 9 e3 ♘b4 10 ♕e2 b5 11 ♘fe5 ♘fd5 12 ♘a5 c5 13 ♘ac6 ♘xc6 14 ♘xc6 ♕c7 15 ♘xe7+ ♕xe7 16 dxc5 ♕xc5 17 ♗d2 ♕c2 18 ♗b4! ♕xe2+ 19 ♔xe2 ♖e8 20 ♗a5 with a clear advantage to White because of his bishops.

8 0-0!?

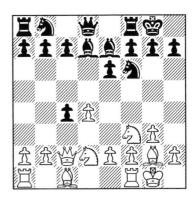

This nonchalant delay in recapturing on c4 was designed to confuse my ageing Russian opponent with some nasty complications. Against someone younger and less well schooled, a more standard move might be more suitable:

a) 8 ♘e5 ♘c6 9 ♕xc4 ♘xe5 10 dxe5 ♘d5 11 0-0 ♗c6 12 ♕g4 ♕d7 13 ♘f3 f5 14 exf6 ♘xf6 15 ♕d4 ♕xd4 16 ♘xd4 ♗xg2 17 ♔xg2 was a bit better for White in E.Miroshnichenko-A.Rychagov, Russian Team Ch. 2005.

b) 8 ♕xc4 ♗c6 9 0-0 a6 10 ♕c2 a5 11 e4 ♘a6 12 a3 ♗b5 13 ♖d1 ♗e2 14 ♖e1 ♗xf3 15 ♘xf3 c5 16 ♖d1 cxd4 17 ♘xd4 gave White a nice game in N.Sulava-V.Kostic, Bad Wörishofen 2000.

8...♗c6 9 e4!? b5

Black feels obliged to hold on to the

extra pawn, lest White get compensation without a sacrifice.

10 ♖e1

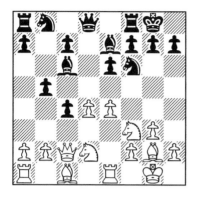

10...♗b7

It might have been better to play 10...♘a6, developing a piece while threatening ...♘a6-b4. An intriguing way to meet this would be 11 a3 ♗b7 12 b4!?, giving Black a supported passed c-pawn but leaving the knight on a6 very bad. A sample line is 12...♘b8 13 ♗b2 ♘c6 14 ♖ad1 (14 ♗c3 is also interesting, as 14...a5 can be answered by 15 bxa5 ♘xa5 16 ♖ab1 c6 17 a4) 14...a5 15 d5 exd5 16 exd5 ♘xd5 17 ♘xc4! bxc4 18 ♕xc4 ♘cxb4 19 ♘e5 c6 20 axb4 ♗xb4 21 ♖e4 with a dangerous initiative for the sacrificed pawns.

11 b3 ♘c6

11...cxb3 12 ♘xb3 gives White excellent compensation for his pawn, thanks to his strong centre, control of the c5-square, and the idea of ♘b3-a5.

12 bxc4 ♘xd4 13 ♘xd4 ♕xd4 14 ♖b1

14 e5?! would lead to simplification after 14...♘g4 15 ♘b3 ♕xc4 16 ♕xc4 bxc4 17 ♗xb7 ♖ab8 18 ♗f3 cxb3 etc.

14...c6

At first *Fritz* likes 14...b4, but then changes its mind after 15 e5 ♘g4 16 ♘b3 ♕b6 17 c5 ♕a6 18 c6 ♗c8 19 ♗f3 etc.

15 e5 ♘g4 16 ♘f3 ♕d7

16...♕b6 17 ♘g5 ♗xg5 18 ♗xg5 would leave Black with the problem of what to do about the knight on g4.

17 ♕e4 h5

There's no good solution about where to put his knight. For example 17...♘h6 18 ♗xh6 gxh6 leaves Black's kingside wrecked, while 17...f5 18 exf6 ♘xf6 19 ♕e2 threatens both ♗h3 and ♘e5.

18 h3 ♘h6 19 ♗xh6 gxh6 20 ♖bd1?!

I'm not sure this was the best because of Black's later 21...♗b4 possibility. Either 20 ♕f4 or 20 ♖ed1 might have been stronger.

20...♕c7 21 ♘d4 bxc4?

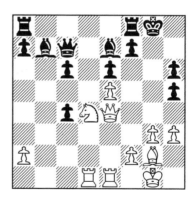

This runs into a bone-crushing reply. Black should have played 21...♗b4!, for example 22 ♖e3 ♖ad8 23 cxb5 c5 24 ♕xb7 ♕xb7 25 ♗xb7 ♖xd4 would see him escape into a drawish endgame.

22 ♘xe6! ♕c8

After 22...fxe6 White gets a winning attack via 23 ♕g6+ ♔h8 24 ♕xh6+ ♔g8 25 ♕g6+ ♔h8 26 ♕xh5+ ♔g8 27 ♕g6+ ♔h8 28 ♖e4 ♗d8 29 ♖xd8! etc.
23 ♘xf8 ♕xf8 24 ♕xc4 1-0

Game 20
N.Davies-S.Collins
Blackpool 2003

---

1 d4 d5 2 c4 e6 3 ♘f3 ♘f6 4 g3 ♗e7 5 ♗g2 0-0 6 ♕c2 c5 7 0-0

7 dxc5 will be examined in the next game.
7...cxd4 8 ♘xd4 ♘c6

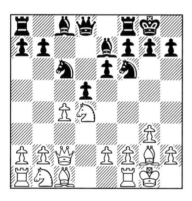

This leads to a kind of reversed Grünfeld Defence, with both sides having chances in a complex middlegame position.

Black has a major alternative in 8...e5, for example 9 ♘f5 d4 (9...♗xf5 10 ♕xf5 ♘c6 11 cxd5 ♘xd5 12 ♘c3! ♘xc3 13 bxc3 gave White the better game in V.Smyslov-M.Peretz, Lugano Olympiad 1968) 10 ♘xe7+ ♕xe7 11 b4!? (11 ♗g5 h6 12 ♗xf6 ♕xf6 13 ♘d2 ♘c6 14 a3 a5 15 b3 ♗f5 was fine for Black in

M.Tratar-R.Zelcic, Zadar 2005; as was 11 b3 ♘c6 12 ♗a3 ♘b4 13 ♗xb4 ♕xb4 14 ♘d2 ♕e7 in E.Miroshnichenko-V.Anand, German League 2004) 11...♗e6 12 ♘d2 ♘a6?! (12...♘c6 looks more natural, but White seems to have an edge after 13 b5! ♘a5 14 ♕a4 ♕c7 15 ♗a3 ♖fd8 16 c5 because of the embarrassment to the knight on a5) 13 a3 ♖ac8 14 ♕d3 ♕d7 15 ♗b2 ♗h3 16 e3 ♗xg2 17 ♔xg2 and White was better because of Black's poorly-placed knight on a6 in H.Koneru-Hou Yifan, Merida 2008.

9 ♘xc6 bxc6 10 b3

White delays the development of his queen's knight, because he wants to see if Black will play ...a7-a5. If he does the knight should go to c3 to stop ...a5-a4, whereas ...♗c8-a6 should be met by putting the knight on d2.

10...a5 11 ♘c3 ♗a6 12 ♖d1 ♕c7 13 ♘a4 ♖ac8

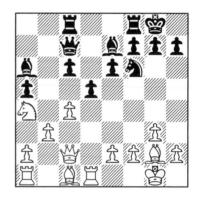

Perhaps Black should just play 13...dxc4, for example 14 bxc4 ♖ab8 15 ♗d2 e5 (15...c5 16 ♖ab1 looks good for White due to the weakness of b5 and a5) 16 ♖ab1 ♖xb1 17 ♖xb1 ♘d7 18 ♕e4

♘f6 19 ♕c2 ♘d7 20 ♗c3 ♗xc4 21 ♗xa5 ♕xa5 22 ♕xc4 and White was slightly better in B.Gulko-J.Hjartarson, Linares 1989.

14 ♗e3 ♘d7

This seems like a good move, after which it's difficult for White to prove very much. In B.Kurajica-P.Van der Sterren, Thessaloniki Olympiad 1984, Black played the committal 14...c5, but would have found himself suffering after 15 cxd5 ♘xd5 (15...exd5 16 ♖ac1 is very pleasant for White) 16 ♗xd5 exd5 17 ♖ac1 ♖fe8 and now just 18 ♖d2 (rather than 18 ♕d2), threatening to capture on c5.

15 ♖ac1 ♕b8 16 ♗d2 ♘b6! 17 ♘b2 a4 18 ♖b1

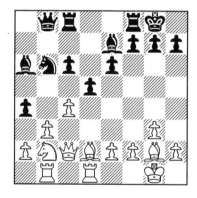

Shadowing Black's queen and trying to keep some tension in the position.

18...a3?!

Ambitious but very committal: the pawn on a3 can easily become weak. The simple move was 18...axb3, when 19 axb3 leaves White slightly more comfortably placed but without any real advantage to speak of.

19 ♘d3 ♘d7 20 ♖dc1?!

The immediate 20 ♕c3 would have been better, intending to meet 20...e5 with 21 ♕a5. This idea only occurred to me on the next move.

20...e5 21 ♕c3 e4 22 ♘f4 ♘f6

22...g5 can be strongly met by 23 ♗h3! ♖fd8 24 ♘h5! etc.

23 ♕a5 ♕a8 24 ♗h3 ♖b8

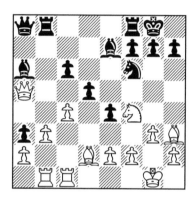

It turns out that 24...♖cd8 would have been preferable, in order to prevent White's bishop from coming to d7 in some lines.

25 cxd5 cxd5

25...♘xd5 is strongly met by 26 ♗d7.

26 ♗c3 ♖fd8 27 ♗e5 ♖b5

As usual 27...g5 is too weakening and White can answer it strongly with 28 ♘g2 g4 (or 28...♗b4 29 ♕a4) 29 ♗xf6 etc.

28 ♕c7 ♗d6?

A miscalculation under pressure. 28...♖e8 was better, though still very pleasant for White after 29 ♕c3.

29 ♗xd6 ♘e8 30 ♕e7 ♘xd6 31 ♖c7 ♖b7 32 ♖bc1 ♖xc7 33 ♖xc7 ♗b5

After 33...♕b8 White can get fancy

with 34 ♘e6!.

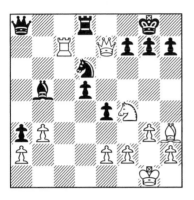

34 ♗e6! ♗e8 35 ♗xd5 ♕b8 36 ♘e6! 1-0

Game 21
L.Le Quang-Z.Azmaiparashvili
Vung Tau 2008

---

1 d4 d5 2 ♘f3 ♘f6 3 c4 e6 4 g3 ♗e7 5 ♗g2 0-0 6 ♕c2 c5 7 dxc5

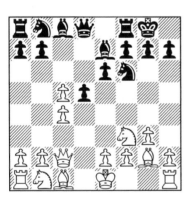

A very interesting alternative to the popular 7 0-0.

7...♕a5+ 8 ♘c3

In a game between two of the big boys, L.Aronian-M.Carlsen, Nice (blindfold rapid) 2008, White played 8

♘bd2, after which 8...♘c6 9 a3 dxc4 10 ♕xc4 ♕xc5 11 0-0 ♕h5 12 h3!? ♗d7 13 g4 ♕d5 14 g5 ♕xc4 15 ♘xc4 ♘d5 16 e4 gave him a slight advantage. This h2-h3 and g3-g4 concept was certain very creative, though I doubt that it would have led to that much after, say, 14...♘e8 15 ♕xd5 exd5. Black's isolated pawn on d5 is compensated for by the weakness of White's kingside pawns.

8...dxc4 9 0-0

In E.Miroshnichenko-E.Gasanov, Minsk 2006, White played 9 ♘d2, when 9...♕xc5 10 ♘a4 ♕a5 11 ♕xc4 ♘c6 12 0-0 ♘e5 13 ♕b3 ♗d7 was really fine for Black whose pieces are getting out very quickly. Not every position with open d- and c-files is good for White in the Catalan; a lead in development is also required.

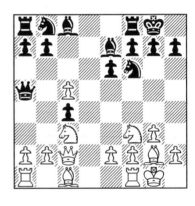

9...♘a6

Black has tried a couple of alternatives here, both of which might be superior:

a) 9...♕xc5 10 ♗g5 (10 ♗e3 ♕h5 11 h3 ♘c6 12 ♖fd1 ♗d7 13 ♘e4 ♖fd8 14 ♕xc4 ♘xe4 15 ♕xe4 ♗e8 16 ♕c2 h6 17 a3 ♕a5 fizzled out to a draw in

J.Ehlvest-A.Vyzmanavin, Lvov 1985) 10...♗d7 (10...♘c6 11 ♗xf6 ♗xf6 12 ♘e4 ♕e7 13 ♘xf6+ ♕xf6 14 ♖fd1 e5 15 ♕xc4 would leave White with a typical Catalan plus due to his strong bishop on g2; Black 'could' recapture with the pawn on move 11, but this would involve considerable danger to his king) 11 ♗xf6 ♗xf6 12 ♘e4 ♕e7 13 ♕xc4 ♗c6 14 ♘xf6+ ♕xf6 15 ♘d4 ♗xg2 16 ♔xg2 ♘d7 17 ♖fd1 ♘b6 18 ♕b3 was only slightly better for White in V.Tukmakov-Z.Ribli, Slovenian Team Ch. 2001.

b) 9...♘c6 10 ♗g5 ♕xc5 11 ♗xf6 ♗xf6 12 ♘e4 ♕e7 13 ♖fd1 b5 (13...♖b8 14 ♘xf6+ ♕xf6 15 ♘d2 e5 16 ♘e4 ♕e7 17 ♕xc4 ♗e6 18 ♕c5 was good for White in E.Miroshnichenko-A.Shneider, Bad Zwesten 2005) 14 a4 ♗a6 15 ♘xf6+ ♕xf6 16 ♖d6 ♖ac8 17 ♘d2 ♘d4 18 ♕d1 ♖cd8 19 ♘e4 ♕e5 20 f4 ♕xd6 21 ♘xd6 ♖xd6 22 e3 ♘f5 23 ♕e1 was agreed drawn at this point in V.Ivanchuk-V.Anand, Linares 2002. Presumably Ivanchuk considered it too risky to continue because of the weakness of his kingside.

10 ♗g5

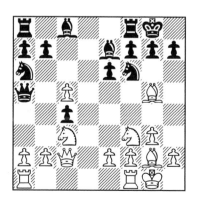

An interesting and dynamic new move from the Vietnamese grandmaster. In earlier games White had played 10 ♘e4, which also seems to give good chances of an edge, for example 10...♘xc5 (10...♘xe4 11 ♕xe4 ♘xc5 12 ♕xc4 ♗d7 13 b4 ♕a4 14 ♗b2 a5 15 ♗xg7! ♔xg7 16 ♕g4+ ♔h8 17 ♕d4+ ♔g8 18 bxc5 ♕xd4 19 ♘xd4 ♗xc5 20 ♘b3 ♗b4 21 ♖fc1! was better for White in M.Krasenkow-P.San Segundo Carrillo, European Ch., Istanbul 2003) 11 ♘xf6+ ♗xf6 12 ♘g5! (12 ♗g5 ♘d7! 13 ♗xf6 ♘xf6 14 ♘d2 c3 15 ♘c4 ♕b4 16 b3 ♘d5 17 ♖fc1 ♗d7 18 ♘e5 ♕d6 19 ♘xd7 ♕xd7 20 ♗xd5 ♕xd5 21 ♕xc3 soon fizzled out to a draw in A.Moiseenko-J.Werle, European Ch., Plovdiv 2008) 12...♗xg5 13 ♗xg5 ♘a4 14 ♗d2 ♕b5 15 ♖fc1! ♕xb2? (if 15...c3 16 bxc3 ♕xe2? 17 ♗f1 ♕g4 18 h3 wins the knight on a4) 16 ♕xb2 ♘xb2 17 a4! ♗d7 18 a5 ♖ad8 19 ♗b4! ♖fe8 20 ♗xb7 ♗b5 21 a6 ♘a4 22 ♖ab1! saw Black struggling for a draw in V.Kramnik-N.Short, Novgorod 1996.

10...♕xc5

10...♗xc5 11 ♗xf6 gxf6 12 ♘d2 would recover the c4-pawn and leave Black's kingside very weak.

11 ♖ac1 ♗d7

Another possibility is 11...♘b4, when 12 ♕b1 ♖d8 13 ♘e4 ♘xe4 14 ♕xe4 ♗xg5 15 ♖xc4 is a sample line showing an ongoing initiative for White.

12 ♗xf6 ♗xf6

Black is evidently reluctant to weaken his kingside with 12...gxf6!?, but in lines such as 13 ♘e4 ♕c7 14

d2!? f5 15 ♕h6 fxe4 16 ♘g5 ♗xg5 17 ♕xg5+ ♔h8 18 ♕f6+ ♔g8 19 ♕g5+ there is nothing more than a draw for White. So perhaps this was a better way, as now White gets a highly typical Catalan initiative.

13 ♘e4 ♕e7 14 ♘xf6+ ♕xf6 15 ♕xc4 ♖fd8 16 ♕b3 ♗c6 17 ♘e1!

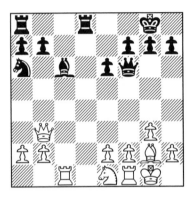

A noteworthy manoeuvre: White exchanges the defender of b7 and prepares to bring his knight to the excellent d3-square.

17...♗xg2 18 ♔xg2 b6 19 ♘d3 ♕d4 20 ♕c4 ♕xc4 21 ♖xc4 ♖d6 22 ♖fc1

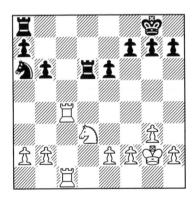

This position is even more unpleasant for Black than it might seem. The

big problem is that the knight on a6 cannot get back into the game.

22...♖ad8 23 b4 ♖d5 24 ♖c8 ♖f8 25 ♖1c3 ♖d4 26 ♖8c4 ♖d5?

26...♖xc4 27 ♖xc4 f6 would have been best, trying to defend along the second rank. Of course White can further improve his position by bringing his king forward.

27 ♖a3 b5 28 ♖c6 ♘b8 29 ♖c7 a6 30 ♖ac3 g6 31 ♖a7 ♖d4 32 ♖cc7 ♖c4 33 ♘c5 e5

The pawn on b4 is immune, as after 33...♖xb4 there follows 34 ♘xe6 ♖e8 35 ♘g5 etc.

34 a3 ♖c3 35 e3 h5 36 h4

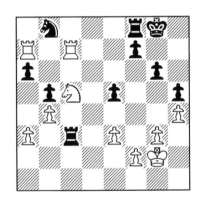

36...♖c4?

Losing without much further ado. 36...♖xa3 is still answered by 37 ♘e6, but here Black can make more of a fight of it with 37...♘c6 38 ♘xf8 ♘xa7 39 ♘d7 a5 40 ♖xa7 axb4 41 ♖b7. Admittedly this final position is resignable anyway.

37 ♖ab7 e4 38 ♖b6 a5 39 ♖cb7 axb4 40 axb4 1-0

The sorry knight on b8 cannot be saved.

Game 22
E.Gleizerov-I.Tsesarsky
Kursk 1987

1 d4 ♘f6 2 c4 e6 3 g3 d5 4 ♗g2 ♗e7 5 ♘f3 0-0 6 ♕c2 ♘a6!?

6...♘c6 7 0-0 ♘b4 8 ♕d1 would come to the same thing.

7 0-0 ♘b4 8 ♕d1 dxc4

In R.Vera-J.Vilela, Cuba Ch. 1985, Black varied with 8...c5, but didn't entirely solve his opening problems there either. The game continued 9 a3 ♘a6 10 cxd5 ♘xd5 11 ♘c3 ♘ac7 12 ♘xd5 ♘xd5 13 dxc5 ♗xc5 14 e4 (14 ♘e5!? looks like another promising approach) 14...♘b6 15 ♕c2 ♗e7 16 a4 ♗d7 17 ♘e5 ♗e8 18 ♖d1 ♖c8! 19 ♕b3 with ongoing pressure for White.

9 ♘a3 c5 10 ♘xc4

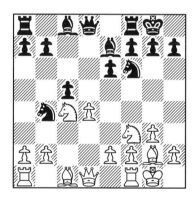

V.Gavrikov-J.Speelman, 3rd match-game, London 1985, was agreed drawn at this point, though this was more because of the match situation than the position.

10...b5

This sharp move doesn't work out too well; but even after the sensible 10...♘c6 White has a clear advantage with 11 dxc5 ♗xc5 12 ♕b3.

11 ♘fe5! ♘fd5

11...♖b8? 12 a3! would attack the crucial defender of the c6-square.

12 a3 bxc4 13 axb4 cxd4

After 13...cxb4 14 ♘xc4 a5 15 e4 ♘f6 16 ♖e1 White would have a clear advantage because his central pawns are very strong.

14 ♘xc4?!

Not bad, but there was a strong case for getting rid of Black's dark-squared bishop with 14 ♘c6, for example 14...♕c7 15 ♘xe7+ ♕xe7 16 ♕xd4 ♗b7 17 ♕xc4 gives White ongoing pressure thanks to his bishop pair.

14...♗f6! 15 ♗f4!

Intending ♗f4-d6-c5, when the d4-pawn would be very hard to protect.

15...♖e8 16 ♗d6

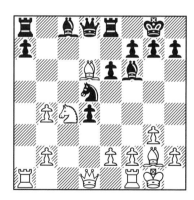

16...♗b7

In his notes Gleizerov suggested the ingenious 16...♗a6!? 17 ♖xa6 ♕c8, though it seems White is better after 18 ♖a5 ♕xc4 19 ♕d2, intending ♗d6-c5 and ♖f1-a1.

17 ♗c5 ♕b8 18 ♗xd4 ♗xd4 19 ♕xd4 ♘xb4 20 ♘d6!?

Once again White is fishing in troubled waters, and on this occasion it pays off big time. After 20 ♗xb7 ♕xb7 21 ♘d6 Black has the excellent resource of 21...♖ed8! 22 ♕xg7+ ♔xg7 23 ♘xb7 ♖d2 with enough counterplay for a draw.

20...♗xg2??

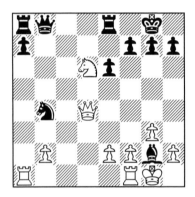

Did Black miss the fact that after White's next move he's threatened with mate on g7? Or did he assume that White had to recapture the bishop on g2, allowing ...♘b4-c2? Either way, this move is a blunder.

The right way to play it was via 20...♖d8!, when 21 ♕xb4 (21 ♗xb7 is answered by 21...♕xb7!) 21...♗xg2 22 ♕xb8 ♖axb8 23 ♘xf7 (23 ♔xg2 ♖xd6 24 ♖xa7 ♖d2 is a dead draw) 23...♗xf1! 24 ♘xd8 ♗xe2 25 ♘xe6 ♖xb2 26 ♖xa7 ♗f3!, and now 27 ♖xg7+ ♔h8 28 ♖xh7+ ♔g8! (28...♔xh7? 29 ♘g5+ would be good for White) 29 ♖g7+ is an unusual draw by perpetual check.

21 ♘xe8 ♕xe8 22 ♖fc1! 1-0

The terrible truth becomes clear: after 22...♘c6 23 ♕a4 ♗d5 White wins a whole piece with 24 e4.

Game 23
O.Kalinin-J.Zeberski
Polish Team Championship 2008

---

1 d4 d5 2 c4 e6 3 ♘f3 ♘f6 4 g3 ♗e7 5 ♗g2 0-0 6 ♘c3

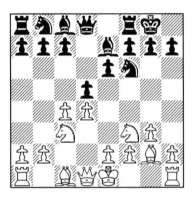

This is quite an interesting option for White which can transpose into lines covered in other chapters. White nonchalantly develops a piece while inviting his opponent to take on c4.

6...dxc4

After 6...♘bd7 White has another interesting option in 7 ♕d3!?, for example 7...c5 (7...c6 8 0-0 is covered in Chapter 7) 8 cxd5 ♘xd5 9 0-0 ♘b4 10 ♕b1 ♘f6 11 dxc5 ♗xc5 12 ♗g5 ♘bd5 13 ♘xd5 exd5 14 ♕c2 gave White a nagging edge in A.Karpov-A.Sokolov, Brussels 1988.

7 ♘e5

7 0-0 would transpose into the 7 ♘c3 line in the previous chapter.

7...♘c6

This is the same concept as in the 6 0-0 dxc4 7 ♘e5 line, again covered in the last chapter, but the fact that White has played ♘c3 instead of 0-0 means there are some differences. 7...c5, is examined in the next game.

8 ♗xc6 bxc6 9 ♘xc6 ♕e8 10 ♘xe7+ ♕xe7 11 ♕a4 c5 12 ♕xc4 cxd4 13 ♕xd4 ♖d8!

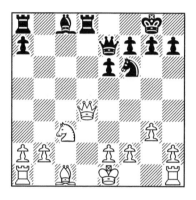

This hasn't been played very much but it looks like a good move.

13...e5 has been the more popular choice, for example 14 ♕h4 ♖b8 15 0-0 ♖b4 16 e4 h6 (16...♗b7 17 f3 ♕c5+ 18 ♔g2 ♘d5?! 19 ♘xd5 ♗xd5 was strongly met by 20 g4! ♗c6 21 ♖e1 ♕d4 22 ♕f2 in S.Shipov-A.Goldin, Russian Ch., St Petersburg 1998) 17 f3 (another possibility is 17 b3!?, when 17...♖d4 18 ♗e3 ♖d3 19 ♖ac1 ♖fd8 gives Black ongoing compensation because of his active pieces and the awkward position of White's queen; instead 17 ♖e1 ♖d8 18 f3? ♖d3 19 ♔g2 ♕b7! 20 ♖e2 ♗g4! 21 fxg4 ♘xe4 22 ♖xe4 ♖xe4 23 ♔h3 ♖e1 led to a spectacular win for Black in T.Markowski-A.Onischuk, Polanica

Zdroj 1999) 17...♖d8 18 g4 ♗a6 19 ♖e1 ♖d3 20 ♕f2 ♕d7 21 ♗e3 ♕b7 22 ♖e2 ♖xe3! 23 ♖xe3 ♖xb2 24 ♕e1 h5 25 g5 ♘h7 26 h4 ♘f8 27 ♖b1 ♘g6 and Black had a strong initiative for the sacrificed exchange in B.Gelfand-R.Ponomariov, Moscow (blitz) 2007.

14 ♕h4 ♖b8 15 0-0 ♖b4 16 e4 h6 17 f3 ♖d3

In A.Matnadze-N.Bojkovic, Antalya (blitz) 2002, Black tried 17...♗a6, after which 18 ♖f2 ♖db8?! (18...♖d3 looks better) 19 g4 ♕c5 20 ♔g2 ♘h7 21 ♖d2 ♘g5 22 ♕f2 saw White gradually unravel.

18 g4 ♗a6 19 ♖f2 ♕c5 20 ♔g2 ♘h7

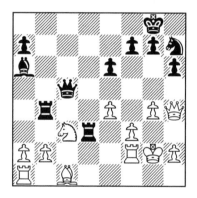

This move has various ideas, such as bringing the knight to g6 via f8 or preparing ...f7-f5. 20...♕d4 was another way to try and keep White tied up.

21 ♕g3

A waste of time. Instead, 21 ♖c2! makes sense, preparing ♕h4-f2, though Black probably gets enough counterplay via 21...f5 22 gxf5 exf5 23 ♕f2 ♕d6 24 ♕g3 ♕c6 etc.

21...♘f8 22 a3?!

This seems nothing more than a

gratuitous weakening of the light squares. Even now 22 ♖c2! looks like a good move. Presumably White took fright at the prospect of 22...♖xe4, but after 23 ♘xe4 ♕xc2+ 24 ♕f2 ♕c6 25 ♗e3 he gets his pieces comfortably mobilized with approximate equality.

22...♖b3 23 ♖c2??

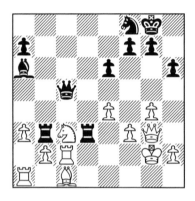

The right idea but in the wrong tactical setting. What follows is a good illustration of the dangers of this position, whatever its objective merits.

23...♖bxc3! 24 bxc3 ♖xc3 25 ♖f2

25 ♖xc3 ♕xc3 wins material because 26 ♖b1 ♕c2+ forks the king and rook.

25...♖xc1 26 ♖xc1 ♕xc1 27 ♕d6 ♗c4

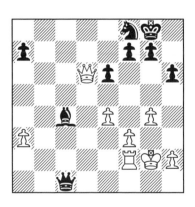

As Black's pieces get coordinated it's only a question of time before White's game collapses.

28 h4 ♘g6 29 h5 ♘f4+ 30 ♔h2 ♘e2 31 ♔h3 ♕e1 32 ♕h2 ♘f4+! 0-1

Game 24
L.Psakhis-H.Stefansson
Winnipeg 1997

1 d4 ♘f6 2 c4 e6 3 g3 d5 4 ♗g2 ♗e7 5 ♘f3 0-0 6 ♘c3 dxc4 7 ♘e5 c5 8 dxc5

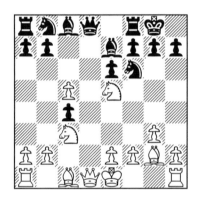

8...♕c7

Black has slightly the worst of it after 8...♕xd1+ 9 ♘xd1 ♗xc5 (9...♘bd7?! 10 ♘xc4 ♘xc5 11 ♘c3 ♗d7 12 ♘a5 ♘d5 13 ♘xd5 exd5 14 ♗xd5 ♖ac8 15 0-0 b6 16 ♘c4 ♗e6 17 ♘e3 ♖fd8 18 ♖d1 left White with an edge in V.Korchnoi-T.V.Petrosian, 3rd matchgame, Ciocco 1977) 10 ♘xc4 (10 ♗d2 ♘c6 11 ♗xc6 bxc6 12 ♖c1 ♗a6 13 ♘xc4 ♖fd8 was more or less equal in V.Korchnoi-N.Short, Hastings 1988/89) 10...♘c6 11 0-0 (11 ♗e3 ♗b4+! 12 ♗d2 ♗xd2+ 13 ♘xd2 ♗d7 14 ♘c4 ♖fd8 15 ♘c3 ♔f8 16 ♘d6 ♖ab8 17 0-0-0 ♘e8 petered out to a draw in V.Korchnoi-T.V.Petrosian, 9th matchgame, Ciocco 1977) 11...♗d7 12 ♗e3 ♗e7 13 ♘c3, for example 13...♖ac8?! (13...♖fd8 14 ♖ac1 is only slightly better for White) 14 ♖ad1 ♖fd8 15 ♗f4 ♗e8 16 ♘d6 ♗xd6 17 ♗xd6 and White's pair of bishops gave him a clear advantage in R.Scherbakov-R.Gavriliuk, USSR 1988.

9 ♘xc4

Not 9 c6?! ♘xc6 10 ♘xc6 bxc6 11 ♕a4 because of 11...♘d5! and Black obtained strong play in E.Kristiansen-B.Parma, Havana Olympiad 1966.

9...♗xc5

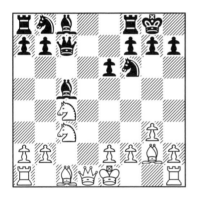

This entails the risky win of a pawn. A more solid option is 9...♕xc5, though Black needs to defend accurately here. For example 10 ♕b3 ♘c6 11 ♗e3 ♘d4 (11...♕h5?! 12 h3 ♘a5 13 ♘xa5 ♕xa5 14 0-0 ♗c5 15 ♗xc5 ♕xc5 was played in A.Beliavsky-L.Portisch, Reggio Emilia 1991, and now 16 ♖fd1 would have been the simplest way to keep an edge) 12 ♗xd4 ♕xd4 13 0-0 ♖b8 (13...♕c5 14 ♖ad1 ♖b8 15 ♕b5! ♕xb5 16 ♘xb5 ♗d7 17 ♘bd6 b6 18 ♖d2 ♖fd8 19 ♖fd1 left Black under pressure in A.Beliavsky-

R.Hübner, Munich 1991) 14 ♖fd1 ♕c5 15 ♖ac1 ♗d7 16 ♘e4 ♕b5 17 ♕d3 ♖fd8 18 ♘ed6 ♕a6 19 ♘e3 b5 20 ♕a3 ♕b6 21 ♘c8 ♖xa3 22 ♘xb6 ♗b2 23 ♘xd7 ♖xd7 24 ♖xd7 ♗xc1 25 ♖xa7 ♗xe3 26 fxe3 b4 and Black's precise defence had maintained equality in B.Gelfand-J.Speelman, Linares 1991.

10 0-0 ♗xf2+

This looks incredibly risky to me, but part of Black's problem is that he doesn't really have great alternatives. For example 10...♘c6 is well met by 11 ♗f4 e5 12 ♗g5, controlling d5, while 10...♖d8 11 ♗f4! ♕e7 12 ♕c2 leaves White with a clear lead in development.

11 ♖xf2 ♕xc4 12 ♖xf6! gxf6 13 ♗h6 ♘d7!

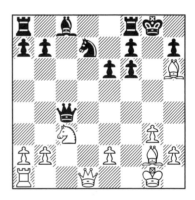

A new move from Stefansson, and by far the best chance for Black. In B.Ivkov-K.Robatsch, Vinkovci 1968, Black played 13...♘c6 but succumbed rapidly following 14 e3! ♖d8 15 ♕h5 e5 16 ♘e4 ♕e6 17 ♕h4 1-0; and in F.Gheorghiu-G.Varabiescu, Romania 1969, Black lasted only slightly longer with 13...♕c5+ 14 e3 f5 15 ♖c1! ♕e7 16

♕d4 f6 17 ♗xf8 ♕xf8 18 ♘b5! ♘d7 19 ♘c7 ♖b8 20 ♘xe6 ♕e7 21 ♖c7 ♔h8 22 ♘c5 1-0.

14 ♘e4

After 14 ♗xf8 ♔xf8 (if 14...♘xf8 15 ♕d8) 15 ♕d6+ ♔e8!? 16 ♖d1 ♕c5+ 17 ♕xc5 ♘xc5 18 ♘b5 ♔e7 19 ♖c1 ♘d7 Black hangs on by the skin of his teeth.

14...♕b4!

On 14...♖d8 White wins with 15 e3 f5 (or 15...♔h8 16 ♘d6 etc) 16 ♕h5 f6 17 ♘d6 ♗g4 18 ♕f7+ ♔h8 19 ♕e7 etc.

15 ♖c1 f5

As Lev Psakhis pointed out in his notes, 15...♖d8? is refuted by 16 ♘xf6+ ♔h8 17 ♕d3! ♕b6+ 18 ♗e3 ♘xf6 19 ♕c3! ♕d6 20 ♕xf6+ ♔g8 21 ♖f1! ♖d7 22 ♖f4 ♔f8 23 ♖g4 etc. But the greedy 15...♕xb2 is quite a tough nut to crack, and I (together with *Fritz*) can't find anything better than the complex 16 ♖c2 ♕b6+ 17 e3 f5 18 ♘d6 ♕d8 19 ♖d2 ♘e5 20 ♘c4 ♘d7 21 ♗xf8 ♕xf8 22 ♘e5 ♘xe5 23 ♖d8, winning Black's queen with all the winning chances in the endgame.

16 ♘d6

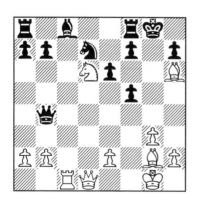

Psakhis expressed regret over this

move, preferring instead 16 ♗xf8. But this seems far from clear either, for example 16...♘xf8 (if 16...♔xf8 17 ♕d6+ ♕xd6 18 ♘xd6 ♘b6 19 ♖c7 gives White a good endgame, while 16...♕xf8 17 ♘d6 ♕d8 18 ♕d4 leaves Black tied up and threatened with ♕h8+ followed by a knight fork on f7) 17 ♘f6+ ♔g7 (17...♔h8 18 ♕d8 ♕b6+ 19 ♕xb6 axb6 20 ♖c7 is another bad endgame for Black) 18 ♕d8 ♕b6+ 19 ♕xb6 axb6 20 ♘e8+ ♔g6 and Black is still fighting.

16...♘e5!

After 16...♖d8 there follows 17 ♘xc8 ♖dxc8 (if 17...♕xb2 18 ♖c2 ♕f6 19 ♕c1 covers the knight on c8 and threatens 20 ♗g5) 18 ♖xc8+ ♖xc8 19 ♕xd7 ♕b6+ 20 ♔f1 ♖d8 21 ♕a4 when White has all the chances.

17 ♗xf8 ♕b6+ 18 e3!

18 ♔h1 ♘g4 19 ♘xc8 ♘f2+ 20 ♔g1 ♘h3+ 21 ♔h1 ♘f2+ is an immediate perpetual check.

18...♕xe3+ 19 ♔h1 ♘g4 20 ♖c2

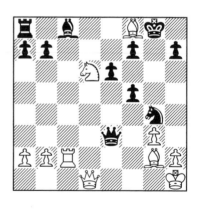

20...♔xf8

20...♘f2+?! is good for White after 21 ♖xf2 ♕xf2 22 ♗h6 ♗d7 23 ♕c1 f6 24 ♗e3 ♕e2 25 ♗xb7 etc.

21 ♘xc8 ♘f2+ 22 ♖xf2 ♕xf2 23 ♗xb7

23 ♕c1!? seems to be adequately met by 23...♕d4.

23...♖b8 24 ♕d8+ ♔g7 25 ♕g5+ ♔h8!

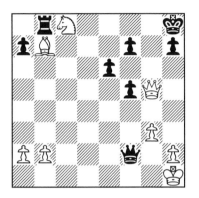

And not 25...♔f8? because of 26 ♕h6+ ♔e8 (or 26...♔g8 27 ♘e7+ ♔h8 28 ♕f6 mate) 27 ♗c6+ ♔d8 28 ♕f8+ ♔c7 29 ♕d6+ ♔xc8 30 ♕d7 mate.

26 ♕d8+ ♔g7 27 ♕g5+ ♔h8 ½-½

An amazing fighting game, brilliantly conducted by both players.

Summary

The move 6 ♕c2 is one of White's most interesting options if he does not want to become embroiled in main line theory. With accurate play it looks as if Black's position is okay after 6...c5 7 0-0 or 7 dxc5, but this can be said about most openings.

After 6 ♘c3 Black again gets his fair share of the chances with 6...dxc4 7 ♘e5 ♘c6, but this calls for the kind of precise and energetic play that's easier when one has studied a lot of theory in detail. Very few Black players under 2700 will have gone into this in such depth, which makes it an ideal weapon at club level.

Chapter Six

Closed Catalan with 7 ♕c2

1 d4 ♘f6 2 c4 e6 3 g3 d5 4 ♗g2 ♗e7 5 ♘f3 0-0 6 0-0 ♘bd7 7 ♕c2

As I mentioned in the introduction, Closed lines tend to be an instinctive choice for club-level players who meet the Catalan for the first time. They want to 'play it safe' and rightly assume that taking the pawn on c4 will involve them in more of a theoretical battle. This adds to the importance of the material that will be covered here.

I have somewhat non-standard views on the Closed Catalan after having played the White pieces against GM Smbat Lputian some years ago. The game Bogdanovski-Lputian (Game 25) is an excellent template for Black's play in this line, with a kind of French Defence arising in which White's bishop on b2 is not particularly well placed.

This is evidently a cause for concern amongst Catalan experts, and perhaps explains why Mikhail Umansky played

the creative formula of 8 ♖d1 and 9 ♘c3 in his game against me (see Game 26). There is, however, a drawback to this way of going about things, in that Black can meet 8 ♖d1 with 8...♘e4, switching to a Stonewall Dutch formation where White's rook really doesn't belong on d1.

Accordingly I believe that White's simplest and most effective strategy is to play for e2-e4 with 8 ♘bd2. The game Nyback-Lputian (Game 27) is a rare Catalan loss for the great Armenian specialist, and shows that there's something to be said for this formula. It may well be better to put the bishop on a6 as in Tolnai-Almasi (Game 28), but here too I prefer White's prospects.

If the reader requires another game in this variation then please remember Davies-Brown in the introduction. That one is of special importance because Black did what just about every club player does and captured on e4.

The final game in this chapter (Damljanovic-Quillan, Game 29) features 6...♘bd7 7 ♕c2 c5, which tries to exchange both White's d- and c-pawns and thus steer the game towards equality. But as usual there's a problem for Black, in that he makes the Catalan bishop a lot stronger.

Game 25
V.Bogdanovski-S.Lputian
World Team Championship,
Yerevan 2001

1 ♘f3 d5 2 d4 e6 3 c4 ♘f6 4 g3 ♗e7 5 ♗g2 0-0 6 0-0 ♘bd7 7 ♕c2

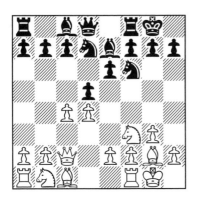

The main alternative here is 7 ♘c3, a gambit line which is covered in the next chapter.

7...c6 8 b3

Although this has been White's most popular move for many years, I don't see it as being particularly testing for Black, especially in view of Lputian's masterful handling of the Black side. My recommended line for White is 8 ♘bd2 followed by a quick e2-e4,

while 8 ♗f4 transposes into Chapter 8, albeit one move earlier, having omitted the moves ...♗b4+ and ♗d2.

8...b6

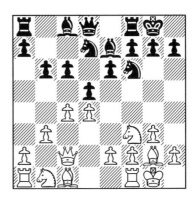

Preparing to develop his queen's bishop on b7 or a6.

Note that the transposition into a Stonewall formation with 8...♘e4 is not as effective in this position as after, say, 8 ♖d1. A.Delchev-G.Giorgadze, Pula 1997, continued 9 ♘bd2 f5 10 ♘e1 ♘xd2 11 ♗xd2 ♘f6 12 ♘d3 ♗d7 13 a3! ♗e8 14 ♗b4 with the better game for White because of his light square control.

On the other hand Black has an interesting alternative in 8...b5!?, which probably deserves more outings than it has had so far. A good model of how to treat this move came in P.Haba-E.Prandstetter, Czech League 1990, which proceeded 9 c5 ♘e4 10 ♗b2 f5 11 ♘e1 ♗g5 12 ♘d3 a5 13 a3 ♕e8 14 e3 ♕h5 15 ♘d2 ♘df6 16 ♘f3 with the better game for White. But I wouldn't consider this the final word in such a strategically rich variation.

9 ♖d1

White can also play 9 ♗b2, for example Z.Kozul-S.Lputian, World Team Ch., Lucerne 1997, went 9...♗a6 10 ♖d1 (10 ♘bd2 ♖c8 11 ♖ac1 c5 12 ♕b1 dxc4 13 ♘xc4 ♗b7 14 dxc5 ♗xc5 was equal in T.Markowski-S.Lputian, European Ch., Warsaw 2005) 10...♖c8 11 ♘c3 ♕c7!? (White gets the initiative after 11...dxc4 12 ♘e5 ♘xe5 13 dxe5 ♘d7 14 ♘e4 ♕c7 15 ♘d6 ♖cd8 16 f4 ♘c5 17 ♘xc4 ♘b7 18 ♗e4 as in D.Paulsen-B.Schmidt, German League 1982, though 12...cxb3 13 axb3 ♘b8 is a possibility) 12 e4 (12 ♘d2 can be answered by 12...c5) 12...dxc4 (12...dxe4 13 ♘xe4 ♘xe4 14 ♕xe4 is just good for White thanks to his central space) 13 ♕e2 b5 14 bxc4 b4! (14...bxc4 15 ♘d2 ♘b6 16 a4 will lead to the recovery of the pawn on c4 with the better game for White) 15 ♘b1 ♘b6 (15...c5 16 d5 exd5 17 exd5 ♘b6 18 ♘e5 isn't clear either) 16 ♘bd2 ♘a4 17 ♖ab1 (17 ♘b3? is answered by 17...♗xc4!) 17...c5! 18 ♖dc1 (not 18 d5? because of 18...♘xb2 19 ♖xb2 exd5 20 exd5 ♘xd5 etc) 18...♖fd8 19 dxc5 ♘xb2 20 ♖xb2 ♕xc5 and Black was better because of his superior pawn structure and pair of bishops.

Another possibility is 9 ♘c3 ♗a6 10 ♘d2 (10 ♗f4!? ♖c8 11 ♖fd1 ♕e8 12 e4 dxc4 13 ♘d2 e5 14 dxe5 ♘g4 15 ♘xc4 ♗xc4 16 bxc4 ♗c5 17 ♖d2 ♘gxe5 ½-½ was far from clear in A.Beliavsky-Z.Almasi, Groningen 1994; while 10 ♖d1 ♖c8 11 e4 dxc4 12 ♘e5 ♘xe5 13 dxe5 ♘d7 14 ♗e3 ♕c7 15 f4 ♘c5 saw Black doing well in T.Grabuzova-S.Lputian, Internet blitz 2004) 10...b5 11 ♖e1 bxc4 12 bxc4 dxc4 13 ♕a4 ♕c8 14

♕xc6 (14 ♘xc4 is better, though Black can counterattack with 14...c5!? 15 ♗xa8 cxd4 which might have been something White was concerned about) 14...♘b6 15 ♖b1 ♕d8 16 e3 ♘fd5 17 ♘xd5? (17 ♗xd5 was mandatory, though this gives Black a strong initiative after 17...exd5 18 ♘xd5 ♕xd5 19 ♖xb6 ♕xc6 20 ♖xc6 ♗b5 21 ♖c7 ♗b4 etc) 17...exd5 18 ♗h3 f5 left White struggling to save his queen in R.Sukharisingh-R.Vaganian, German League 1996.

9...♗a6

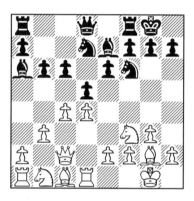

This is better than the passive 9...♗b7, for example 10 ♘c3 b5!? 11 c5 b4 12 ♘a4 a5 13 ♘b2 ♗a6 14 ♘d3 ♗xd3 15 exd3 ♘e8 16 a3 was good for White in Y.Razuvaev-S.Lputian, USSR Ch., Vilnius 1980. At that dim and distant time Lputian was still learning his craft.

10 ♘bd2 ♖c8

Black can also try the immediate 10...c5!?, for example 11 e4 (11 ♗b2 ♖c8 looks okay for Black) 11...dxc4 (11...♖c8 transposes to the next note) 12 ♘xc4 (12 bxc4 cxd4 13 e5 ♘g4 14 ♕e4 h5 15 h3 ♘c5 left White struggling in R.Hübner-V.Anand, Dortmund 2000) 12...cxd4 13 ♘xd4 ♖c8 14 ♕e2 ♕c7 15 ♗f4 ♗xc4 16 bxc4 e5 17 ♘f5 ♘c5 18 ♗d2 ♘e6 19 ♗c3 ♗c5 gave Black a solid game in V.Filippov-A.Galkin, Russian Ch., St Petersburg 1998.

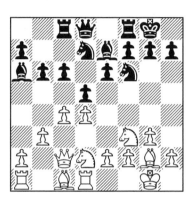

11 e4 ♗b7

Lputian likes to maintain the tension in this line, arguing that it can be difficult for White to improve his position.

Black has an alternative in 11...c5, but this leaves him struggling against White's initiative in a position with a symmetrical pawn structure. For example 12 exd5 exd5 13 ♘f1 (13 ♗b2 ♗b7 14 ♕f5 dxc4 15 ♘xc4 b5 16 ♘e3 ♗e4 17 ♕f4 c4 18 d5 c3 19 ♗xc3 ♖xc3 20 d6 ♖c5 21 dxe7 ♕xe7 was equal in I.Polovodin-S.Lputian, Irkutsk 1983) 13...cxd4 (13...dxc4!? 14 d5 ♘e8 15 bxc4 ♘d6 16 ♘e3 ♖e8 17 ♗f1 b5 gave Black counterplay in A.Delchev-L.B.Hansen, Istanbul Olympiad 2000) 14 ♘xd4 b5 15 ♘e3 bxc4 (15...♘b6 16 ♕d2 bxc4 17 ♕a5 ♗b7 18 ♕xa7 ♗a8 19 ♘ef5 ♗c5 was I.Stohl-A.Kosten, German League 2001,

when White could have won on the spot with 20 ♘e6!) 16 ♘xd5 ♘xd5 17 ♗xd5 cxb3 18 ♕xb3 required great accuracy from Black in I.Stohl-V.Dydyshko, Polish Team Ch. 2000.

12 ♗b2 ♕c7!?

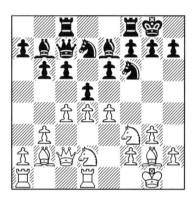

13 ♖ac1

In N.Davies-S.Lputian, Isle of Man 2003, I tried 13 e5 against the maestro, but after 13...♘e8 14 ♘f1 (14 cxd5 cxd5 15 ♕d3 ♕b8 16 ♖ac1 ♘c7 17 h4 ♗a6 18 ♕b1 ♘b5 was fine for Black in D.Fridman-S.Lputian, Internet blitz 2004) 14...♕b8 15 cxd5 cxd5 16 ♕d2 a5 17 ♘e1 ♘c7 his pieces were getting into play on the queenside without obvious progress for White on the other side of the board. It was this game, and the post mortem that followed, that taught me about Black's chances in this variation and Lputian's mastery of it.

13...♕b8 14 e5 ♘e8 15 ♘f1

After 15 h4 Black can prevent ♘f3-g5 with 15...h6 before launching the traditional counterattack following 16 ♘f1 c5.

15...♘c7 16 ♘e3

In this position 16 h4 can be answered b 16...♖fd8 17 ♘g5 ♘f8.

16...♖fd8 17 cxd5 cxd5 18 ♕b1 ♗a6 19 h4 ♕b7 20 a3 ♗b5 21 ♘g5 ♘f8

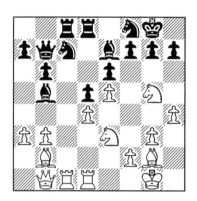

Very economical defence, after which it's difficult to see further progress for White on the kingside. Having played similar positions in the King's Indian Attack I don't like the fact that White's dark-squared bishop is on b2, far away from the action.

22 ♘h3 a5! 23 a4 ♗e8

23...♗a6 would also be playable here. From e8 the bishop can often emerge on the kingside after an advance of Black's f-pawn.

24 ♕a1 ♘a6 25 ♗f1 ♘b4 26 ♘f4 ♘d7 27 ♘d3 ♘c6

Here, too, Lputian is keeping as much tension in the position as possible, because he wants to win. 27...♘xd3 28 ♗xd3 ♘b8 29 ♗a3 ♗xa3 30 ♕xa3 ♘a6 would be rather too equal for his liking.

28 ♘c2 ♘db8 29 ♗a3 ♘a6 30 ♗xe7 ♕xe7 31 ♘de1 ♘ab8 32 ♘a3 f6!?

A pawn lever that is highly reminiscent of the French Defence. Not only does Black attack the white centre, he

makes room for his light-squared bishop to come out on the kingside.

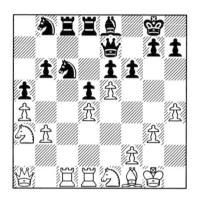

33 exf6 ♕xf6 34 ♘b5 ♘a6 35 ♘d3 ♘ab4 36 ♘f4

White cannot simplify with 36 ♘xb4 ♘xb4 37 ♖xc8 ♖xc8 38 ♘d6 because of the powerful reply 38...♖c2!.

36...♗g6 37 ♗h3 ♗f5 38 ♗xf5 ♕xf5 39 ♕b2 e5 40 dxe5 ♘xe5 41 ♕e2?!

A slip under pressure. White should blockade the d-pawn with 41 ♘d4, when 41...♕g4 42 ♕e2 ♕xe2 43 ♘fxe2 ♘ed3 44 ♖c3 seems to hold.

41...♖xc1 42 ♖xc1 d4! 43 ♖d1 d3 44 ♕e3 ♕g4 45 ♘c3 ♘f3+ 46 ♔g2?!

I get the impression that the clock

might have been playing its part here. 46 ♔f1 was a better try.

46...♘xh4+ 47 ♔f1?

And 47 ♔h2 was better here, though Black would still be well on top. A sample line is 47...♘f3+ 48 ♔g2 ♘g5 49 f3 ♕f5 with ongoing pressure.

47...♘f3?!

Not the best. Black should play 47...♖f8, when 48 ♕e6+ ♕xe6 49 ♘xe6 ♖c8 50 ♘b5 ♘f3 leaves him with an extra pawn.

48 ♔g2?

48 ♕xb6 was correct, regaining the pawn while retaining the possibility of trading queens with 49 ♕e6+.

48...♘g5 49 ♘xd3

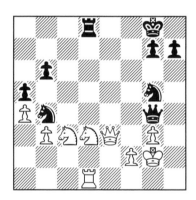

49...♖f8?

Missing an immediate win with 49...♘c2! 50 ♕f4 ♕h3+ 51 ♔g1 ♘d4 etc. Now White is right back in the game.

50 ♘f4 h6 51 ♖d2 ♕c8 52 ♘cd5 ♘xd5 53 ♖xd5 ♕c6 54 ♕d3 ♕b7 55 ♔g1

55 f3 is also fine for White.

55...♕c6 56 ♕g6 ♕b7 57 ♖xg5?

Presumably White missed something when he played this move. Simply 57 ♕d3 is equal.

57...hxg5 58 ♘e6 ♖c8 59 ♔h2

59 ♘xg5 ♖c1+ leads to mate next move.

59...♕f7 0-1

The queens must come off, after which the endgame is hopeless for White.

Game 26
M.Umansky-N.Davies
Correspondence 2004

---

1 d4 ♘f6 2 c4 e6 3 g3 d5 4 ♗g2 ♗e7 5 ♘f3 0-0 6 0-0 ♘bd7 7 ♕c2 c6 8 ♖d1

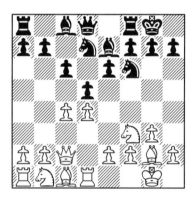

8...b6

The usual formula, though the early placement of White's rook on d1 presents Black with another very interesting option, which is to play the position as a Stonewall Dutch formation via 8...♘e4. For example, 9 ♘e1 (9 ♘bd2 f5! 10 a4?! ♕e8 11 a5 a6 12 b3 ♕h5 13 ♘f1 ♔h8 14 ♗a3! ♗xa3 15 ♖xa3 ♘df6 16 ♘e5 ♗d7 17 f3 ♘d6 18 ♕d2 ♖ad8 19 ♖aa1 ♗c8 20 c5?! ♘f7 21 ♕e3 g5! gave Black attacking chances on the kingside in R.Naranja-B.Ivkov, Palma Interzonal

1970) 9...f5 10 ♘d3 ♗f6 11 e3 ♔h8 12 f3 ♘g5 13 ♘d2 ♖e8 14 ♖b1 b6 15 b4 ♗b7 16 c5 ♘f7 17 f4 g5 with chances for both sides in M.Sorokin-V.Kosyrev, St Petersburg 2001.

9 ♘c3

The exotic 9 a4 seems to leave Black with a number of good options, such as 9...♗a6 (9...♗b7 10 a5 c5 11 a6 ♗c6 12 ♘e5 ♘xe5 13 dxe5 ♘e8 14 cxd5 exd5 15 ♘c3 ♘c7 regrouped nicely for Black in K.Nika-A.Botsari, Athens 1988; and 9...a5 looks solid enough too) 10 b3 ♖c8 11 a5 b5 12 c5 b4!? 13 ♗d2 (13 ♗f4 is well met by 13...♘e4 14 ♘e1 e5!) 13...♗xe2 14 ♖e1 ♗a6 15 ♗xb4 ♘e4 16 ♘e5 ♘xe5 17 dxe5 ♖b8 was very good for Black in M.Hackel-R.Vaganian, German League 1999.

9...♗a6 10 ♘e5

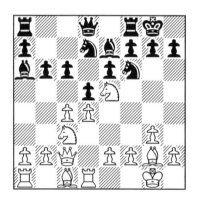

I think this is by far the most dangerous option. After other moves Black seems to hold his own fairly comfortably, for example:

a) 10 b3 ♖c8 11 e4 (11 ♗b2 ♕c7 12 ♖ac1 ♖fd8 13 cxd5 cxd5 14 ♕b1 ♕b8 was fine for Black in C.Collins-T.Ward, Detroit 1990) 11...dxc4 12 ♕e2 b5 13

bxc4 b4 14 ♘a4 c5 15 e5 ♘d5 16 a3 ♘7b6 gave White problems in A.Shchekachev-T.Wirschell, Antwerp 1996.

b) 10 ♘d2 ♖c8 (10...b5 11 b3 ♘b6 is also possible, for example 12 c5 b4 13 cxb6 bxc3 14 ♘b1 axb6 leaves Black with fewer pawn islands) 11 e4 c5 12 exd5 cxd4 13 dxe6 dxc3 14 exd7 ♕xd7 15 ♘e4 cxb2 16 ♗xb2 ♖xc4 17 ♘xf6+ ♗xf6 18 ♖xd7 ♖xc2 led to a drawn endgame in C.Bernard-M.Godena, Cannes 1996.

c) 10 cxd5 cxd5 11 ♗f4 (11 ♘e5 ♖c8 12 ♗f4 b5 13 a3 ♕b6 gave Black a comfortable game in A.Iljushin-A.Graf, Novgorod 1999) 11...b5 12 a3 ♕b6 13 b4?! ♖fc8 14 ♕d3 ♖c4 was better for Black in P.Govciyan-A.Muller, Cannes 1999. White should not have given the c4-square away as he did with his 13th move.

10...♖c8

In earlier games Black took on e5 and found himself under serious pressure, for example 10...♘xe5 11 dxe5 ♘d7 (11...♘g4 is well met by 12 cxd5 cxd5 13 ♕a4, for example 13...♗c4 14 b3 b5 15 ♕a6! ♗b4 16 ♗d2 ♗xc3 17 ♗xc3 ♗xe2 18 ♗a5 ♕g5 19 ♖d2, trapping Black's light-squared bishop) 12 cxd5 cxd5 13 ♗f4 b5 (13...g5 wins the e5-pawn but would weaken Black's kingside horribly) 14 e4 d4?! (this is not good, but after 14...b4 White has many attractive possibilities, one of them being a piece sacrifice via 15 ♘xd5!? exd5 16 exd5) 15 ♖xd4 ♕c7 16 ♖ad1 ♘b6 17 a3 left Black in an unenviable position in V.Tkachiev-R.Vaganian, Neum (blitz) 2000.

11 ♕a4 ♘b8

Despite the retrograde appearance of this move I did not see a particularly good alternative. I was also fortified by the Reshko-Korelov encounter in the next note, but Umansky had an improvement ready.

12 b3!

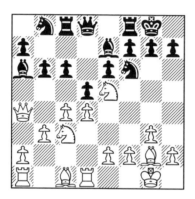

An excellent move which is far from easy to meet. In A.Reshko-A.Korelov, Leningrad 1963, White played 12 e4, but then 12...dxc4 (12...b5 is not bad here either) 13 ♗e3 ♕c7 14 ♘f3 b5 left White struggling to get enough play for his pawn.

12...♘e8

After 12...♘fd7 White gets the better of it with simply 13 ♗a3 ♘xe5 14 dxe5, while after 12...b5 he can try 13 ♘xb5 cxb5 14 cxb5 ♗b7 15 ♕xa7 ♖c7 16 ♗f4 ♗d6 17 a4 with some powerful passed pawns on the queenside for the sacrificed piece.

13 ♗a3

Black can meet 13 e4 with 13...♘d6, the point being that 14 exd5 is answered by 14...b5 15 ♘xc6 ♖xc6 16 ♘xb5 ♗xb5 17 cxb5 ♖c2 with counterplay.

13...b5

White is also better after 13...♗xa3 14 ♕xa3 ♕d6 15 ♕a4, while 13...♘d6 14 ♗b4 f6 (or if 14...b5 15 cxb5 cxb5 16 ♕a3) 15 ♘d3 dxc4 is refuted by 16 ♘c5!.

14 ♗xe7 ♕xe7 15 ♘xb5!?

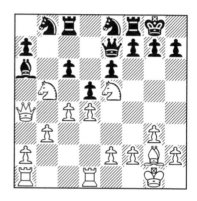

Umansky is a highly creative player, here coming up with a really brilliant idea that cost me months to defend against! Both 15 cxb5 cxb5 16 ♘xb5 ♕b7 17 ♘a3 ♗xe2 and 15 ♕a5 bxc4 16 bxc4 f6 are okay for Black.

15...f6

After 15...cxb5 16 cxb5 ♗b7 17 ♕xa7 White's passed pawns would be difficult to handle because of the passivity of Black's pieces.

16 ♘xc6!

The point of his previous move; White now obtains three pawns for the sacrificed piece, in a position in which it is far from easy for Black to defend.

16...♖xc6 17 cxd5 ♖b6

In this position I didn't like the look of 17...♗xb5 18 ♕xb5 ♘c7 19 ♕b7 exd5 20 ♖dc1.

18 ♘c3 e5!

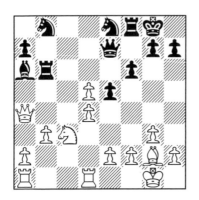

A good move of my own. Black needs to keep the d5-pawn where it is and blockade d6 with a knight.

19 ♖ac1 ♘d6 20 e4 ♗c8

There's no longer any future for the bishop on a6, so I made room for a rook or knight to use this square.

21 h3

Ruling out ...♗c8-g4 while preparing ♔g1-h2.

21...♖b7 22 ♕a3 ♖c7 23 f4 exd4

I also considered the immediate 23...g5, but after 24 dxe5 fxe5 25 f5 Black is stymied on the kingside.

24 ♖xd4 g5 25 ♔h2 gxf4 26 gxf4 ♔h8 27 ♘e2

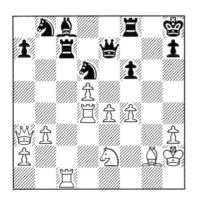

With his king feeling something of a breeze, White brings the knight over in reinforcement and exchanges a pair of rooks.

27...♖xc1 28 ♕xc1 ♖g8 29 ♘g3 ♘d7 30 ♖d1

Not 30 ♕c7? due to 30...♘b5.

30...♕g7 31 ♕e3

31 ♕c3 can be answered by 31...♕h6, hitting f4.

31...♘b6

In retrospect I'm not sure this was the best as the knight doesn't do much on the queenside. 31...♘f8 was an interesting alternative, one of the points being the variation 32 ♖g1 ♘g6 33 ♘h5 ♕h6 34 ♘xf6 ♖f8 35 e5 ♘xe5 36 ♕xe5 ♖xf6 etc.

32 ♕f2 ♗d7 33 ♖e1 ♕h6 34 ♖e3

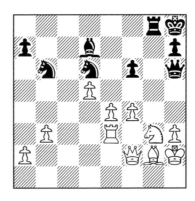

One of the problems White faces here is that if he advances his pawns he makes Black's pieces more active. For example, in this position 34 e5 ♘f5 35 ♘xf5 ♗xf5 36 e6 can be met by 36...♘xd5.

34...♕h4 35 a4

Here, too, 35 e5 can be met by 35...♘f5, for example 36 e6 ♘xe3 37

♕xe3 ♗c8 38 ♘f5 ♕h5 39 ♘e7 ♖xg2+ 40 ♔xg2 ♘xd5 etc.

35...♘f7 36 ♘h1

And not 36 e5? because of 36...♘h6!, suddenly threatening ...♘g4+.

36...♕h6

Black doesn't want to exchange queens with 36...♕xf2 as his counterplay lies in the weakness of White's king.

37 a5 ♘c8 38 e5

38 ♘g3 ♕h4 39 ♘h1 ♕h6 would repeat, while after something like 38 ♖g3 ♖e8 39 ♖c3 ♘fd6 40 ♖e3 ♘e7 Black's knights would start to get frisky.

38...fxe5 39 fxe5 ♘xe5!

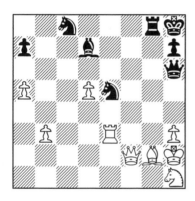

Getting rid of White's monster pawns and forcing a draw.

40 ♖xe5 ♕d6 ½-½

41 ♕f4 ♖f8 42 ♕g3 ♖g8 is a repetition.

Game 27
T.Nyback-S.Lputian
European Club Cup,
Kallithea 2008

---

1 d4 d5 2 c4 e6 3 ♘f3 ♘f6 4 g3 ♗e7 5 ♗g2 0-0 6 0-0 c6 7 ♕c2 ♘bd7 8 ♘bd2

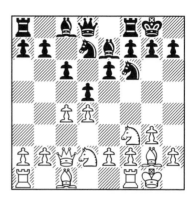

As I mentioned earlier, I think this plan is good for White. He wants to play simply e2-e4 and will decide the fate of his queen's bishop later.

8...b6 9 e4 ♗b7 10 ♖e1

Once again a simple and direct way to play it. Instead, 10 b3 leads to the kind of positions examined in Game 25 (Bogdanovski-Lputian), for example 10...♖c8 11 ♗b2 ♕c7 12 ♖fe1 dxe4 13 ♘xe4 c5 14 ♘xf6+ ♗xf6 15 ♖ad1 cxd4 16 ♘xd4 a6 was equal in B.Thorfinnsson-H.Danielsen, Differdange 2008.

10...♖c8 11 e5 ♘e8 12 cxd5 cxd5 13 ♕a4

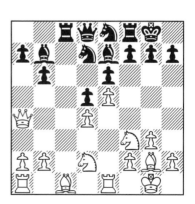

13...♘c7

Other moves have been tried here, for example:

a) 13...a5 14 ♗f1 (14 ♘b1!?, intending to put the knight on c3, looks interesting) 14...♘b8 15 ♗d3 ♗a6 16 ♗b1 ♘c6 17 ♘f1 ♗b4 18 ♗d2 f5 was none too promising in V.Filippov-L.Portisch, European Cup, Chalkidiki 2002.

b) 13...a6 14 ♘f1 b5 15 ♕d1 ♘b6 16 h4 a5 17 ♕d3 ♗a6 18 ♘g5 g6 left Black with serious weaknesses on the kingside in C.Horvath-I.Vukovic, Zalakaros 2006.

14 ♘f1 b5 15 ♕d1 a5

In Z.Izoria-E.Agrest, Las Vegas 2003, Black played 15...b4, but after 16 h4 ♘b8 17 ♗g5 ♘c6 18 ♘e3 White was building up nicely on the kingside without Black having much counterplay on the other flank.

16 h4 a4 17 ♘1h2 ♖a8

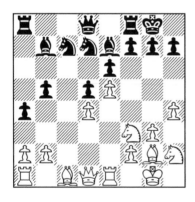

The first sign that things aren't going too well for Black. He wants to play ...b5-b4 but must first defend the a4-pawn.

18 ♗f1 b4 19 ♗d3 f5 20 exf6 ♘xf6

20...gxf6? 21 ♗f4 would make it difficult for Black to defend his e6-pawn.

21 ♗f4 ♘e4 22 ♘g5 ♗xg5 23 hxg5 ♘xg5

If anything this helps White further develop his initiative. 23...a3 would have made it more difficult.

24 ♕h5 ♘e4 25 f3 ♘f6 26 ♕h4!?

Playing for mate. White would also be better after 26 ♕e5, for example 26...♗a6 27 ♗xa6 ♘xa6 28 ♕xe6+ ♔h8 29 ♖ac1 keeps up the pressure.

26...♗a6 27 ♗c2!?

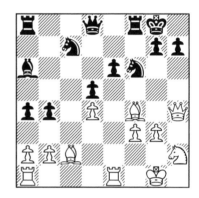

Still trying for mate. 27 ♗xh7+ ♘xh7 28 ♕xd8 ♖fxd8 29 ♗xc7 would recover the pawn but produce a drawish endgame.

27...b3

I suspect that after 27...♘b5 White would have played the calm 28 ♖ad1, protecting the pawn on d4, while keeping his light-squared bishop on the b1-h7 diagonal.

28 axb3 axb3 29 ♗b1 h6

It's hard to believe that 29...h5 would have been better, but at least it prevents White's next powerful move.

30 ♘g4 ♘ce8

After 30...♘xg4 31 ♕xg4 ♖f7 32 ♖c1

♘b5 33 ♗e5 I don't see any good moves for Black.

31 ♗xh6!

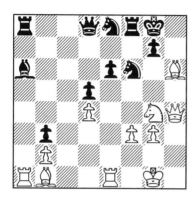

31...♘xg4

Or 31...gxh6 32 ♘xh6+ ♔g7 33 ♖xe6, when Black is defenceless against the many threats.

32 ♕xg4 ♕f6

32...♕d7 33 ♗f4 ♘f6 34 ♕xe6+ ♕xe6 35 ♖xe6 would leave White a pawn up in the endgame.

33 ♗g5 ♕xf3 34 ♕xe6+ ♕f7 35 ♗f4 ♕xe6 36 ♖xe6 ♗c8 37 ♖xa8 ♗xe6 38 ♖b8

Winning a vital pawn.

38...♘f6 39 ♖xb3 ♘e4 40 ♖b6 ♗f5 41 ♗a2 ♘f6 42 b4 ♔f7 43 b5 ♖h8?

Losing immediately. 43...♗e4 would have been more tenacious.

44 ♖xf6+! gxf6 45 b6 1-0

Game 28
T.Tolnai-I.Almasi
Hungarian Team
Championship 2003

---

1 g3 ♘f6 2 ♗g2 d5 3 ♘f3 e6 4 0-0 ♗e7

5 c4 0-0 6 d4 ♘bd7 7 ♕c2 c6 8 ♘bd2 b6 9 e4 ♗a6

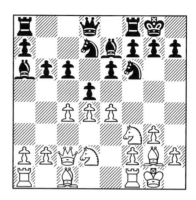

An alternative to 9...♗b7, examined in the previous game.

10 e5!?

The traditional way of playing such positions was to try and lock the bishop on a6 out of the game with 10 b3, which leads back into Bogdanovski-Lputian (Game 25) after 10...♖c8 11 ♖d1. Tolnai's treatment is more promising I think.

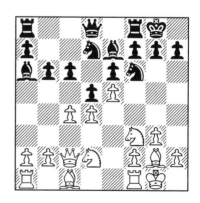

10...♘e8 11 ♖e1 ♖c8 12 ♕a4

It's still not too late to revert to b2-b3 plans with 12 b3, when A.Shirov-S.Azarov, European Club Cup, Kemer

2007, proceeded 12...c5 13 ♗b2 ♘c7 14 ♖ad1 b5 15 dxc5 ♗xc5 16 cxd5 ♘xd5 17 ♕b1 ♗b4 18 ♖e4!? ♗e7 19 ♖g4!? ♕c7 20 ♘e4 ♕c2 21 ♕a1 h5 22 ♘d4 ♕c7 23 ♖g5 ♗xg5 24 ♘xg5 ♖fe8 25 ♗xd5 exd5 26 e6 fxe6 27 ♘gxe6 ♕b6 28 ♘f4 ♘f6? 29 ♘f5 with a massive attack. Frankly I think that the position after 17 ♕b1 was as dull as dishwater for White and that the way things subsequently erupted was more a function of Mr Shirov's remarkable abilities than anything else.

12...♘b8 13 cxd5 cxd5 14 ♘f1

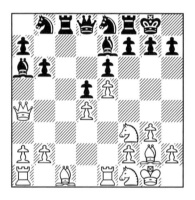

This is a 'new move' from Tolnai, but I suspect he was making it up as he went along and just made a logical move.

In an earlier game, S.Chloupek-M.Zlatohlavek, Czech Team Ch. 1991, White played 14 ♗f1, after which 14...♗xf1 15 ♘xf1 ♕d7 16 ♕xd7 ♘xd7 17 ♗d2 ♘c7 18 ♖ac1 ♘a6 led to a much easier endgame for Black, the exchange of a couple of minor pieces easing his cramp.

Besides Tolnai's move I think that White has another interesting possibility in 14 ♘b1, intending to bring the knight to c3. After 14...♕d7 15 ♕xd7 (15 ♕d1 ♘c6 16 ♘c3 is also possible) 15...♘xd7 16 ♘c3, White again enjoys more space in the endgame.

14...♕d7 15 ♕xd7 ♘xd7

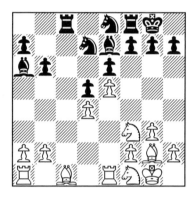

Despite the simplification brought about by the exchange of queens, White is slightly better here. The key factor once more is his extra space and the possibility of advancing his kingside pawns.

16 ♗d2 ♘c7 17 ♘e3

White could also play 17 ♖ac1, the point being that 17...♘b5 is simply met by 18 a4 ♘c7 19 ♘e3.

17...♗d3 18 ♖ec1 a5

White can answer 18...♗e4 with 19 ♖c3, for example 19...♘b5 20 ♖xc8 ♖xc8 21 a4 ♘c7 22 ♖c1 with ongoing pressure, but this would have been a better way for Black to play it.

19 ♘e1 ♗e2 20 f4 a4?!

Giving White the b4-square, though Black's position is far from easy in any case. For example, 20...♘b5 21 ♔f2 ♘xd4 22 ♗c3 ♘b5 23 ♔xe2 d4 leaves White with a clear advantage after 24 ♗d2 dxe3 25 ♗xe3.

21 ♔f2 ♗a6 22 ♘1c2 ♘b8 23 ♗b4 ♗xb4 24 ♘xb4

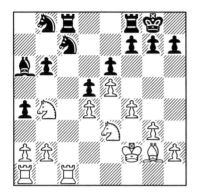

White is clearly better thanks to his strong knight on b4 and extra space.

24...♗b5 25 ♘d1 ♘ca6 26 ♘xa6 ♗xa6 27 ♘c3 ♖c4 28 ♔e3 ♖fc8 29 a3 ♖4c7 30 ♗f3 g6 31 ♗d1 ♘c6

Attempting to protect the a4-pawn with 31...b5 would lead to a total paralysis after 32 ♗e2 ♖c6 33 ♖ab1 ♔f8 34 ♘a2 ♔e7 35 ♖c3 etc.

32 ♘xa4 ♘xd4 33 ♖xc7 ♘f5+ 34 ♔d2 ♖xc7 35 ♘xb6

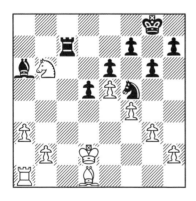

Emerging a pawn up, and the win in sight.

35...♖b7 36 ♘a4 d4 37 b4 ♘e3 38 ♘c5

♘c4+ 39 ♔e1 ♖a7 40 ♘xa6 ♖xa6 41 ♗e2 ♖xa3 42 ♖xa3 ♘xa3 43 ♗d3 1-0

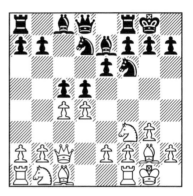

> ## Game 29
> ## B.Damljanovic-G.Quillan
> Granada 2007

1 ♘f3 ♘f6 2 c4 e6 3 g3 d5 4 d4 ♗e7 5 ♗g2 0-0 6 0-0 ♘bd7 7 ♕c2 c5!?

An attempt to equalize in the centre which surfaces now and then, but Damljanovic's play in this game makes it look rather unpalatable.

8 ♖d1

In one of my own games I responded with 8 dxc5, N.Davies-I.Shrentzel, Tel Aviv 1993, continuing 8...♘xc5 9 ♘c3 dxc4 10 ♘e5 ♘d5 (10...♗d7 11 ♘xc4 ♖c8 12 ♖d1 ♘a4 was okay for Black in J.Flesch-A.Lein, Ordzhonikidze 1964, and this may be a better way for him to play it) 11 ♖d1 ♘b4 12 ♕b1 ♕c7 13 ♗f4 g5 14 ♘g6 gxf4 15 ♘b5 ♕b6 16 ♘xe7+ ♔g7 17 ♘xc8 (17 ♘d6 ♘cd3 18 exd3 ♕xd6 19 ♘xc8 ♖axc8 20 dxc4 keeps an edge too) 17...♖axc8 18 ♘d6 ♖cd8 19 ♘xc4 ♕c7

20 ♕c1 ♖xd1+ 21 ♕xd1 f6 22 ♕c1 b5 23 ♘a3 with the better game for White.

8...cxd4 9 ♘xd4 e5 10 ♘f5 d4 11 e3

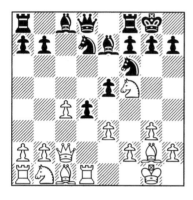

11...dxe3 12 ♘xe7+

White can also play 12 ♗xe3 immediately, when 12...♖e8 13 ♘xe7+ ♕xe7 14 ♘c3 was very pleasant for White in J.Sylvan-R.Cannon, Copenhagen 2007, due to his bishops, space and queen-side pawn majority.

12...♕xe7 13 ♗xe3 ♘g4 14 ♗c1 ♘c5 15 h3 ♘f6 16 ♗e3 ♗e6 17 b3 ♖ac8 18 ♘c3 b6 19 ♖d2

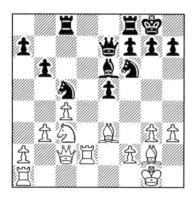

White has a nice plus here, again because of his bishop pair and queen-side pawn majority.

19...a5 20 ♖ad1 ♖fd8 21 g4 ♘e8 22 ♘e4 ♖xd2 23 ♖xd2 f6 24 f4 exf4 25 ♗xf4 ♗f7 26 ♘c3

Emphasizing the weakness of the d5-square now that his dark-squared bishop has been activated.

26...♗g6 27 ♕d1 ♘e4?

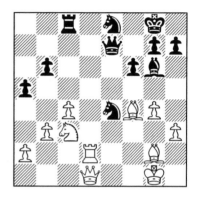

Trying to escape the torture but stepping into a series of pins.

28 ♕e1 ♕c5+ 29 ♗e3 ♕c6 30 ♗f2 ♘8d6 31 ♖xd6! ♕xd6 32 ♘xe4 ♕e6 33 ♘c3 ♕d6 34 ♕e3 ♖e8 35 ♗d5+ ♔h8 36 ♕xb6 ♕f4 37 ♕d4 ♕g5 38 ♗c6 1-0

Summary

Rather than becoming embroiled in positions akin to the Bogdanovski-Lputian game, there's a very strong case for keeping it simple with 8 ♘bd2 followed by 9 e4. I do understand that this cuts across conventional wisdom and many years of established theory, but if White gains space on the king-side with e4-e5, I really don't want my dark-squared bishop sitting on b2.

Chapter Seven

Closed Catalan with 7 ♘c3

1 d4 ♘f6 2 c4 e6 3 g3 d5 4 ♗g2 ♗e7 5 ♘f3 0-0 6 0-0 ♘bd7 7 ♘c3

The Closed Catalan with 7 ♘c3 can be reached via a number of different move orders, which is why this chapter is quite important. Besides the regular Catalan there is, for example, 1 d4 d5 2 c4 e6 3 ♘c3 ♘f6 4 ♘f3 ♗e7 5 g3 0-0 6 ♗g2 ♘bd7 7 0-0.

Black's set-up appears to make perfect sense against a knight on c3, because it seems that he can try to take the c4-pawn and then defend his ill-gotten gains with ...♘d7-b6. White certainly wouldn't want to play c4xd5, as after ...e6xd5 Black liberates his c8-bishop.

It turns out, however, that if Black does take on c4, White can obtain compensation by playing e2-e4 and getting a broad pawn centre. In Ivanisevic-Lepelletier (Game 30) Black broke the centre up with 8...c5, but this is very risky because of 10 e5!? (rather than 10 exd5 as played in the game). In Jirka-Brener

(Game 31) Black was successful in taking on c4 and then hanging on to the pawn, but White can play the middlegame better, with 14 h3 for example and long-term positional compensation.

White also has another approach – protecting the pawn with ♕d1-d3 before Black takes it. I personally don't like this much because the queen seems exposed on d3. Jozsef Horvath evidently disagrees (see Game 32, Horvath-Manole), but Bauer-Timofeev (Game 33) rather confirms my view. Once Timofeev had a grip on the position it seemed very difficult for White to do anything, so this is an argument for 9 e4.

1 d4 ♘f6 2 c4 e6 3 ♘c3 d5 4 ♘f3 ♗e7 5

g3 0-0 6 ⍦g2 dxc4

6...⍦bd7 7 0-0 c6 8 ♕d3 will be examined in Games 32 and 33.

7 0-0 ⍦bd7

Reaching a position that we'll be dealing with via the move order 3 g3 d5 4 ⍦g2 ⍦e7 5 ⍦f3 0-0 6 0-0 ⍦bd7 7 ⍦c3 dxc4.

8 e4 c5

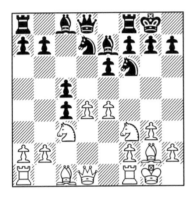

Trying to free his game rather than hold onto the extra pawn. 8...c6 is examined in the next game.

9 d5

Some other moves:

a) 9 ♕e2?! cxd4 10 ⍦xd4 ⍦e5 11 ⍦d1 ⍦d3 12 ⍦e3 e5 13 ⍦f3 ♕a5 was good for Black in B.Khotenashvili-T.Gasparian, Tbilisi 2007.

b) 9 e5 ⍦d5 10 ⍦e4 (it's difficult to believe that 10 ⍦xd5 exd5 would offer White enough play) 10...b5 11 dxc5 ⍦xc5 12 ⍦xc5 ⍦xc5 13 ⍦g5 ⍦e7 14 ♕g4 ⍦b8 15 ⍦d1 ♕c7 left White struggling to generate enough for his pawn in M.Bach-F.Hegeler, Hamburg 1997.

c) 9 ⍦f4!? is interesting, for example 9...cxd4 (9...⍦b6 10 a4 cxd4 11 ⍦xd4 a6 12 a5 ⍦bd7 13 e5 ⍦d5 14 ⍦xd5 exd5 15

⍦f5 ⍦c5 16 ⍦xe7+ ♕xe7 17 ⍦xd5 was better for White in M.Sorokin-E.Pigusov, Voronezh 1988) 10 ♕xd4 ⍦b6 (instead 10...⍦c5 11 ♕xc4 ♕d3 12 ♕b4 a5 13 ♕b6 ⍦cxe4 14 ⍦e5 ♕d6 was V.Ragozin-G.Levenfish, Leningrad 1936, when 15 ♕xd6 ⍦xd6 16 ⍦fd1 would have kept a strong initiative for the pawn, even in the endgame; while after 10...e5 11 ⍦xe5 ⍦xe5 12 ♕xe5 ⍦e6 13 ⍦d5 ⍦d7 14 ⍦xe7+ ♕xe7, as in Nguyen Anh Dung-I.Csom Budapest 1999, 15 ♕d6 would also have been good for White) 11 ♕e3 ♕d3 was V.Ragozin-A.Budo, Leningrad 1936, and now 12 ⍦fd1 ♕xe3 13 ⍦xe3 followed by ⍦d2 and ⍦f1 (as necessary) would recover the pawn on c4 with a slightly better endgame.

9...exd5

Black must be careful to avoid 9...⍦b6?, which loses a piece to 10 d6 ⍦xd6 (or 10...♕xd6 11 ♕xd6 ⍦xd6 12 e5) 11 e5 etc. Quite a few players have fallen for that one!

10 exd5

White has a dangerous alternative here in 10 e5!?,

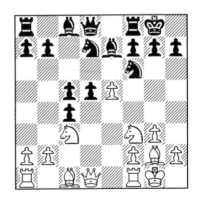

for example 10...♘g4 (10...♘e8 11 ♕xd5 ♘b6 12 ♕e4 ♕d3 is well met by 13 ♗e3, as 13...♕xe4 14 ♘xe4 ♘d7 15 ♖ac1 b5 16 ♖fd1 gives White a strong initiative) 11 ♕xd5 ♘b6 12 ♕e4 (12 ♕xd8!? ♖xd8 13 h3 ♘h6 14 g4 was also promising for White in M.Czerniak-A.Lev, Israeli Ch. 1976, the game proceeding 14...f6 15 a4 ♘f7 16 e6 ♗xe6 17 ♖e1 ♘e5 18 ♘xe5 fxe5 19 ♖xe5 ♔f7 20 a5 ♘c8? 21 a6! with White winning quickly) 12...♕d3 (12...f5 should be answered by 13 ♕f4, for example 13...h6 14 h3 ♗g5 15 ♘xg5 hxg5 16 ♕xg5 ♘xe5 17 a4! is a typical and strong idea) 13 h3 ♕xe4 (13...♘h6 14 ♖d1 ♕xe4 15 ♘xe4 ♗e6 was R.Martin Canfran-A.Picanol Alamany, Barcelona 2001, when 16 ♗g5 ♖fe8 17 ♗xe7 ♖xe7 18 ♘xc5 ♗d5 19 ♖ac1 would have recovered the pawn with the better game) 14 ♘xe4 ♘h6 (14...♗f5 15 ♘d6 ♘h6 16 ♘xb7 ♗d3 was played in G.De Fotis-W.Browne, US Open, Aspen 1968, and now 17 ♖e1 would have set Black more problems) 15 ♗e3 (15 g4!? is interesting, to shut the knight on h6 out of the game) 15...♘f5 16 ♗xc5 ♘a4 17 ♗xe7 ♘xe7 18 b3 ♘b6 19 ♘d4 and White had a strong initiative in A.Skripchenko-M.Congiu, French Women's Ch., Besancon 2006.

10...♘b6

10...♗d6 11 ♗g5 h6 12 ♗xf6 ♘xf6 13 ♘d2 ♗e5 14 ♘xc4 ♗d4 15 ♘b5 ♗g4 16 ♕d2 ♘xd5 17 ♘xd4 cxd4 18 ♕xd4 gave White some pressure in A.O'Kelly de Galway-G.Stoltz, Dortmund 1951, due to the strong Catalan bishop on g2.

11 ♘e5 ♗d6 12 f4

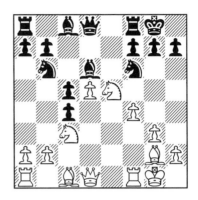

It doesn't seem as good to protect the knight with 12 ♖e1, for example 12...♖e8 13 f4 ♗f5 14 h3 ♗d3 15 ♘xd3 cxd3 16 ♖xe8+ ♕xe8 17 ♕xd3 ♕e1+ 18 ♔h2 c4 gave Black the initiative in I.Kan-A.Kotov, USSR Ch., Leningrad 1939.

It's also worth pointing out that 12 ♗f4? loses a piece to 12...g5!, as this has been played in at least one game!

12...♖e8 13 ♕f3

This natural and aggressive move seems to have been a novelty. Earlier White focused on 13 a4, for example 13...a5 (13...♗xe5 14 fxe5 ♗g4 15 ♕e1!? ♘fxd5 16 a5 ♘xc3 17 ♕xc3 gave White active play in B.Nikcevic-F.Van Hasselt, Paris 1994) 14 ♘b5 (14 h3 h5 15 ♕f3 ♕c7 16 ♗d2 ♗d7 17 ♘xd7 ♕xd7 left Black solid enough in K.Miton-S.Zavgorodniy, Moscow 2002) 14...♗xe5 (14...♗f5 15 ♖e1 ♘g4 16 ♘xg4 ♖xe1+ 17 ♕xe1 ♗xg4 18 ♗d2 was better for White in M.Petursson-M.Dutreeuw, San Bernardino 1989) 15 fxe5 ♖xe5 16 ♗f4 ♖xd5 17 ♗xd5 ♘bxd5 18 ♗c7 ♕e8 19 ♖e1 ♕c6 20 ♗e5 wasn't clear in V.Ragozin-L.Rudakovsky, USSR Ch., Moscow 1940.

13...♖xe5!?

This might be a bit of an overreaction, though Black does get some compensation here. Moves such as 13...♕c7 and 13...♗d7 look solid enough, with play along the lines of Miton-Zavgorodniy, given in the previous note.

14 fxe5 ♗xe5 15 h3 ♗d7 16 ♗f4 ♗d4+ 17 ♔h2?!

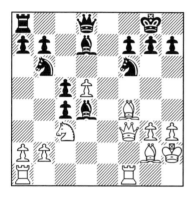

In view of the possible reply, White should have played 17 ♗e3, when 17...♕e7 18 ♖ae1 ♗xc3 19 bxc3 ♘fxd5 20 ♗g5! ♕f8 produces a sharp position in which both sides have chances.

17...♕f8?!

It seems that both players might have missed 17...♘fxd5 18 ♘xd5 ♗c6, recovering the piece with a good game for Black.

18 ♖ae1 ♖e8

Another possibility was 18...♗xc3 19 ♕xc3 ♘fxd5, for example 20 ♗xd5 ♘xd5 21 ♕xc4 ♗c6 with two pawns for the exchange and a solid enough position.

19 g4 ♘c8?!

19...♗xc3 20 bxc3 ♘fxd5 is still quite

playable, and indeed probably Black's best. After the passive text Black gradually drifts into an inferior position.

20 a4 b6 21 ♕g3 a6 22 d6 ♖xe1 23 ♖xe1 ♘e8 24 ♘d5 ♔h8?

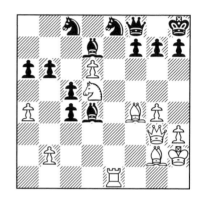

For better or worse Black had to go for 24...♘exd6, for example 25 ♗xd6 ♕xd6 26 ♕xd6 ♘xd6 27 ♘xb6 ♗e6 produces an endgame which is probably tenable with accurate play. Now White crawls into his guts.

25 ♘e7 ♘a7?

After this Black is completely lost. The best chance lay in 25...g5!? 26 ♗xg5 ♘exd6, at least getting rid of White's passed d-pawn.

26 ♗e5

26 ♕f3! intending 27 ♕b7 seems even stronger.

26...♘f6 27 g5 ♘e8

27...♗xe5 28 ♕xe5 ♘h5 29 a5 would decisively undermine Black's queenside pawns.

28 ♗d5 1-0

Black doesn't have any good moves and is threatened with 29 ♖f1, amongst other horrors.

Game 31   **J.Jirka-I.Brener**   Brno 2007

1 d4 ♘f6 2 c4 e6 3 g3 d5 4 ♗g2 ♗e7 5 ♘f3 0-0 6 0-0 dxc4 7 ♘c3 ♘bd7 8 e4 c6

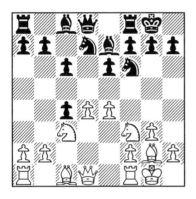

Aiming to hold on to the c4-pawn.

9 a4

White might also consider just 9 ♕e2 b5 10 ♖d1, relying on his central pawns for compensation.

9...a5

Stopping the further advance of White's a-pawn and 'sealing' the weakness on b4. But there other possibilities here:

a) 9...b6 10 ♕e2 ♗a6 11 ♖d1 ♕c8 12 d5 (12 ♗g5 ♗b4! 13 ♘d2 h6 14 ♗f4!? ♖e8! 15 ♖ac1 was V.Inkiov-I.Farago, European Team Ch., Skara 1980, when 15...e5! 16 dxe5 ♘xe5 17 ♗xe5 ♖xe5 18 f4 ♗c5+ 19 ♔h1 ♘g4! would have been better for Black according to Farago) 12...exd5! 13 exd5 (13 e5?! is good for Black after 13...♘e4 14 ♘xe4 dxe4 15 ♕xe4 ♘c5) 13...♖e8 14 dxc6 ♘c5 15 ♘b5

(15 ♘e5!? is worth considering, for example 15...♗f8 16 ♗g5 ♘d3 17 ♗xf6 gxf6 18 ♕g4+ ♕xg4 19 ♘xg4 ♔g7 20 c7 ♖ac8 21 ♘d5 etc) 15...♘d3 (15...♘b3 is strongly met by 16 ♘g5 ♘xa1 17 ♕xc4 ♖f8 18 ♗f4 with more than enough for the exchange) 16 ♖xd3! cxd3 17 ♕xd3 ♕xc6! seems to leave White with nothing better than 18 ♘fd4 (instead 18 ♘g5 ♖ad8! 19 ♕b3 ♘d5 20 ♗e3 was I.Zaitsev-P.Lukacs, Dubna 1979, and now 20...♗b7! would have been good for Black) 18...♕c5 19 ♗xa8 ♖xa8 20 ♗e3 ♕d5 21 ♕f5, when he is slightly worse in the coming endgame.

b) 9...e5

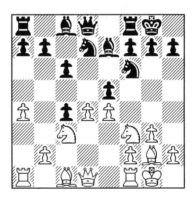

10 dxe5 (both 10 ♘xe5?! ♘xe5 11 dxe5 ♘g4, and 10 d5 ♗b4 are quite good for Black) 10...♘g4 11 ♗f4 (11 e6?! fxe6 12 ♘d4 can be met by 12...♘de5, the point being that 13 f4 is refuted by 13...♗c5!) 11...♕a5 12 e6 (12 ♘d5!? cxd5 13 exd5 ♖e8 14 h3 is possible) 12...fxe6 13 e5! (13 ♕e2 ♘ge5 14 ♘d4! ♘d3! 15 ♘xe6 ♖f6 16 ♗c7 ♕b4 17 ♘d4 ♗c5! 18 ♘c2 ♕xb2 19 ♘d1 ♕b3 20 ♘de3 ♘7e5 was good for Black in V.Topalov-V.Kramnik, Linares 1997; while after 13

♗d6!? ♗xd6 14 ♕xd6 ♘de5 15 ♘xe5 ♘xe5 16 ♖ab1! ♖d8 17 ♕e7 ♘g6 18 ♕a3 e5 19 b4!, as in G.Sosonko-J.Van der Wiel, Wijk aan Zee 1987, then 19...cxb3 20 ♕xb3+ ♔h8 21 ♖fd1 ♗g4 would have left White struggling to justify his play) 13...♘dxe5 14 ♘xe5 ♘xe5 15 ♕h5 ♗d6! (15...♖f5 16 ♕e8+ ♗f8 17 ♗e4 ♘f7 18 ♗xf5 ♕xf5 19 ♖ae1 e5 20 ♗xe5 was good for White in E.Mochalov-L.Yagupov, Orel 1999) 16 ♘e4 ♖f5 17 ♕e8+ ♖f8 18 ♕h5 ♖f5 19 ♕e8+ ½-½ V.Topalov-G.Kasparov, Sarajevo 2000.

10 ♕e2 b6 11 ♖d1 ♗a6 12 ♗f4 ♗b4

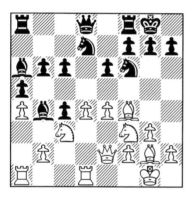

Black has succeeded in holding the c4-pawn, but where does he go from here? The problem is that he lacks a clear plan. Black has tried a couple of other moves:

a) 12...♖a7 13 d5! cxd5 14 ♘d4 ♘c5!? 15 ♘c6 ♕d7 16 ♘xa7 ♕xa7 17 exd5 exd5 18 ♗xd5 ♘d3 was L.Szabo-G.Forintos, Budapest 1970, and now 19 ♗e3 looks like White's most solid option with the better game.

b) 12...♖e8 13 ♘d2 ♖c8 14 ♘xc4 ♘d5 15 ♗d2 ♘b4 16 ♗e3 (16 ♖ac1 would keep things going) 16...♘d5 17 ♗d2

♘b4 ½-½ was G.Sosonko-P.Van der Sterren, Dutch Ch., Hilversum 1987.

13 ♕c2

The immediate 13 d5 seems playable here, for example 13...cxd5 14 exd5 e5 15 ♘xe5 ♖e8 16 d6 wasn't clear in L.Hansen-S.Hamann, Danish Junior Ch. 1988.

13...♖e8

C.Bauer-S.Conquest, Bilbao (rapid) 2004, provided a good illustration of how White should handle this type of position, the game proceeding 13...♖a7 14 h3 h6 15 g4 ♗e7 16 ♗e3 ♕c8 17 g5 hxg5 18 ♗xg5 ♖e8 19 e5 ♘h5 20 ♗xe7 ♖xe7 21 ♘e4 with ongoing compensation for the pawn. In the main game I don't think White chooses an especially good plan.

14 ♖d2

Hereabouts White starts to go the wrong way. I think he should play like Bauer in the previous note with 14 h3 followed by 15 g4.

14...♕c8 15 ♖ad1 ♖a7 16 h4

Here, too, I prefer 16 h3 followed by g3-g4.

16...b5 17 ♗h3 bxa4

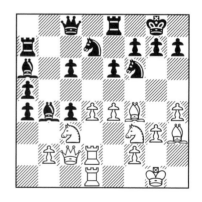

Black is doing well now as White's pieces are all a bit loose. Jirka decides to sacrifice the exchange but never looks like having enough.

18 ♘xa4 ♗xd2 19 ♖xd2 h6 20 g4 ♕b7 21 ♘c3 ♕b3 22 ♕c1?

22 g5 is a better try, but with a material deficit one can understand White's eagerness to avoid the exchange of queens.

22...♘xe4 23 ♖c2

And not 23 ♘xe4? ♕xf3 etc.

23...♘xc3 24 ♖xc3 ♕b5 25 ♘d2 e5 26 ♖e3 ♖aa8 27 dxe5 ♘c5

Black decides that 27...♘xe5 28 ♕e1 f6 29 g5 would give White more counterplay.

28 ♗f1 ♘d3 29 ♗xd3 cxd3 30 h5

After an immediate 30 g5 Black can block the kingside with 30...h5, so White must first preclude this possibility if he wants to make a breakthrough.

30...♖ad8 31 ♖g3 ♕a4 32 ♘f3 ♕c2 33 ♕e1 ♕e2 34 ♕xa5 ♗c4 35 g5

White presses on with his attack, but Black comes first through the centre.

35...d2! 36 ♘xd2 ♕e1+ 37 ♔g2

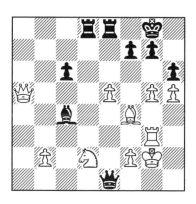

37...♗f1+! 38 ♔g1

If 38 ♘xf1 ♕xa5 wins the queen.

38...♗h3+ 39 ♔h2 ♕xf2+ 40 ♔xh3 ♕xf4 41 ♘f3 ♖d3 42 ♔g2 hxg5 0-1

Game 32
Jo.Horvath-V.Manole
Aschach Donau 2007

1 d4 ♘f6 2 ♘f3 d5 3 c4 e6 4 ♘c3 ♗e7 5 g3 0-0 6 ♗g2 ♘bd7 7 ♕d3 c6 8 0-0

4 g3 ♗e7 5 ♗g2 0-0 6 0-0 ♘bd7 7 ♘c3 c6 8 ♕d3 would be the Catalanesque route to this position.

8...b6

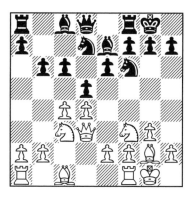

8...a6 is a solid option that we'll look at in the next game.

9 ♖d1

This is a good way to encourage Black's bishop to come out to a6.

Instead, O.Romanishin-K.Bischoff, Essen 2001, featured the interesting 9 b3 a5!?, after which 10 ♖d1 ♗a6 11 ♗b2 b5!? 12 cxb5 cxb5 13 ♘xb5 ♘e4 14 a4 ♖b8 15 ♖dc1 ♕b6 16 ♗f1 ♗xb5 17 axb5 ♕xb5 18 ♕xb5 ♖xb5 19 ♖c7 ♖d8 led to a draw.

In V.Korchnoi-T.V.Petrosian, Moscow 1975, White played 9 e4 ♗a6 10 b3 ♖c8 11 ♗f4 (11 ♖d1 would lead back into the main game), which Petrosian should have answered by 11...c5! 12 exd5 exd5 13 ♘b5 dxc4 14 bxc4 ♗xb5 15 cxb5 ♘d5, with a good game for Black.

9...♗a6 10 b3 ♖c8

10...c5 11 e4 ♖c8 would come to the same thing.

11 e4 c5

The critical line, though other moves have also been tried:

a) 11...dxe4 12 ♘xe4 ♘xe4 13 ♕xe4 leads to a typical Catalan position that can arise from other lines. White is better because of his extra space, for example 13...b5 14 ♕c2 bxc4 15 bxc4 ♕a5 16 ♗d2 ♗b4 17 ♗f4 ♗e7 18 ♖ab1 left Black uncomfortably placed in V.Mikhalevski-L.Ravi, Calcutta 2001.

b) 11...♕c7 12 ♗f4 ♕b7 13 e5! ♘e8 14 a4! ♕b8 15 ♗g5 ♗xg5 16 ♘xg5 g6 17 g4 led to a strong kingside attack in D.Yevseev-S.Azarov, Minsk 2000.

12 exd5 exd5 13 ♘b5!?

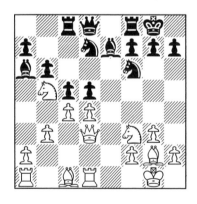

An interesting sideline which de-

serves more attention. Other possibilities are as follows:

a) 13 ♗b2 dxc4 14 bxc4 cxd4 15 ♘b5 ♗xb5 16 cxb5 ♘c5 17 ♕xd4 ♕xd4 18 ♘xd4 ♘a4 19 ♘f5 ♗c5 (19...♖fe8 20 ♗d4 was good for White in O.Romanishin-D.Ciric, Dortmund 1976) 20 ♗xf6 gxf6 21 ♖d7 ♘c3 22 a4 ♖cd8 23 ♖xa7 ♖d2 gave Black enough counterplay and led to a draw in G.Gross-S.Roy Chowdhury, Prague 2008.

b) 13 dxc5 dxc4 14 bxc4 ♘xc5 (14...♖xc5!? 15 ♘b5 ♗xb5 16 cxb5 ♖d5 17 ♘d4 ♘e5!? 18 ♕c3 ♗c5! 19 ♗b2 ♖d6 20 ♖d2 ♕d7 21 ♖ad1 ♕g4 22 h3! ♗xd4 23 hxg4 ♗xc3 24 ♗xc3 ♖xd2 25 ♖xd2 ♘exg4 26 ♗c6 gave White much the better endgame in E.Gleizerov-D.Barua, Calcutta 2002) 15 ♕f1 ♕e8 16 ♘b5?! (16 ♘d4 is stronger, with a tiny edge) 16...♘ce4 17 ♘fd4 ♗c5 18 ♗b2 ♕e5 19 ♕e2 ♗xb5 20 cxb5 was E.Gleizerov-R.Perez, Malaga 2001, and now just 20...♖fe8 would have given Black fully equal play.

13...dxc4

This seems to be better than capturing on d4 as White's pieces would then be very active. M.Petursson-G.Sigurjonsson, Icelandic Team Ch. 1995, saw 13...cxd4 14 ♘fxd4 ♗c5 (14...♘c5 was played in M.Praszak-T.Luther, Koszalin 1997, which White should probably have met with 15 ♕f5, getting away from the bishop on a6 – Black seems to be under some pressure here) 15 ♘xa7 dxc4 16 ♕f1 b5 17 ♘xc8 ♕xc8 18 ♗f4 and Black had inadequate compensation for the exchange.

14 bxc4 ♗xb5 15 cxb5 c4 16 ♕f5

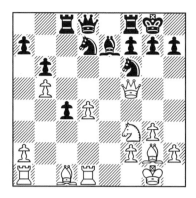

16...g6?!

It's probably better not to weaken the kingside. In H.Wirthensohn-H.Eis, German League 1993, Black played 16...♖e8, when 17 ♗g5 g6 18 ♕h3 ♘e4 19 ♗xe7 ♕xe7 gave him an excellent game. Maybe White can improve with 17 ♗f4, avoiding exchanges.

17 ♕c2 ♕c7 18 d5 ♗d6?

Black really shouldn't allow the white knight to come to c6 as it does in the game. 18...♗c5 was stronger, so as to meet 19 ♘d4 with 19...♗xd4 20 ♖xd4 ♕c5. I would still prefer White, but Black is fighting at least.

19 ♘d4 ♘e5 20 ♘c6 ♘xc6?

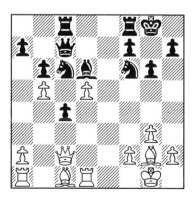

Black should probably do anything rather than give White this supported passed pawn on c6, for example 20...♖fe8 looks like a better fighting chance.

21 dxc6 ♖cd8 22 ♗b2 ♘g4 23 ♕xc4

The fall of the c4-pawn is the beginning of the end. Black will be unable to blockade the c6-pawn forever, especially when White sets up threats elsewhere on the board.

23...h5 24 ♗h3 ♘e5 25 ♕c3 f6 26 ♖d5 ♗c5 27 ♖ad1 ♖xd5 28 ♖xd5 ♕e7 29 ♔g2 g5 30 ♗f5 g4 31 ♕e1 ♖e8 32 ♗xe5 fxe5 33 ♕e4 ♖f8 34 ♖xe5 1-0

Game 33
C.Bauer-A.Timofeev
Spanish
Team Championship2007

---

1 d4 d5 2 c4 e6 3 ♘c3 ♗e7 4 ♘f3 ♘f6 5 g3 0-0 6 ♗g2 ♘bd7 7 ♕d3 c6 8 0-0 a6

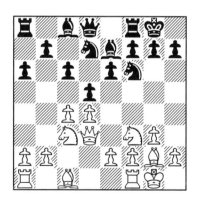

Aiming for ...b7-b5 is an interesting plan, not least because White cannot easily bring a knight in contact with the potentially weak c5-square. Besides this and 8...b6 (as in the previous game), another idea worth noting is 8...♕a5 9 e4 (9 b3 may be better) 9...♕a6. V.Mihajlovic-B.Tadic, Yugoslav Team Ch. 2002, continued 10 b3 dxc4 11 bxc4 e5 (11...♘b6!?) 12 dxe5 ♘g4 13 ♗f4 ♘c5 14 ♕c2 ♘e6 15 h3 ♘xf4 16 gxf4 ♘h6 17 f5 with much the better game for White because of the badly-placed knight on h6. But as noted, both sides may be able to improve on this.

9 ♗f4

Presumably Black intended to meet 9 e4 with the Meranesque 9...dxc4 (9...dxe4 10 ♘xe4 ♘xe4 11 ♕xe4 simply leaves White with a nice space advantage) 10 ♕xc4 b5 11 ♕e2 (11 ♕xc6 ♖a7 12 ♗f4 ♗b7 will win back the important e4-pawn) 11...♗b7 12 ♖d1, as in I.Macejovsky-M.Nabelek, Ostrava 2002, when 12...b4 13 ♘a4 ♕a5 14 b3 c5 seems to gain adequate counterplay. Nevertheless, I think this is the critical line, as in the game White seems to run out of ideas within a few moves.

9...♘h5 10 ♗e3 f5

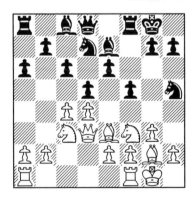

Now switching to a stonewall for-

mation, more characteristic of the Dutch than the Catalan. It looks as if Black has lost time, but White's 'extra' development seems to be ineffective in this type of position, what with his queen on d3 and bishop on e3.

11 ♖ad1 b5 12 c5

12 cxd5 cxd5 would leave White's pieces poorly placed, but it's not clear what they're doing on these squares after the text move either.

12...♗f6 13 ♗f4 ♘xf4 14 gxf4 a5 15 a3 b4

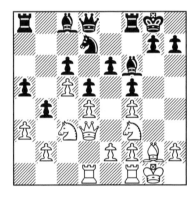

Black already has the initiative. Of course White needn't lose from this position, but the opening certainly hasn't gone well for him.

16 ♘a2 bxa3 17 ♕xa3 ♗a6 18 ♕e3 ♖e8 19 ♖d2 ♖b8 20 ♖a1 h6 21 ♕c3?!

The queen is exposed on c3. 21 ♘c1 looks like a better idea, intending to bring the knight to d3.

21...♗c4 22 ♘e5 ♘xe5 23 dxe5 ♗e7 24 b4 ♗xa2 25 ♖dxa2 axb4

Black is already winning here, but he faces stiff resistance in his attempts to convert it to a point on the scoreboard.

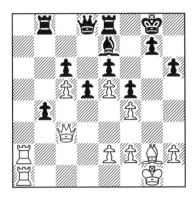

26 ♕d4 ♖b5 27 ♖c1 b3 28 ♖b2 ♕a5

Black can even play 28...♗xc5 29 ♕d3 ♕b6 etc.

29 ♕d3 ♖eb8 30 ♕g3 ♔h7 31 ♔h1 ♖xc5 32 ♖g1 ♕c3 33 ♗f3 ♗f8

33...g5! would, paradoxically, have been a good way to safeguard Black's king. After 34 fxg5 hxg5 35 ♕h3+ ♔g7 there's no further danger and the e5-pawn is hanging.

34 ♕g6+ ♔h8 35 ♖bb1 ♕d2?

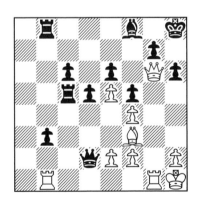

This could have spoiled everything. Time-trouble?

36 ♕xe6?

Missing 36 ♖xb3!, when 36...♖xb3? 37 ♕e8 ♔g8 38 ♗h5 creates trouble.

36...b2 37 ♕xf5 ♖c4 38 ♕g6 ♕xf4 39 e6 ♕f6 40 ♕g3 ♖a8 41 ♗h5 ♖e4 42 ♕c7 ♖a1 43 ♕b8 ♖b4 44 ♕e8 ♖xb1 45 ♖xb1 ♔h7 46 f3 g6 47 e7 ♕xe7

And not 47...♗xe7? because of 48 ♗xg6+ ♕xg6 49 ♕xe7+ ♔g8 50 ♕d8+ ♔f7 51 ♕d7+ ♔f8 52 ♕d8+ ♔g7 53 ♕e7+ ♔h8 54 ♕f8+ ♔h7 55 ♕e7+ etc with a draw by repetition.

48 ♕xg6+ ♔h8 49 ♗g4 ♕h7 50 ♕f6+ ♔g7 51 ♕d8+ ♔g8 52 ♕d6 ♖xg4! 53 fxg4 ♕e8

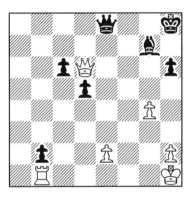

54 ♔g1?

54 ♕f4 would have been more tenacious.

54...♕e4 55 ♖xb2 ♕d4+ 56 e3 ♕xb2 57 ♕xc6 ♕b1+ 58 ♔f2 ♕e4 59 h3 ♔h7 60 ♕d7 ♔g6 61 ♔e2 ♗f6 62 ♕d6 ♕e5 63 ♕d7 ♔g5 64 ♕f7 ♔h4 65 ♕g6 ♗g5 66 ♕d3 ♕e4 0-1

Summary

I am somewhat sceptical about the ♕d1-d3 ideas and would advise White to steer clear of them. On the other hand, the sacrifice of the c4-pawn seems to offer White fair compensation.

Chapter Eight

Closed Catalan with 4...♗b4+

1 d4 ♘f6 2 c4 e6 3 g3 d5 4 ♗g2 ♗b4+

Setting up a Closed Catalan after first playing 4...♗b4+ 5 ♗d2 ♗e7 is quite an interesting treatment by Black. He argues that White's bishop on d2 would actually be better placed on c1, and given my recommendation of ♘bd2 and e2-e4 against the Closed, this appears justified.

White can handle this line in several different ways, of which the most popular is 6 ♘f3 0-0 7 0-0 ♘bd7 8 ♗f4 c6 9 ♕c2, as in the first three games of the chapter. White seems to have some pressure after 9...b6 (Vaganian-Gyimesi, Game 34), and Vaganian also gave a good demonstration of how to deal with 9...♘h5 (Vaganian-Kalashian, Game 36). But 9...a5 (Gelfand-Kamsky, Game 35) shows just how tough Black position can be if he doesn't create any new weaknesses.

Instead of 8 ♗f4 White can also put the bishop on g5 and Kaidanov-Stefansson (Game 37) also gave evidence of a slight edge for White. But this development is more likely to lead to simplification, and indeed Stefansson would have been close to equality with 15...♘xe5 instead of 15...♗xg2.

Last but not least we come to Carlsen-Stubberud (Game 38) in which White plays 5 ♘bd2 rather than 5 ♗d2. With the knight on f3 here (instead of the bishop on g2) this is a pawn sacrifice since Black can play 5...dxc4 transposing into lines covered in the next chapter (see Games 42 and 43). But Carlsen's opponent took the pawn a move later, after which it was easily recovered with a great game for White.

Game 34
R.Vaganian-Z.Gyimesi
Antwerp 2008

---

1 ♘f3 ♘f6 2 c4 e6 3 g3 d5 4 d4 ♗b4+ 5

♗d2

By far the most popular reaction, though 5 ♘bd2 also merits consideration (see Game 38).

5...♗e7 6 ♗g2 0-0 7 0-0 c6 8 ♗f4 ♘bd7 9 ♕c2 b6

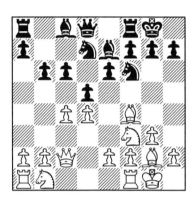

For 9...a5 see the next game, while 9...♘h5 is examined in Game 36.

10 ♖d1

It's difficult to get anywhere by just playing down the c-file, for example 10 cxd5 cxd5 11 ♖c1 (11 ♕c6 ♗a6 12 ♘c3 ♕c8 13 ♕a4 b5!? 14 ♘xb5 ♕c6 15 ♘c3 ♕xa4 16 ♘xa4 ♗xe2 was fine for Black in J.Nogueiras-W.Browne, Linares, Holland 1994; as was 11 ♗c7 ♕e8 12 ♘c3 ♗b7 13 ♖fc1 ♘b8! 14 a4 ♘c6 15 ♘b5 ♕d7 16 ♘e5 ♘xe5 17 ♗xe5 ♖fc8 in J.Plachetka-J.Ambroz, Czech Ch., Frenstat 1982) 11...♗b7 12 ♘c3 (12 ♘bd2 ♖c8 13 ♕d1 a6 14 ♖xc8 ♕xc8 15 ♖c1 ♕a8 16 ♘e5 ♖c8 17 ♘xd7 ♘xd7 18 ♘f3 ♖xc1 19 ♕xc1 ♕c8 petered out to equality in M.Mchedlishvili-Zhang Zhong, Manila 2008) 12...♖c8 13 ♕d3 (13 ♕d1 ♘e8 14 ♖c2 g5 15 ♗d2 ♘d6 16 ♖ac1 f6 17 ♘e1 f5 was again fine for Black in U.Andersson-E.Bareev, Ubeda

1997; as was 13 ♕b3 a6 14 a4 ♖c6 15 ♘a2 ♕a8 16 ♖xc6 ♗xc6 17 ♘b4 ♗b7 18 ♘d3 ♖c8 19 ♘de5 h6 in J.Smejkal-A.Yusupov, Thessaloniki Olympiad 1988) 13...a6 14 a4 ♖c6 15 ♖c2 ♕a8 16 ♖ac1 ♖fc8 17 ♘d2 ♗b4 18 ♘a2 ♖xc2 19 ♖xc2 ♗e7 and Black had no problems whatsoever in A.Wojtkiewicz-Y.Seirawan, Tilburg 1992.

Another possibility is 10 ♘bd2, as played in G.Kaidanov-A.Ivanov, Chicago 1995. The game proceeded 10...♗a6 11 ♖fe1 ♘h5 12 ♗e5!? ♖c8 13 cxd5 cxd5 14 ♕a4 ♗b7 15 ♕xa7 ♗c6 16 ♕a6 f6, and now Kaidanov later suggested 17 ♗h3! fxe5 18 ♗xe6+ ♔h8 19 ♘xe5 ♗b4 20 ♘xc6 ♖xc6 21 ♕b5, assessing this as better for White. There are of course many unanswered questions in this line.

10...♗b7

Black can also play 10...♗a6, for example 11 ♘e5 (if 11 cxd5 cxd5 12 ♘c3 b5! 13 a3 ♖c8 with the initiative) 11...♘xe5 (11...♕c8 12 cxd5 ♘xe5 13 d6! ♘g6 14 dxe7 ♘xe7 15 e4 was good for White in Y.Razuvaev-G.Borgo, Saint Vincent 2000; but 11...♖c8 12 ♕a4 ♘b8! 13 ♘d2! b5 14 cxb5 cxb5 15 ♕b3 ♕b6 was fine for Black in V.Tukmakov-A.Korotylev, Geneva 2001) 12 dxe5 ♘d7 13 cxd5 cxd5 14 e4 ♖c8 15 ♘c3 d4 16 ♖xd4 ♕c7 17 ♖ad1 ♖fd8 18 h4 h6 19 h5 ♗c5 20 ♖4d2 ♗e7 21 ♖d4 ♗c5 22 ♖4d2 was agreed drawn at this point in A.Lastin-V.Yemelin, Russian Team Ch. 2004.

11 ♘e5

White has also played 11 ♘c3, but this doesn't appear to trouble Black unduly after 11...♖c8 (11...dxc4 is well met by 12 ♘d2) 12 b3 c5! (12...♘h5 13 ♗c1 f5 14 ♗b2 ♗d6 15 e3 ♘hf6 16 ♘e2 ♘e4 17 ♘f4 ♕e7 18 ♘e5! ♘xe5 19 dxe5 ♗b8 20 a4! g5 21 ♘d3 g4 22 ♘f4 ♕f7 23 a5 gave White the initiative in M.Marin-R.Pogorelov, Andorra 1994) 13 cxd5! cxd4! (13...♘xd5? 14 ♘xd5 ♗xd5 15 e4! cxd4 16 ♕e2 ♗b7 17 ♘xd4 gave White a plus in R.Dautov-Z.Gyimesi, Germany-Hungary match, Budapest 2004, one of the points being that 17...e5? is met by 18 ♘f5 exf4 19 ♕g4 ♗f6 20 ♖xd7! etc) 14 ♘xd4 (if 14 d6 ♗xf3 15 ♗xf3 ♖xc3 16 dxe7 ♕xe7 17 ♗d6! ♖xc2 18 ♗xe7 ♖e8 is fine for Black) 14...♘xd5 15 ♗xd5 ♗xd5 16 ♕d3 ♘f6! etc.

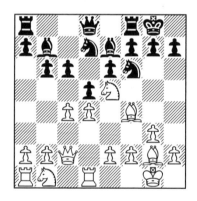

11...♖c8 12 ♘c3 ♘h5 13 ♗c1

This seems to be better than 13 ♗d2. For example, in D.Fridman-A.Yusupov, Essen 2002, Black replied with 13...♘hf6, after which 14 e4 c5 15 exd5 cxd4 16 ♘c6 ♗xc6 17 dxc6 ♘e5 18 ♘b5 ♘xc6 19 ♗f4 ♕d7 20 ♖ac1 ♗c5 21 ♗xc6 ♖xc6 22 ♗e5 ♕e7 23 ♘xd4 led to equality.

13...♘hf6

13...♕c7 14 ♘xd7 ♕xd7 15 e4 dxc4 16 ♕e2 ♘f6 17 ♕xc4 c5 18 dxc5 ♕c7 19 ♕e2 ♗xc5 20 ♗f4 e5 21 ♗g5 was agreed drawn in S.Ernst-I.Stohl, German League 2007.

Instead, in R.Fridman-R.Van der Burght, Dutch Team Ch. 2005, Black steered the game in the direction of a stonewall formation with 13...f5, but after 14 ♘xd7 ♕xd7 15 ♕a4 ♕c7 16 ♗f3 White held the initiative, as 16...♘f6 can be answered by 17 ♕xa7! ♖a8 18 ♗f4 etc.

14 e4 dxc4

In C.Lingnau-I.Farago, Senden 2003, Black played 14...c5, but after 15 exd5 cxd4 16 ♘xd7 ♕xd7 17 ♖xd4 exd5 18 cxd5 ♗c5 19 ♖h4 h6 20 ♗h3 ♕e7 he could count himself fortunate that White didn't respond with 21 ♗xh6! gxh6 22 ♕d2 ♘h7 23 ♕xh6 f5 24 ♗xf5 ♖xf5 25 ♕g6+ etc.

15 ♘xc4 b5 16 ♘e3 ♕b6

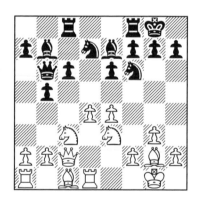

17 b3

The aggressive 17 f4!? was tried in V.Filippov-Z.Izoria, European Ch., Istanbul 2003, whereupon Black might have considered the immediate

17...c5!?. Instead he played 17...♖fd8, when the game reeled on 18 e5 ♘d5 19 ♕f2 f5 20 g4 g6 21 gxf5 gxf5 22 a4 b4 23 a5 ♕c7 24 ♘cxd5 cxd5 25 ♗d2, with White having the better of it because of his space.

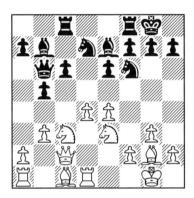

17...♖fd8

An earlier game, A.Wojtkiewicz-Zhang Zhong, Internet blitz 2004, went 17...♖fe8 18 h4 c5 19 d5 exd5 20 ♘exd5 ♗xd5 21 ♘xd5 ♘xd5 22 ♖xd5 ♘f6 23 ♖d1 c4 with good counterplay for Black. I rather suspect that Vaganian would have played 18 ♗b2, as he does after 17...♖fd8. With sensible play White should be slightly better here because of his nice central pawn configuration.

18 ♗b2 ♘f8 19 a4 a6

And not 19...♖xd4? because of the reply 20 ♖xd4 ♕xd4 21 ♘cd5 ♕c5 22 b4! etc.

20 ♕e2 ♘g6 21 h4

Reminiscent of Wojtkiewicz's play against Zhang Zhong, this kingside pawn advance is going to be much stronger now that Black has put his knight on g6.

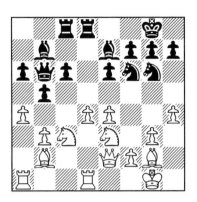

21...h6

21...♖xd4? is still bad due to 22 ♖xd4 ♕xd4 23 h5 ♘f8 24 ♘cd5 ♕c5 25 b4 etc.

22 axb5 axb5 23 e5 ♘e8

Going very passive, but he probably didn't like 23...♘d5 because of 24 ♘exd5 cxd5 (24...exd5 would give White a menacing kingside pawn majority) 25 h5 ♘f8 26 ♕xb5 ♕xb5 27 ♘xb5 ♖c2 28 ♗a3.

24 ♘e4 c5 25 dxc5 ♗xc5 26 ♖xd8 ♖xd8 27 ♘xc5 ♗xg2 28 ♘xe6

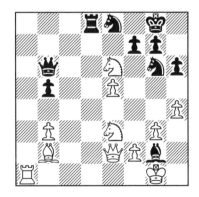

This wins a pawn, though the position gets quite exciting due to the exposure of White's king.

28...♕xe6 29 ♔xg2 ♘xe5 30 ♕xb5 ♘d3 31 ♖d1 ♘f4+ 32 ♔f3

And not 32 gxf4?! because of 32...♖xd1 33 ♘xd1 ♕g4+ etc.

32...♖xd1 33 ♘xd1 ♘d5 34 ♕c4 ♘d6 35 ♕g4 ♘f5 36 ♕e4 ♕d7 37 ♔g2

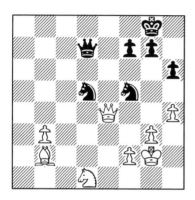

Getting back to relative safety.

37...h5 38 ♘c3 ♘f6 39 ♕a8+ ♔h7 40 ♘e4 ♘d5 41 ♘g5+ ♔g6 42 ♕a4 ♕b7 43 ♔h2 ♘de7 44 ♕c4 f6 45 ♗xf6 ♕b6 46 ♗e5 ♕xf2+ 47 ♔h3 ♔h6 48 ♘e4 ♕e1?

This could have lost immediately. 48...♕g1 was better, though Black is still just a pawn down after 49 ♕a6+ g6 50 ♕a1.

49 ♗f4+?

White could have saved himself a lot of trouble with 49 ♕e6+ g6 50 ♗f4+ ♔g7 51 ♕e5+ ♔f8 (or 51...♔g8 52 ♘f6+) 52 ♕b8+ ♔f7 (52...♔g7 53 ♗e5+ leads to mate next move) 53 ♘g5+ ♔g7 54 ♗e5+ etc. He eventually brings home the point anyway, but with considerably more effort.

49...♔h7 50 ♘g5+ ♔h8 51 ♔g2 ♕b1 52 ♕a4 ♕c2+ 53 ♔h3 ♕c8 54 ♕c4 ♕b7 55 ♔h2 ♕b6 56 ♔g2 ♕b7+ 57 ♔f2 ♕b6+ 58 ♔f1 ♕b7 59 ♔e1 ♕h1+ 60 ♔d2

♕g2+ 61 ♔c1

61...♘c6?

Black should have tried 61...♘xg3. Is White still winning here? I don't know.

62 ♕e4 ♕f1+ 63 ♔b2 ♕f2+ 64 ♔b1 ♕g1+?

It would have been better to play 64...♕f1+, though White's king gets to run away via 65 ♔c2 ♕f2+ 66 ♔c3 ♕c5+ 67 ♔d3 ♕b5+ 68 ♕c4 etc.

65 ♗c1 ♘ce7 66 ♕a8+ ♘g8 67 ♕f3 ♕xg3?

Losing on the spot. 67...♘fh6 would have been more tenacious.

68 ♘f7+ ♔h7 69 ♕xf5+ g6 70 ♘g5+ 1-0

Game 35
B.Gelfand-G.Kamsky
FIDE Grand Prix, Sochi 2008

---

1 ♘f3 ♘f6 2 c4 e6 3 g3 d5 4 d4 ♗b4+ 5 ♗d2 ♗e7 6 ♗g2 0-0 7 0-0 c6 8 ♗f4 ♘bd7 9 ♕c2 a5!?

A somewhat bizarre-looking semi-waiting move, with which Black keeps options of ...b7-b6 plans, a stonewall formation with ...♘h5 and ...f7-f5, or a queenside expansion via ...b7-b5.

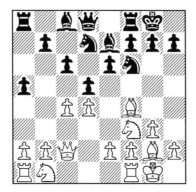

10 ♖d1

In P.Eljanov-K.Asrian, Russian Team Ch. 2008, White played 10 ♘bd2, but after 10...♘h5 could then only drop his bishop back to e3 rather than the neater c1-square. The game continued 11 ♗e3 b6 (11...f5!? seems playable here) 12 cxd5 cxd5 13 ♘e5, and now Black might have considered 13...♘xe5 14 dxe5 ♗a6, the idea being that 15 g4 can be met by 15...♖c8 16 ♕a4 b5 17 ♕d1 d4 etc.

10...♘h5 11 ♗c1 b5 12 ♘e5 ♗b7 13 ♘xd7 ♕xd7 14 c5 f5

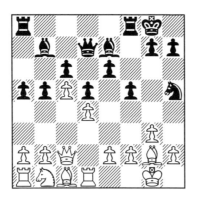

This looks very solid. If White can't find anything better then 9...a5 must be considered very reasonable.

15 ♘d2 ♕c7 16 ♘f3 ♗f6 17 ♗g5 ♖ae8 18 ♕d2

18 ♗xf6 ♘xf6 19 ♘e5 ♘g4 would lead to the prompt ejection of White's well-placed knight. You need more than a knight on e5 to break through a stonewall.

18...♗c8 19 ♖ac1 ♗xg5 20 ♕xg5 ♘f6 21 ♕f4 ♕xf4 22 gxf4

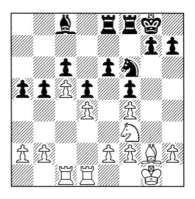

Of course White is 'better' in this endgame, but where does he break through?

22...♖e7 23 ♘e5 ♗d7 24 ♖d3 ♖a8 25 ♖h3 ♗e8 26 e3 ♖c7 27 ♖g3 ♖e7 28 ♗f1 ♖c7 29 ♗d3 ♔f8 30 ♔f1 ♖d8 31 ♔e2 ♖a7 32 ♖cg1 ♖c7 33 f3 ♘h5 34 ♖g5 ♘f6 35 ♖5g3 ♘h5 36 ♖g5 ½-½

> ### Game 36
> **R.Vaganian-D.Kalashian**
> Armenian Team
> Championship 2008

1 ♘f3 ♘f6 2 c4 e6 3 g3 d5 4 d4 ♗b4+ 5

♗d2 ♗e7 6 ♗g2 0-0 7 0-0 c6 8 ♕c2 ♘bd7 9 ♗f4 ♘h5 10 ♗c1 f5

Setting up a stonewall looks like the most consistent follow-up, though Black has tried other moves here too:

a) 10...♘hf6 could result in a draw by repetition after 11 ♗f4 ♘h5 12 ♗c1 ♘hf6 etc, though White can play one of the moves covered in the previous chapter such as 13 b3 or 13 ♘bd2.

b) 10...b5?! is well met by 11 ♘e5!, for example 11...♗b7 (if 11...♘xe5? 12 dxe5 bxc4 13 g4 wins a piece) 12 ♘xd7 ♕xd7 13 c5 a5 14 ♘d2 b4 15 ♘f3 ♗a6 16 ♖e1 f5 17 b3 ♕b7 18 a3 ♘f6 19 ♘g5! ♕c8 20 axb4 axb4 21 ♗d2 was good for White in E.Dizdarevic-N.Short, European Cup, Solingen 1988.

c) 10...♗d6?! is answered by 11 e4 dxe4 12 ♘g5 ♘hf6 13 ♘c3, recovering the e4-pawn with a typical space advantage.

11 b3

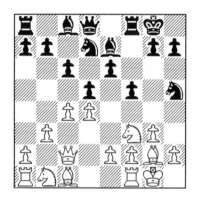

11...g5

This looks like the move of a wild man, though with the centre closed such things are possible. Quite a few alternatives have been tried here:

a) 11...♗d6?! 12 ♗a3 ♗xa3 13 ♘xa3 costs Black a tempo because his dark-squared bishop moved before being exchanged. The game A.Khalifman-R.Lau, Dordrecht 1988, continued 13...♕e7 14 ♕b2 a5 15 ♘c2 ♘hf6 16 ♘ce1 b6 17 ♘d3 ♗b7 18 ♖ac1 ♖fc8 19 ♘fe5 ♘xe5 20 ♘xe5 c5 21 ♖fd1 ♖c7 22 ♘d3 when Black's pawn structure was starting to look a bit exposed.

b) 11...♘df6 12 e3 ♗d7 13 ♗a3 ♗xa3 14 ♘xa3 ♘e4 15 ♘b1 ♗e8 16 ♘e5 ♕g5!? 17 ♘c3 ♘hf6 18 ♖ae1 ♕h6 19 f3 ♘g5 20 ♘d3!? ♗d7 21 ♕c1 ♘f7 22 ♕a3 b6 23 ♘e5 ♗e8 24 f4 was better for White at this stage in V.Korchnoi-M.Chandler, Hastings 1988/89.

c) 11...♘hf6 is well met by 12 ♘g5, when Black has to retreat his knight with 12...♘b8.

d) 11...b6 12 cxd5 cxd5 13 ♕c6 looks devastating, though White gets no more advantage than two rooks for his queen after 13...♘df6 14 ♕xa8 ♕c7 15 ♗d2 ♗a6 16 ♕xf8+ ♗xf8 17 ♖c1 ♕b7 18 ♘c3 etc.

e) 11...b5!? is an interesting line, for example 12 cxd5 cxd5 13 ♕c6 ♕b6 14 ♕xa8!? (14 ♕xb6 axb6 15 ♗g5 ♗d6 16 ♖c1 ♗b7 would offer both sides chances in the endgame) 14...♘b8 15 ♗d2! ♗b7 16 ♗a5! ♕a6 17 ♕xb8 ♖xb8 18 b4! ♗d8!? 19 ♗xd8 ♖xd8 20 ♘bd2 ♕d6 21 a3 ♘f6 22 ♘b3 ♘d7 23 ♘c5 gave White compensation for the queen in V.Salov-P.San Segundo Carrillo, Madrid 1996.

12 ♗a3

Logically exchanging Black's better bishop so as to leave him with the one that's blocked in by pawns. In E.Bareev-Y.Balashov, Russian Ch., Elista 1996, White played it another way with 12 e3, after which 12...g4 13 ♘e5 ♘xe5 14 dxe5 ♘g7 15 ♘c3 h5 16 ♗b2 h4 17 ♖ad1 ♕e8 18 f3 hxg3 19 hxg3 ♕g6 wasn't clear.

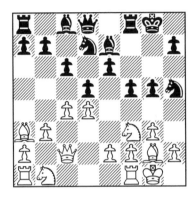

12...g4

I've often seen stonewallers play this move, the argument being that it becomes more difficult for White to break through with f2-f3 followed by a later e2-e4. The drawback is that it leaves Black without any chance of counterplay on the kingside.

13 ♘e5 ♗xa3 14 ♘xa3 ♘xe5 15 dxe5 ♕e7 16 ♕b2 ♗d7 17 e3 ♘g7 18 ♖fc1 h5 19 b4 a6 20 ♘b1 h4 21 a4 ♔f7 22 ♘d2 ♖h8 23 b5!

A key pawn lever, prising open files.

23...hxg3 24 hxg3 axb5 25 axb5 ♖xa1

If Black does nothing, say with 25...♔g6, White could just improve his position with 26 ♕d4. This is why he tries to shoot his way out of trouble, the only problem being that White has the bigger gun.

26 ♖xa1 cxb5

After 26...♕d8 White could play 27 b6, intending ♖a1-a7 followed by ♘d2-b3-c5 (or a5), which is very very nasty for Black.

27 cxd5 exd5 28 ♗xd5+ ♔g6 29 ♗xb7 ♘e6 30 ♗g2 ♖d8 31 ♖a6 ♗c8 32 ♖b6 ♕d7 33 ♘f1 ♔h6 34 f4

White had another powerful option in 34 e4.

34...gxf3 35 ♗xf3 ♔g6 36 ♖d6 ♕e8 37 ♕h2 ♔g7 38 ♕h4 ♕f8

Or 38...♖xd6 39 ♕f6+ ♔h7 40 exd6 etc.

39 ♖b6 ♔g8 40 g4 f4?

Letting White's king's bishop into the game with deadly effect. 40...♖e8 would have put up a bit more of a fight.

41 ♗e4 ♔f7 42 ♕f6+ ♔g8 43 ♖xe6 ♗xe6 44 ♕g5+ 1-0

44...♔h8 45 ♕h4+ leads to mate, while blocking the check with 44...♕g7 would lose the rook on d8.

> ## Game 37
> ## G.Kaidanov-H.Stefansson
> ## Lubbock 2008

1 d4 ♘f6 2 c4 e6 3 g3 d5 4 ♘f3 ♗b4+ 5 ♗d2 ♗e7 6 ♗g2 0-0 7 0-0 c6 8 ♗g5

A very natural-looking move. The only issue is whether or not it's that effective, as it can easily lead to exchanges.

8...♘bd7

After 8...dxc4 9 ♘e5, White would recover his pawn with a good game.

9 ♘bd2 b6 10 ♕c2

In A.Kuligowski-W.Browne, Wijk aan Zee 1983, White chose instead to play 10 ♖c1, but after 10...♗b7 11 cxd5 exd5 12 ♘e1?! ♖e8 13 ♘d3 ♘e4! 14 ♗xe7 ♕xe7 15 ♖e1 ♖ad8 Black already had an excellent game.

Instead of playing down the c-file Kaidanov plans to gain space with e2-e4, which is usually the more promising procedure. But the drawback here is that more pieces are exchanged, on account of White's bishop being on g5.

10...♗b7 11 e4 dxe4 12 ♘xe4 c5 13 ♘xf6+ ♗xf6 14 ♗xf6 ♕xf6 15 ♘e5

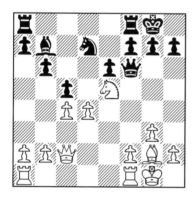

15...♗xg2?!

This looks okay at first sight, but I'm not sure that this is really the case. Instead I suspect Black should play 15...♘xe5 16 dxe5 (16 ♗xb7 ♘f3+ 17 ♗xf3 ♕xf3 18 dxc5 bxc5 looks more or less equal) 16...♕e7 17 ♗xb7 ♕xb7. It's true that White will be slightly better after putting a rook on d1, but this position looks easier to defend that the one Black gets in the game.

16 ♘xd7 ♕f3

16...♕xd4 isn't good because of 17 ♖fd1 ♕e4 18 ♕xe4 ♗xe4 19 ♘xf8 ♗xf8

20 ♖d7 etc.

17 ♘xf8 ♖xf8 18 ♕b3

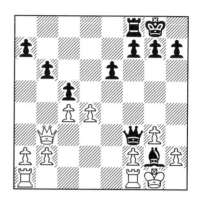

18...cxd4

Probably the right decision. At first sight it looks as if Black can reach a safe endgame via 18...♕xb3 19 axb3 ♗xf1, but after 20 ♔xf1 his troubles become rather evident. For example, after 20...♖a8 there is 21 dxc5 bxc5 22 ♖a5 ♔f8 23 ♖b5 intending ♖b7, when Black would not have an easy time of it.

19 ♖fd1 e5 20 ♕xf3 ♗xf3 21 ♖d3 ♗e2 22 ♖d2 ♗xc4

There was another possibility in 22...d3, but then White can bring his king forward with 23 f3 f5 24 ♔f2. It's not clear he can win, but certainly he has what chances that are going.

23 ♖e1 f6 24 f4 ♗xa2 25 fxe5 fxe5 26 ♖xe5 ♖d8 27 ♖e4 d3 28 ♖a4 ♗b3 29 ♖xa7

Now it's clear that White is on top. Where did Black go wrong? Move 15 perhaps?

29...♗c2 30 ♖c7 ♖d5 31 ♔f2 ♖e5 32 ♔f3 h6 33 ♖c4 ♖b5 34 b4 ♖e5 35 ♖e4 ♖d5 36 ♔e3 ♔h7 37 ♖d4 ♖e5+ 38 ♖e4 ♖d5 39 ♖c4 ♖f5 40 ♔d4 ♖f6 41 ♔c3

♔g6 42 ♖c7 ♖f5

42...♔h7 would have been more tenacious as now White gets a pair of rooks off.

43 ♖c6+ ♖f6 44 ♖xf6+ ♔xf6 45 ♖f2+ 1-0

Black won't be able to defend both the b6-pawn and his kingside.

Game 38
M.Carlsen-O.Stubberud
Tromsø 2007

---

1 d4 ♘f6 2 c4 e6 3 g3 d5 4 ♘f3 ♗b4+ 5 ♘bd2 0-0 6 ♗g2 dxc4

One of several moves that Black can try. The others are as follows:

a) 6...b6 7 0-0 ♗b7 8 cxd5 exd5 (8...♗xd5 9 ♕c2 ♗xd2 10 ♗xd2 ♘c6 was tried in Kir.Georgiev-B.Abramovic, Yugoslav Team Ch. 2002, and now the most economical move is probably 11 ♗c3 with the better game for White because of his bishop pair) 9 ♘e5 ♖e8 (9...♗d6 10 ♘df3 c5 11 b3 ♘a6 12 ♗b2 ♖c8 13 ♖c1 ♖c7 14 ♖e1 ♖e8 was J.Ehlvest-J.Timman, Manila Olympiad 1992, when 15 e3 was probably best; Black's position is probably harder to play because of the responsibilities imposed by his hanging pawns, though it's not clear that he's worse here) 10 ♘dc4 h6 11 a3 ♗f8 12 b4 ♘e4 13 ♘e3 ♘d7 14 ♗b2 ♗d6 15 f3! ♘ef6 16 f4 gave White the initiative in D.Gurevich-L.Psakhis, Beersheba 1993.

b) 6...c5 7 dxc5 ♗xc5 8 0-0 ♘c6 9 a3 a5 10 cxd5 exd5 11 ♘b3 ♗b6 12 ♘bd4 ♖e8 13 b3 (13 ♗e3 can be met by the

dangerous 13...♖xe3!?, as in A.Raetsky-V.Tukmakov, Biel 1994; Najdorf was probably aware of this when he played 13 ♖e1 in M.Najdorf-C.Merlo, Argentine Ch., Buenos Aires 1960, with White having the better game after 13...♘e4 14 ♗e3 ♗g4 15 ♕d3 ♘d6 16 ♘xc6 bxc6 17 ♗xb6 ♕xb6 18 ♕d4) 13...♗g4 (13...♘xd4 14 ♘xd4 ♗xd4 15 ♕xd4 ♖xe2 16 ♗g5 gives White more than enough for the pawn) 14 ♗b2 ♘e4 15 ♖c1 ♕d6 16 ♕d3 ♖ad8 17 e3 h6 18 ♖c2 and White had some pressure in M.Petursson-I.Jelen, Ljubljana 1981.

7 ♕c2 ♘c6 8 ♕xc4

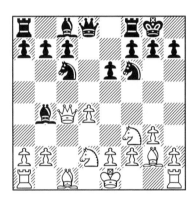

8...♘e4

Trying to exchange an extra set of minor pieces, but White maintains persistent pressure.

A better way to play it is with 8...♕d5, though there, too, White maintains an edge because of his extra space and Catalan bishop. For example, 9 0-0 ♗xd2 (9...♖d8 10 e3 ♕xc4 11 ♘xc4 ♗d7 12 a3 ♗f8 13 b4 ♘e7 14 ♘fe5 gave White a pleasant positional plus in N.Birnboim-S.Tatai, Israel-Italy match, Trento 1987) 10 ♕xd5 exd5 11 ♗xd2

♖e8 12 e3 ♘e4 13 ♖fc1 a5 14 ♗e1 ♗f5 15 ♘d2 ♘f6! 16 a3 (16 ♖c5!?) 16...a4 17 ♖c3 ♖a6 18 f3 h5 19 h3 ♖b6 20 g4 hxg4 21 hxg4 ♗g6 22 b4 left White with an ongoing edge in the endgame in V.Mikhalevski-N.Rashkovsky, Biel 2001.

9 ♕d3 ♘xd2 10 ♗xd2 ♕e7

In an old game G.Shainswit-O.Ulvestad, US Ch., South Fallsburg 1948, Black tried 10...♗xd2+ 11 ♕xd2 ♕d6 but failed to equalize. The game continued 12 ♕c3 ♖d8 13 e3 ♗d7 14 0-0 ♘b4 15 a3 ♘d5 16 ♕c2 h6 17 ♖ac1 ♖ac8 18 ♖fd1 with White having persistent pressure.

11 0-0 ♖d8 12 ♗xb4 ♘xb4 13 ♕c4 ♘d5 14 ♖ac1 c6 15 ♖fd1

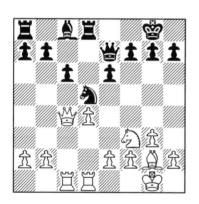

Black's game is solid enough but very passive. Young Carlsen gradually improves his position in masterful style.

15...♗d7 16 ♘e5 ♗e8 17 ♘d3 ♘b6 18 ♕c3 ♘d7 19 ♕a5 ♕d6 20 e3 f6 21 b4 a6 22 ♘c5 ♘xc5 23 bxc5

Black's backward pawn on b7 is defensible, but in the long term he'll have trouble defending on the other flank

because of White's extra centre pawn. Carlsen is in no hurry.

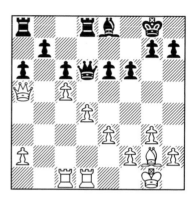

23...♕e7 24 ♖b1 ♗g6 25 ♖b4 ♖d7 26 ♖d2 ♖c8 27 h4 ♖cc7 28 ♕a4 ♗f7 29 ♕d1 g6 30 ♖bb2 ♔g7 31 ♖bc2 ♖d8 32 ♕a1 ♖cd7 33 ♗h3 ♖d5 34 e4 ♖5d7 35 ♕c3 ♖c7 36 a3 ♕f8 37 ♖d3 ♕e7 38 ♖e2 ♖cd7 39 ♖ee3 ♖c7 40 f4 ♕f8 41 ♖e1 ♔g8 42 ♔h2 ♖e8 43 ♖de3 ♖ce7 44 ♖1e2 e5

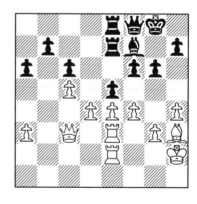

Finally Black's nerve goes and he tries to do something, so that White's advantage crystallizes into direct pressure on the kingside.

45 dxe5 fxe5 46 f5 ♖d8 47 ♖f3 ♖d4 48 fxg6 hxg6 49 ♖ef2 ♕e8

After 49...♖xe4? there follows 50 ♖xf7! ♖xf7 51 ♗e6 etc.

50 ♕e3 ♔g7?!

50...♗c4 was a better try, but probably forlorn after 51 ♖f6 intending 52 ♕g5.

51 h5! 1-0

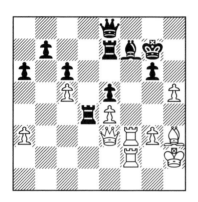

White is crawling in with ♖f6 and ♕g5, and there's not a thing Black will be able to do about it.

Summary

Played in the right setting 4...♗b4+ is not a bad line and one can sense White's frustration in the game Gelfand-Kamsky. But it's only an option against particular White move orders.

Obviously Black can't use this against Flank Opening move orders, as 1 ♘f3 d5 2 c4 e6 3 g3 ♘f6 4 ♗g2 ♗b4 wouldn't even be check! And if Black tries it after 1 d4 ♘f6 2 c4 e6 3 g3 d5 4 ♗g2 ♗b4+ he must seriously reckon with 5 ♘d2, because 5...dxc4 would lose a piece to 6 ♕a4+.

Chapter Nine

Open Catalan with 5...♝b4+

1 d4 ♞f6 2 c4 e6 3 g3 d5 4 ♝g2 dxc4 5 ♞f3 ♝b4+

This line is related to the previous chapter because Black can sometimes play 4...♝b4+ and follow up with ...d5xc4. This is most apparent when White blocks the check with 5 ♞d2 as in Games 42 and 43 (Davies-Wilczek and Umansky-Rause), though in my game Black had to play 5...♞c6 before taking on c4 (5...dxc4 would have been met by 6 ♕a4+). This is one of the joys of playing ♝f1-g2 before ♞g1-f3, though it may not be possible if one wishes to steer clear of other things.

The first three games feature 6 ♝d2, and then Black meeting this with either 6...a5 (Ivanchuk-Alekseev and Kramnik-Topalov, Games 39 and 40) or 6...♝xd2+ (Nakamura-Serper, Game 41). All these games are quite interesting and double-edged, which perhaps explains why 5...♝b4+ has been receiving some high-level attention.

After 6...a5 my personal preference would be for Ivanchuk's 7 0-0 and then looking more closely at 9 ♞e5 or 10 ♞e5. And after 7 ♕c2 I'd be more inclined to try (7...♝xd2+) 8 ♞bxd2 than Kramnik's 8 ♕xd2. There again, he's 2700+ whilst I'm currently 2500-, and part of the reason may be that I don't value pawns enough!

Given my apparent disregard for the little guys, my choice of 5 ♞d2 (Davies-Wilczek, Game 42) becomes easier to understand. White wants to make 5...♝b4+ look like a loss of time and invites Black to win a pawn at the cost of several tempi. Frankly, I think I had great compensation in this game and even managed to 'prove' my point by winning. I'm not as convinced that White has enough in Umansky-Rause (Game 43), though he managed to do the business in the end.

This chapter is rounded off with the 5 ♞c3 of Almasi-Balogh (Game 44), which strictly speaking should probably be categorized as a Nimzo-Indian. I can't say that I'm particularly enthralled by White's prospects in this line, but it does look like a playable option.

Game 39
V.Ivanchuk-E.Alekseev
Foros 2008

---

1 ♘f3 d5 2 d4 ♘f6 3 c4 e6 4 g3 dxc4 5 ♗g2 ♗b4+ 6 ♗d2 a5 7 0-0

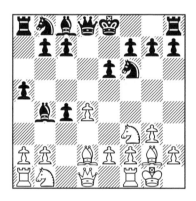

A nonchalant reply. For 7 ♕c2 see the next game.

7...0-0

Black shouldn't try defending the c4-pawn before White spends a move to attack it. After 7...b5? 8 a4! ♗xd2 (8...c6 is met by 9 axb5 ♗xd2 10 ♘fxd2!) 9 ♘fxd2 ♖a7 10 axb5 ♕xd4 11 ♘a3 ♗b7 12 ♗xb7 ♖xb7 13 ♘dxc4 White was clearly better in P.Genov-J.Kuzev, Bulgarian Ch. 1995.

In A.Shirov-V.Korchnoi, Carlsbad 2007, Black played it in another way with 7...♘c6 8 e3 0-0 9 ♕e2 e5, but after

10 ♘xe5 ♘xe5 11 dxe5 ♘g4 12 f4 ♗f5 (if 12...♕d3 13 ♕xd3 cxd3 14 ♘c3 ♗c5 15 ♖ae1, followed by h2-h3 and g3-g4, will shut out Black's h6-knight) 13 e4 ♕d4+ 14 ♔h1 ♗c8 15 ♘c3 ♖d8 (another possibility is 15...♗c5, but this too doesn't look promising for Black after, for example 16 h3 ♘f2+ 17 ♔h2 ♖d8 18 ♘d5 ♕xb2 19 ♖fb1 ♕a3 20 ♕xc4 etc) 16 ♖ad1 ♗xc3 17 bxc3 ♕d3 18 ♗f3 ♕xe2 19 ♗xe2 White had a clear advantage.

8 ♗g5

Black can meet 8 ♕c2 with 8...b5, for example 9 a4 bxa4 10 ♖xa4 ♗b7 11 ♗xb4 axb4 12 ♖xa8 ♗xa8 13 ♘bd2 c5 14 dxc5 ♕a5 15 ♕xc4 ♗d5 16 ♕d4 ♖d8 17 ♘c4 ♗xc4 18 ♕xc4 ♖c8 19 ♘d4 ♖xc5 saw Black equalize in A.Karpov-J.Piket, 4th matchgame, Monte Carlo 1999.

Another high-level game, E.Bareev-V.Kramnik, Monte Carlo (rapid) 2005, varied with 8 ♘c3 ♘c6 9 a3 ♗xc3 10 ♗xc3 ♘d5 11 ♗d2 b5 12 e4 ♘b6 13 ♗e3 ♗b7 14 ♕c2 ♘e7 15 ♖ad1, White having compensation for the pawn.

8...b5

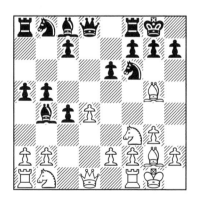

9 a4

Logical, but not the only move. In

V.Kramnik-D.Navara, Prague (rapid) 2008, White played 9 ♘e5, after which 9...♖a6 10 a4 bxa4?! (10...c6 is probably better, transposing into Buhmann-Bartel in the next note) 11 ♘xc4 ♘bd7 12 ♘c3 c5 13 ♘xa4 h6 14 ♗d2 ♕c7 15 ♗f4 left him with an excellent game.

9...c6 10 ♘c3

Another interesting possibility is 10 ♘e5!?, opening the Catalan diagonal. After 10...♖a6 11 ♘c3 h6 12 ♗xf6 gxf6 13 ♘g4 e5 14 e3 ♔g7 15 h3 ♗xc3 16 bxc3 ♕e7 17 ♕c2 a double-edged position arose in the game R.Buhmann-M.Bartel, Polanica Zdroj 2007.

10...♕b6 11 ♗xf6 gxf6 12 axb5 cxb5 13 d5 ♖d8?!

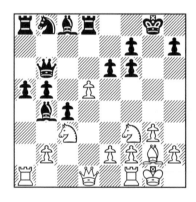

This is incorrect as White stands clearly better after his reply. Black should probably play 13...e5, despite the apparently vulnerability of his king.

14 ♕d4! ♕xd4

On 14...♘d7 there follows 15 dxe6 fxe6 (15...♕xe6 16 ♕h4 threatens ♘f3-d4) 16 ♕g4+ ♔h8 17 ♘g5, winning material.

15 ♘xd4 ♖a6 16 ♘dxb5 ♖b6 17 ♖fd1 e5

18 ♘a3 ♗a6?!

After this White's advantage increases. Black should probably try 18...♗xa3 19 ♖xa3 ♖xb2 20 ♖xa5 ♖c2, when he has better drawing chances than in the game.

19 ♘a4 ♖b7 20 ♖dc1 ♖c7 21 e4 f5 22 exf5 ♘d7 23 ♗f1 ♖dc8 24 ♘c2 ♗f8 25 ♘e3

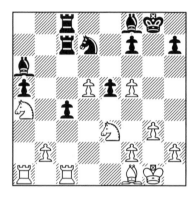

25...e4

Maybe 25...♘c5 would have been better, though after 26 ♘xc5 ♖xc5 27 f6 White would be well in control.

26 ♘c3 ♘c5 27 ♖d1 ♘b3 28 ♖a4 ♗b4 29 d6 ♖b7

On 29...♖c6 White could even play 30 ♖xb4! axb4 31 ♘cd5 as at least a couple of things will be forked by the move ♘d5-e7.

30 ♘cd5 ♔f8 31 ♘xb4 ♗b5 32 ♖a2 axb4 33 ♗xc4!

The loss of this vital pawn spells the beginning of the end. Black can't take twice on c4 because White's d-pawn would queen.

33...♗xc4 34 ♘xc4 ♔g7 35 ♘e3 ♖d8 36 ♖d5 ♖b6 37 ♖a4

37 d7! was also very strong.

37...♘c1!?

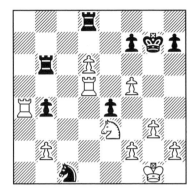

7 ♕c2

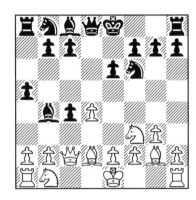

Trying for some counterplay rather than going meekly to his doom. 37...♖bxd6 38 ♖xd6 ♖xd6 39 ♖xb4 leaves Black two pawns down with little hope of a swindle.

38 ♘c4 ♖b7 39 ♖c5 ♘d3 40 ♖c7 ♖b5 41 g4 ♖d5 42 ♖aa7 ♖f8 43 h4 h5 44 g5 ♘e1 45 f6+ ♔g6 46 ♔h2 ♖f5 47 ♖a5 ♖xf2+ 48 ♔g1 e3 49 ♘e5+ ♔h7 50 ♖xf7+ ♖xf7 51 g6+

And not 51 ♘xf7?? ♘f3+ 52 ♔h1 ♖h2 mate.

51...♔h6 52 gxf7 ♖xf6 53 d7 1-0

Game 40
V.Kramnik-V.Topalov
1st matchgame, World
Championship, Elista 2006

---

1 d4 ♘f6 2 c4 e6 3 ♘f3 d5 4 g3 dxc4 5 ♗g2 ♗b4+ 6 ♗d2 a5

It's interesting that Topalov should play a line that Kramnik has also used as Black. David Bronstein first tried this tactic in his 1951 encounter with Mikhail Botvinnik.

Varying from 7 0-0 which featured in the previous game.

Another move White might want to consider is 7 ♘a3!?, for example 7...♗xa3 8 bxa3 0-0 9 ♕c2 b5 10 a4 c6 11 ♖b1 ♗a6 12 a3! ♘bd7 13 0-0 ♖b8 14 ♖fd1 ♕b6 15 e4 h6 16 ♗c3 gave White good compensation for the pawn in M.Marin-L.Psakhis, Internet (rapid) 2005. Psakhis later suggested 8...a4!? to stop White undermining the black queenside with a3-a4 himself. As the cliché goes, it deserves tests.

7...♗xd2+

7...♘c6 brings about a position that is more frequently reached via a Bogo-Indian move order (3...♗b4+ 4 ♗d2 a5 5 g3 d5 6 ♗g2 ♘c6 7 ♕c2 dxc4) and represents a reasonable alternative for Black. After 8 ♕xc4 ♕d5 9 ♕d3 0-0 (9...♕e4 10 ♕xe4 ♘xe4 11 ♗xb4 ♘xb4 12 0-0! was good for White in A.Beliavsky-L.Ljubojevic, Linares 1991, the point being that 12...♘c2 13 ♘e1! ♘xa1 14 ♗xe4 leaves the knight on a1 trapped) 10 ♘c3 ♕h5 11 a3 ♗xc3 12 ♗xc3 b6 13 0-0 ♗a6 14 ♕c2 ♖ac8 15

罩fe1 ♘e7 16 e4 favoured White because of his space and bishop pair in A.Chernin-A.Yermolinsky, Chicago 1998.

8 ♕xd2!?

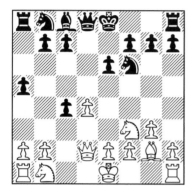

It looks odd to spend another tempo moving the queen, but there's method to this madness. After the natural 8 ♘bxd2 Black can hold onto his extra pawn with 8...b5, though admittedly this position offers White compensation. B.Avrukh-P.Eljanov, Calvia Olympiad 2004, continued 9 a4 c6 10 b3 cxb3 11 ♘xb3 0-0 12 0-0 ♗a6 13 ♘c5 ♘bd7 14 罩fd1 with ongoing play for the pawn, though not sufficient for more than a draw.

8...c6

In A.Wojtkiewicz-B.Gulko, US Ch., San Diego 2006, Black played 8...b6, but after 9 ♘e5 罩a7 10 ♘a3 ♗b7 11 ♗xb7 罩xb7 12 ♘axc4 White was better because of his superior development and extra centre pawn.

9 a4 b5 10 axb5 cxb5 11 ♕g5

Recovering his pawn by forking g7 and b5.

11...0-0

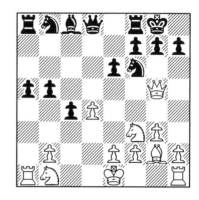

This is certainly the natural decision, making sure his king gets to safety. But there was a case for keeping the queenside intact, say with 11...b4!?. After 12 ♕xg7 罩g8 13 ♕h6 ♗b7 Black has active piece play to compensate for his vulnerable king.

12 ♕xb5 ♗a6

At the time of the game this was a new move, though it has subsequently be tried by several other players. In A.Grischuk-A.Moiseenko, Russian Team Ch. 2006, Black played the dubious 12...♘a6?!, after which 13 ♕xc4 ♘b4 14 ♕b3 e5 15 ♘xe5 罩b8 16 0-0 ♕xd4 17 罩xa5 left White on top.

13 ♕a4

Faced with a new move over the board, Kramnik understandably avoids the sharpest line. In some later games White plunged in with 13 ♕xa5, but this seems to be rather drawish after 13...♗b7 14 ♕xd8 罩xa1! 15 ♕xf8+ (not 15 ♕b6? 罩xb1+ 16 ♔d2 c3+! 17 ♔xc3 ♘d5+ etc) 15...♔xf8 16 0-0 罩a2, for example 17 ♘c3 (17 ♘bd2 ♗xf3! 18 ♘xf3 ½-½ was E.Postny-T.Luther, German League 2007) 17...罩xb2 18 罩b1 罩xb1+

19 ♘xb1 ♘d5 20 ♘e1 ½-½ as in D.Blagojevic-R.Wojtaszek, European Team Ch., Crete 2007.

13...♕b6 14 0-0 ♕xb2 15 ♘bd2 ♗b5 16 ♘xc4 ♗xa4 17 ♘xb2 ♗b5

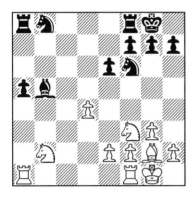

The exchange of queens has brought about a position in which White has one pawn island against Black's two, but then Black has a passed a-pawn. White is probably a bit better, but it isn't much.

18 ♘e5 ♖a7

In A.Zontakh-O.Chebotarev, Lipetsk 2007, Black played his rook one square further with 18...♖a6, after which 19 ♖fe1 a4 20 e3 ♘bd7 21 ♘ec4 ♘d5 22 ♘a3 ♗c6 seemed fine for him, at least at this stage. White may be able to improve on this with 19 ♘bd3, leading to similar play to the next note.

19 ♗f3

In subsequent games White tried to improve with 19 ♘bd3, and this does seem to keep rather more pressure than the text. Kir.Georgiev-D.Pavasovic, Valjevo 2007, continued 19...♘fd7 20 ♖fb1 ♘xe5 21 ♖xb5 ♘xd3 22 exd3 ♖d8 (22...a4 23 ♖a3 ♘d7 24 ♗c6 ♘f6 25 ♖b4

♖d8 26 ♖axa4 ♖xa4 27 ♖xa4 was better for White in E.Gleizerov-T.Luther, Rumanian Team Ch. 2007) 23 d5 a4 24 ♖a3 ♘d7 25 dxe6 fxe6 26 ♖b4 ♘f6 27 ♗c6 ♖a6 28 ♖c4 ♘d7 29 ♗b7 ♖d6 with enough counterplay for equality.

19...♘bd7 20 ♘ec4

20 ♘xd7 doesn't look like much for White after 20...♗xd7 21 ♖a3 and now 21...g5!?, which is similar to Topalov's 21...g5 in the game.

20...♖b8 21 ♖fb1

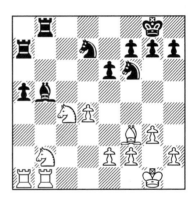

Capturing on a5 would be very drawish after 21 ♖xa5 ♖xa5 22 ♘xa5 ♗xe2 23 ♗xe2 ♖xb2 etc. In V.Potkin-E.Romanov, Krasnoyarsk 2007, White tested a different square for his rook with 21 ♖fc1, but after 21...g5 22 e3 g4 23 ♗d1 ♗c6 24 ♘xa5 ♖xa5 25 ♖xa5 ♖xb2 26 ♖xc6 ♖b1 27 ♔g2 ♖xd1 he certainly didn't stand better.

21...g5!?

An interesting move from Topalov, making room for his king while gaining space on the kingside. It's not going to be easy to find a great square for White's bishop.

22 e3 g4 23 ♗d1 ♗c6 24 ♖c1

And not 24 ♘xa5? because of 24...♗e4!.

24...♗e4 25 ♘a4 ♖b4 26 ♘d6 ♗f3!?

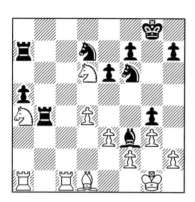

A sharp and ambitious decision that is typical of Topalov's play. Will the pawn on f3 be a weakness or a strength? Certainly it adds to the tension in what could have become a dull endgame.

27 ♗xf3 gxf3 28 ♘c8 ♖a8 29 ♘e7+ ♔g7 30 ♘c6 ♖b3 31 ♘c5 ♖b5 32 h3?!

This seems to be the cause of White's coming difficulties. He should have played 32 ♖a4!?, when 32...♘xc5 33 dxc5 ♘d7 34 ♖ac4 a4 35 ♘d4 gives him a strong c-pawn to balance Black's passed a-pawn.

32...♘xc5 33 ♖xc5

33 dxc5 is met by 33...♘d7, when the c5-pawn can't easily be defended.

33...♖b2

Threatening 34...♘e4.

34 ♖g5+ ♔h6?!

34...♔f8 was better, for example after 35 ♖gxa5 ♖xa5 36 ♘xa5 (and not 36 ♖xa5? ♘e4) 36...♘e4 37 ♖f1 f6 White is completely tied up and can only watch while the black king crawls forward.

35 ♖gxa5 ♖xa5 36 ♘xa5 ♘e4 37 ♖f1 ♘d2 38 ♖c1 ♘e4 39 ♖f1 f6

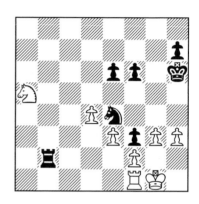

Keeping White's knight out of e5, just as in the 34...♔f8 line, but this time White has a resource.

40 ♘c6 ♘d2 41 ♖d1 ♘e4 42 ♖f1 ♔g6 43 ♘d8!

Had Black's king gone to f8 this wouldn't have been a problem, but now Black has to withdraw his rook to defend e6.

43...♖b6

43...e5!? was well worth considering, both here and later. I won't dwell on this interesting endgame because it is, after all, a book about the opening!

44 ♖c1 h5 45 ♖a1 h4

45...e5!? was possible here too.

46 gxh4 ♔h5 47 ♖a2 ♔xh4 48 ♔h2 ♔h5 49 ♖c2 ♔h6 50 ♖a2 ♔g6 51 ♖c2 ♔f5 52 ♖a2

White can only wait.

52...♖b5 53 ♘c6 ♖b7 54 ♖a5+ ♔g6 55 ♖a2 ♔h5?!

Black finally threatens ...♖b7-g7-g2, but this way of doing it allows White unexpected counterplay. He should have played 55...♔h6, when 56 d5 ♖g7

57 dxe6 ♖g2+ 58 ♔h1 ♔g7! 59 ♖a7+ ♔g6 60 ♘e7+ ♔h6 61 ♖a2 ♘xf2+ 62 ♖xf2 ♖xf2 63 ♘f5+ ♔g6 64 ♘d6 ♖f1+ 65 ♔h2 f2 66 e7 ♖h1+ 67 ♔xh1 f1♕+ will be a draw by perpetual check.

56 d5! e5

Black can probably still play 56...♖g7, but then 57 dxe6 ♖g2+ 58 ♔h1 ♘xf2+ 59 ♖xf2 ♖xf2 60 e7 ♖f1+ 61 ♔h2 ♖f2+ 62 ♔g3 ♖g2+ 63 ♔xf3 certainly leaves White with the chances. Note that 56...exd5 would be bad because of 57 ♘d4, followed by capturing on f3.

57 ♖a4 f5?

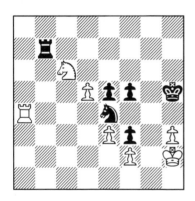

No doubt shocked by the change in events Topalov misses 57...♘xf2 58 ♔g3 e4 59 ♔xf2 ♖b2+ with a draw by perpetual check. Now he's losing.

58 ♘xe5 ♖b2 59 ♘d3 ♖b7 60 ♖d4 ♖b6 61 d6

The simplest way to win, freeing up White's king.

61...♘xd6 62 ♔g3 ♘e4+ 63 ♔xf3 ♔g5 64 h4+ ♔f6

64...♔xh4 is met by 65 ♘c5.

65 ♖d5 ♘c3 66 ♖d8 ♖b1 67 ♖f8+ ♔e6 68 ♘f4+ ♔e5 69 ♖e8+ ♔f6 70 ♘h5+ ♔g6 71 ♘g3 ♖b2 72 h5+ ♔f7 73 ♖e5

♘d1 74 ♘e2 ♔f6 75 ♖d5 1-0

1 d4 ♘f6 2 c4 e6 3 ♘f3 d5 4 g3 dxc4 5 ♗g2 ♗b4+ 6 ♗d2 ♗xd2+

Unusual but interesting. With 5...♗b4+ currently being quite fashionable, we might well see more of it.

7 ♘bxd2 b5

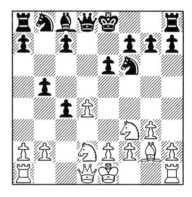

The only logical follow-up. After either 7...0-0 8 ♘xc4 or 7...♕e7 8 ♘xc4 ♕b4+ 9 ♘fd2, White is going to be better because of his superb Catalan bishop on g2 and central pawn majority. Such positions are a joy to play for White, and even more miserable to defend as Black.

8 a4

It seems that Serper has made a speciality of this line, the game V.Strugatsky-G.Serper, Los Angeles 2001, having gone 8 ♘e5 ♘d5 9 b3 ♗b7 10 bxc4 ♘c3 11 ♗xb7 ♘xd1 12 ♖xd1 f6 13 ♗xa8 fxe5 14 dxe5 ♕d4 15 cxb5

♕xe5 with a draw being agreed in this unclear position.

8...c6 9 0-0 ♗b7

In V.Zilberstein-J.Klovans, Tbilisi 1973, Black played 9...0-0, after which 10 e4 ♘bd7 11 e5 ♘d5 12 ♘e4 brought about a messy position where White had compensation for his pawn.

Serper's move looks like a prepared novelty, immediately challenging the long diagonal.

10 ♕c2 0-0 11 b3 cxb3 12 ♘xb3 ♘bd7 13 ♘e5 ♘xe5 14 dxe5 ♘d5 15 ♘c5 ♕e7 16 ♖fc1 a5 17 ♗xd5 exd5 18 ♘xb7 ♕xb7 19 ♕xc6 ♕xc6 20 ♖xc6 b4

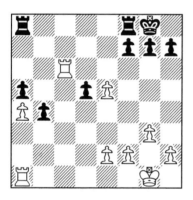

Properly speaking this endgame should be a draw, the strength of Black's b-pawn compensating him for the pawn deficit. But in practice it proves far from easy to play, with White coming close to victory at one point.

21 ♔f1 ♖fc8 22 ♖d6 ♖c5 23 ♖b6 ♖ac8 24 ♖d1 ♔f8 25 ♔e1 ♔e7 26 f4 g6 27 ♖d3 h5 28 ♔d2 ♖8c7 29 ♔e3 ♖d7 30 h3 ♖dc7 31 g4 hxg4 32 hxg4 ♖c3 33 ♖b5 ♖7c5 34 ♖xc3 ♖xc3+ 35 ♔d4 ♖c4+ 36 ♔xd5 ♖xf4 37 ♖xa5 b3 38 e4 ♖f1

A safer line might have been 38...♖xg4, for example 39 ♖a7+ ♔f8 40 ♖b7 ♖g1 41 ♖xb3 ♖a1 42 ♖b4 g5 43 e6 fxe6+ 44 ♔xe6 g4 45 e5 g3 46 ♖f4+ ♔e8 47 ♖g4 ♔f8 48 ♖xg3 ♖xa4 with a draw in sight.

39 ♖a7+ ♔f8 40 ♖b7 ♖d1+ 41 ♔c5 ♖c1+ 42 ♔d4 ♖a1 43 e6 ♖xa4+

And here 43...f6 looks better, keeping White's king out of e5.

44 ♔e5 fxe6 45 ♖xb3?!

Missing what looks like a genuine opportunity via 45 g5!. Black's king would be unable to slip away to h6.

45...♔g7 46 ♖b7+ ♔h6 47 ♖b5 ♔g5 48 ♔xe6+ ♔xg4 49 e5 g5 50 ♔f6 ♖f4+ 51 ♔g6 ♖e4 52 ♔f7 ♔f3 53 ♖b3+ ♔f4 54 e6 g4 55 e7 ♖xe7+ 56 ♔xe7 g3 57 ♔f6 g2 58 ♖b1 ♔f3 59 ♔f5 ♔f2 60 ♔f4 g1♕ 61 ♖b2+ ♔e1 62 ♖b1+ ♔f2 63 ♖b2+ ♔f1 64 ♖b1+ ♔g2 65 ♖xg1+ ♔xg1 ½-½

Game 42
N.Davies-T.Wilczek
Correspondence 2004

---

1 d4 ♘f6 2 c4 e6 3 g3 d5 4 ♗g2

In the other games in this chapter White had already played ♘g1-f3 by this point, and could do so here as well, when 4 ♘f3 dxc4 5 ♗g2 ♗b4+ 6 ♘bd2 ♘c6 reaches the position at move six below. However, there are some advantages to playing 4 ♗g2 first, as we'll see in the next note.

4...♗b4+ 5 ♘d2 ♘c6

One of the points behind 4 ♗g2 is that Black can't play 5...dxc4 because of 6 ♕a4+, winning the bishop on b4. So Black gets his knight out before making this capture.

6 ♘gf3 dxc4 7 0-0 c3

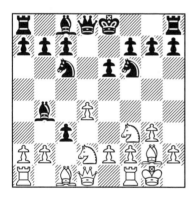

Making sure he keeps the pawn, but White gets a lot of compensation.

Black has a major alternative in 7...♗xd2, when I think White should recapture with the queen. After 8 ♕xd2 (8 ♗xd2 ♘xd4 9 ♘e5! 0-0 10 ♖c1 c5! 11 ♖xc4 ♘d7 12 ♘d3! e5 13 ♘xc5 ♘xc5 14 ♖xc5 ♕e7 15 ♗b4 ♗g4 16 f3 ♗e6 was fine for Black in V.Tukmakov-S.Lputian, Novosibirsk 1986) 8...♖b8 (8...0-0 9 a4 a5 10 ♕c3 ♘b4 11 ♘e5 ♘fd5 12 ♕xc4 b6 13 ♕b3 ♗a6 14 ♖e1 c5 was N.Birnboim-A.Avni, Israeli Ch.

1988, and now 15 e4 ♘f6 16 dxc5 bxc5 17 ♗e3 would have been very promising for White) 9 b3!? cxb3 10 ♗a3! ♘e7 11 axb3 ♗d7 (11...a6 12 ♖ac1 0-0 13 ♕c2 c6 14 e4 gave White nice compensation in P.Haba-A.Hellmayr, Austrian Team Ch. 2001) 12 ♘e5 ♗b5 13 ♖fc1 a6 14 g4!? 0-0 15 g5 ♘e8 16 ♖c3 f6 17 gxf6 ♖xf6 18 ♖d1 ♘d5 19 ♖g3 gave White a strong attack in Z.Kozul-Z.Vukovic, Yugoslav Ch., Banja Vrucica 1991.

8 ♘c4

Another promising possibility is 8 ♘b3, for example 8...cxb2 9 ♗xb2 0-0 10 ♕c2 ♘a5 (10...♕e7 11 ♘e5 ♘a5 12 ♘d3 ♘xb3 13 axb3 c6 14 ♘xb4 ♕xb4 15 ♗a3 was good for White in A.Mikhalevski-A.Bykhovsky, Israeli Team Ch. 1996) 11 ♘c5 ♕e7 12 ♖fd1 b6 13 ♘e5 ♖b8 14 ♘b3 ♘d7 15 a3 ♘xe5 16 axb4 ♘xb3 17 ♕xb3 ♘g4 18 ♖xa7 was terrific for White at this stage in S.Porat-V.Golod, Tel Aviv 2001.

8...0-0

Black has also taken the b2-pawn immediately, lest White withdraw the offer. For example, 8...cxb2 9 ♗xb2 0-0 10 ♕c2 (10 ♕b3 ♗e7 11 ♖fd1 ♕e8 12 ♖ac1 ♘d8 13 ♘fe5 a5 14 e4 was also promising for White in the old game V.Makogonov-G.Kasparian, Parnu 1947) 10...♗e7 (10...♗d7 11 e4 ♘a5 12 ♘e3 ♖c8 13 ♖fd1 ♕e8 14 a4 ♕e7 15 ♘e5 gave White a strong initiative in I.Gaponenko-R.Akopov, Smolensk 1991) 11 ♖ac1 ♘b4 12 ♕b1 ♗d7 (12...c6 13 e4 ♘a6 14 ♖fd1 b6 15 ♘ce5 was also very nice for White in T.Toshkov-N.Spiridonov, Albena 1984) 13 ♘fe5 ♖b8 14 ♘a5 and White had a lot of pressure for the pawn in T.Toshkov-S.Makarichev, Warsaw 1985.

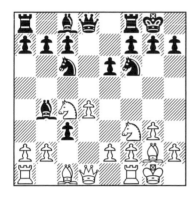

9 ♕d3

There are other moves here:

a) 9 b3 strikes me as being a bit mean spirited as it tries to recover the pawn. After 9...♖b8 (9...♘e4!?) 10 a3 ♗e7 11 ♕c2 b5 12 ♘ce5 ♗b7 13 ♘xc6 ♗xc6 14 ♕xc3 ♗e4 15 ♗b2 ♘d5 16 ♕c1 ♕c8 17 ♘e5 ♗xg2 18 ♔xg2 c5 Black was doing okay in P.Haba-L.Ostrowski, Czech League 1999, and he might have done better trying to hold the pawn.

b) 9 ♖b1 e5 (9...c2 10 ♕xc2 ♘xd4 11 ♘xd4 ♕xd4 12 ♗e3 would give White a strong initiative for the pawn, but 9...♕d5!? looks interesting) 10 bxc3 e4 11 ♘fe5 ♗xc3 12 ♘xc6 bxc6 13 ♗a3 ♖e8 14 ♕a4 ♗g4 15 e3 ♗e2 16 ♖fc1 was good for White due to his superior pawn structure in P.Haba-A.Strauss, Vienna 1998.

c) 9 ♕b3!? is worth considering, for example 9...♘d5 10 e4 cxb2 11 ♗xb2 gives compensation similar to the game.

9...cxb2 10 ♗xb2 ♗e7 11 e4

It seems that this obvious move is a theoretical novelty. In Z.Kozul-L.Ljubojevic, Belgrade 1989, White played 11 ♖ac1 and also had compensation after 11...a5!? 12 ♕b1?! a4 13 e4 a3 14 ♗a1 ♘b4 15 ♖fd1 ♖a4 16 ♘e3.

11...b6 12 a3

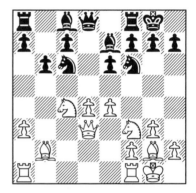

I felt it was worth a tempo to stop any ...♘c6-b4 nonsense. Black now finds it difficult to formulate any kind of plan, whereas White can improve his position almost at leisure.

12...♗b7 13 ♖fe1 a5 14 ♖ad1 a4 15 d5 ♘a5

15...exd5? 16 exd5 ♘a5 is bad due to 17 ♘g5 (threatening 18 ♗xf6) 17...g6 18 d6! etc.

16 ♘e3 ♘b3?!

I think this may be a mistake, as there's just not enough time to transfer the knight to c5 effectively. 16...♗c5 might have been a better try, but then one of White's options is to recover his sacrificed pawn with 17 ♕c2 ♕e7 18 ♕xa4, while keeping the better position.

17 ♕c2 ♕c8

And this could well be the decisive

mistake, though White generates tremendous pressure in any case. I think Black should play 17...exd5, when I was considering lines like 18 ♘f5!? (18 exd5 is a simple way to play it, with very strong pressure against the black king) 18...♗c5 19 ♘xg7! ♔xg7 20 exd5 h6 21 ♘g5 hxg5 22 ♕f5 with a winning attack.

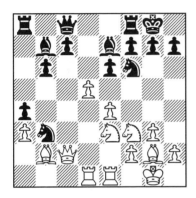

18 ♗h3 ♘c5 19 ♘g5

Setting up threats against e6 and h7.

19...♘e8

On 19...h6 I was intending 20 dxe6 fxe6 21 ♘xe6 ♘xe6 22 ♘d5 ♖e8 23 ♘xc7 etc.

20 dxe6 fxe6 21 ♘xe6 ♘xe6 22 ♕c4 ♔f7 23 ♘d5! b5

After 23...♗a6 White should maintain his pressure on the a2-g8 diagonal with 24 ♕a2.

24 ♕xb5

One of the secrets of attacking chess is to know when to start taking material rather than attempt to land a haymaker.

24...♗a6

And not 24...c6 because of 25 ♗xe6+ ♔xe6 26 ♘f4+ etc.

25 ♕a5 ♗e2

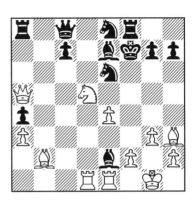

I considered several alternatives for Black in this position:

a) 25...♗b7 26 ♕c3 ♗f6 27 e5 ♗g5 28 ♕c4 threatens 29 f4.

b) 25...♖b8 26 ♗d4 ♗c4 27 ♘xe7 ♔xe7 28 ♕h5 traps Black's king in the centre.

c) 25...c5 26 ♘b6 ♕c7 27 ♖d7 ♗c4 28 ♕xa8 ♕xb6 29 ♖b7 ♕d6 30 ♕xa4 puts White ahead on material while maintaining a huge attack.

d) 25...♗g5 26 ♕c3 threatens 27 ♕e5 amongst other things.

26 ♗xe6+

Cashing in.

26...♕xe6

26...♔xe6 is met by 27 ♘f4+ ♔f7 (or 27...♖xf4 28 ♕d5 mate) 28 ♕d5+ followed by mate next move.

27 ♕xa8 ♗xd1 28 ♘xe7 ♗b3 29 ♘c6

Gaining time through the threat of 30 ♘d8+.

29...♔g8 30 ♘d4 ♕c4 31 ♕c6

The exchange of queens will reduce Black's counterplay, which is why I chose it instead of other promising lines.

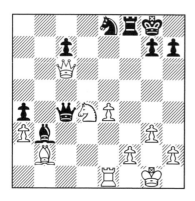

31...♘d6 32 e5 ♕xc6 33 ♘xc6 ♘c4 34 ♗c1 ♖a8 35 f4 ♘a5

Hoping for salvation in an opposite-coloured bishop endgame. But even this is not enough.

36 ♘xa5 ♖xa5 37 f5 ♖d5 38 ♔f2 ♖d1 39 g4 h5 40 h3

White needs to keep his pawns together.

40...♖xe1 41 ♔xe1 ♔f7

Black can't attack the pawns with 41...hxg4 42 hxg4 g6 43 e6 gxf5 44 gxf5 ♗c2 45 f6 ♗f5 because 46 f7+ ♔g7 47 ♗h6+ would lead to promotion of the f-pawn.

42 ♗g5 ♔e8

After 42...g6 there follows 43 e6+ ♔e8 44 gxh5 gxh5 45 ♔d2 ♗d5 46 ♔e3 and White protects the pawns, while 42...hxg4 43 hxg4 g6 44 e6+ ♔e8 45 ♔d2 is similar.

43 e6 ♗d5 44 ♔f2

After this everything is clear: White can protect his pawns with his king and prevent any blockade by keeping them on light squares.

44...c5 45 ♔g3 hxg4 46 hxg4 ♔f8 47 ♗e3 c4 48 ♗c5+ ♔g8 49 ♗b4 g6 50 ♔f4

gxf5 **51 gxf5 ♔h7 52 ♔e5 ♗c6 53 f6 1-0**

Game 43
M.Umansky-O.Rause
World Correspondence
Championship 2004

1 d4 d5 2 c4 e6 3 ♘f3 ♘f6 4 g3 ♗b4+ 5 ♘bd2 dxc4 6 ♗g2 b5

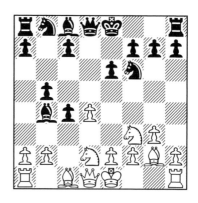

Setting about holding the c4-pawn in the most direct way. Note again that this line would not be possible against a 3 g3 and 4 ♗g2 move order, as 5...dxc4 loses a piece to 6 ♕a4+. However, 1 d4 d5 2 c4 e6 3 g3 has its own issues because of 3...dxc4! 4 ♘f3 c5! 5 ♗g2 ♘c6!. On the other hand, Black cannot play this way if he's already put his knight on f6, which often happens on move one.

Other moves seen here:

a) 6...a5 7 0-0 b5 8 ♘b1!? a4 9 ♘e5 ♖a6 10 a3 ♗e7 11 ♘c3 c6 12 e4 0-0 13 ♗e3 ♘bd7 14 f4 gave White compensation in Z.Kozul-A.Saric, Nova Gorica 2007, though this all looked very weird and messy.

b) 6...0-0 7 0-0 ♗d7 8 ♘xc4 ♗c6 9 ♘ce5 ♗d5 10 a3 ♗e7 11 ♗g5 gave White a comfortable and risk-free edge in J.Kraai-Zhang Zhong, Beijing (blitz) 2008.

7 0-0

The move 7 a4 was played in a rare loss for the young Norwegian star, Magnus Carlsen. The game M.Carlsen-I.Ivanisevic, European Team Ch., Crete 2007, went 7...c6 8 ♕c2 ♗b7 9 0-0 0-0 10 e4 ♘bd7 11 e5 ♘d5 12 ♘e4 h6 13 ♗d2 with compensation for the pawn, but maybe not enough.

My own feeling is that White should be much more violent and direct in this kind of line, rather than sitting back and trying to let the compensation manifest itself.

7...0-0 8 a4 c6 9 axb5

Another possibility is 9 ♘e5, when R.Buhmann-R.Jedynak, French Team Ch. 2007, was agreed drawn after 9...♘d5 10 e4 ♘f6 11 ♘df3 ♗b7 12 ♕e2 ♘bd7 13 ♖d1 a6 14 ♗g5 ♗e7.

9...cxb5 10 ♘h4 ♘d5 11 e4

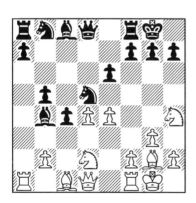

11...♘c7

There's also a case for 11...♘f6, after

which White would probably play 12 e5 ♘d5 13 ♘e4 intending 14 ♕g4. I wouldn't attempt to assess this before seeing some more trials by strong players.

12 e5 ♕xd4 13 ♕h5 g6 14 ♕g5 a5 15 ♘e4 ♘d7 16 ♗f4 ♘d5 17 ♕h6 ♖d8

Black had an alternative in the move 17...♗e7, when White should play 18 ♗g5 ♖e8 19 ♗xe7 ♖xe7 20 ♘g5 ♘f8 21 ♘hf3 ♕xb2 22 ♖fb1, once again with a powerful initiative as his pieces bounce off Black's queen into the attack.

18 ♘g5 ♘f8 19 ♘hf3 ♕xb2?!

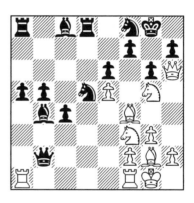

Maybe 19...♕d3 would have been better, but after 20 ♖fd1 ♕e2 21 ♖ab1 White still has a strong initiative and is only one pawn down.

20 ♖fb1 ♕e2?

Losing the queen. Black had to try 20...♕c2, even though it allows White to play 21 ♘d4 ♕c3 22 ♘xb5, breaking up the pride of Black's position, his queenside pawns.

21 ♗f1 ♕c2 22 ♘d4 ♕xb1 23 ♖xb1 ♘xf4 24 ♘c6! ♗b7 25 ♘xd8 ♖xd8 26 gxf4 c3 27 h4!

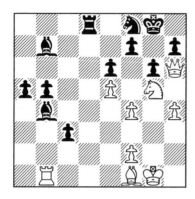

27...♖d2

One of the points behind White's last move is that 27...c2 28 ♖c1 ♖d2 can be answered by 29 f5 exf5 (29...gxf5 30 ♕f6 is terminal) 30 h5 threatening ♘xh7.

28 f5 exf5 29 ♖xb4! axb4 30 e6! fxe6 31 ♘xh7! ♘xh7 32 ♕xg6+ 1-0

After 32...♔h8 there follows 33 ♕e8+ ♔g7 34 ♕e7+ ♔g8 35 ♕xe6+ ♔g7 36 h5 c2 37 h6+ ♔f8 38 ♕xf5+ ♔e8 39 ♕e5+ ♔d7 (or 39...♔f7 40 ♕f4+) 40 ♗h3+ ♔c6 41 ♗g2+ ♔d7 42 ♕xb5+ with a winning attack. White is picking everything up with check.

Game 44
Z.Almasi-C.Balogh
Heviz 2008

---

1 ♘f3 ♘f6 2 c4 e6 3 d4 d5 4 g3 dxc4 5 ♗g2 ♗b4+ 6 ♘c3

This would not be my choice and this game is given largely to show how Black should play against it. Having said that the line has been used by some very strong players, albeit some-

times via the move order 1 d4 ♘f6 2 c4 e6 3 ♘c3 ♗b4 4 g3 d5 5 ♗g2 0-0 6 ♘f3 dxc4, which qualifies it as a '4 g3 Nimzo'.

6...0-0 7 0-0 ♘c6

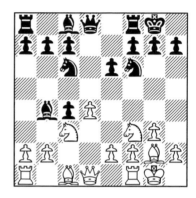

In O.Renet-M.Sharif, Marseilles 1986, Black played 7...c5, but was under pressure after 8 dxc5 ♘c6 (8...♗xc5 9 ♕a4 gives White the initiative) 9 ♕a4 ♕a5 10 ♕xa5 ♘xa5 11 ♘e5 ♗xc5 12 ♖d1.

8 ♗g5

White has tried other moves here:

a) 8 ♖e1 ♘d5 9 ♕c2 ♗e7! was B.Gulko-A.Yusupov, Linares 1990, and now White's best was probably 10 a3, so as to play e2-e4 without having to worry about a black knight going to b4 and then d3.

b) 8 a3 ♗a5 9 ♗g5 h6 10 ♗xf6 ♕xf6 11 ♕a4 ♗b6 12 e3 ♘a5 13 ♘e5 ♕e7 14 ♘e4 ♖d8 15 ♘xc4 ♗d7 16 ♕c2 ♘xc4 17 ♕xc4 ♗c6 was about equal in M.Illescas-A.Yusupov, Linares 1990.

8...h6

Black can also consider 8...♗e7, for example 9 e3 (9 ♕a4!? ♘xd4 10 ♖fd1 looks like a more interesting try)

9...♘d5 10 ♗xe7 ♕xe7 11 ♘d2 ♘b6 12 ♕e2 ♘a5 13 ♕h5 f5 14 e4 ♘c6! was already better for Black in E.Ubilava-G.Agzamov, Sevastopol 1986.

9 ♗xf6 ♕xf6 10 e3

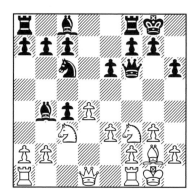

10...♖d8

Another possibility is 10...♖b8, when Z.Kozul-A.Delchev, Nova Gorica 2005, continued 11 ♘d2 ♘a5 12 ♕h5 (12 ♕a4 ♕e7 13 a3 ♗xc3 14 bxc3 b6 left White struggling to equalize in G.Fish-I.Khenkin, German Ch., Altenkirchen 2005), and now 12...♕f5 (rather than the 12...b6 played in the game) 13 ♕xf5 exf5 seems to leave White struggling.

11 ♕e2

Alternatives are no improvement:

a) 11 ♘e4 ♕e7 (11...♕f5!?) 12 a3 ♗d6 13 ♘fd2 e5 14 ♘xc4 exd4 15 exd4 ♗f5 16 ♘c3 ♕f6 17 ♘d5 ♕xd4 led to equality in J.Ehlvest-A.Yermolinsky, Moscow 2005.

b) 11 ♕a4 ♗d7 12 ♕c2 ♗d6 13 ♖fd1 ♖ac8 14 ♕e2 e5 15 ♕xc4 exd4 16 ♘xd4

♘xd4 17 ♖xd4 ♗e5 18 ♖xd7 ♖xd7 19 ♗h3 ♖cd8 saw Black rather more than equalize in Z.Kozul-G.Dizdar, Croatian Ch., Split 2008.

11...e5 12 ♕xc4 exd4 13 ♘d5

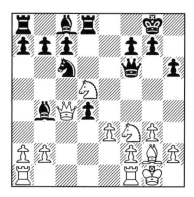

It looks like White might be pressing, but the position soon fizzles out to stone cold equality.

13...♕d6 14 ♘xb4 ♗e6 15 ♕b5 ♕xb4 16 ♕xb4 ♘xb4 17 ♘xd4 ♗d5 18 ♖fc1 c6 19 b3 a5 20 a3 ♘a6 21 ♖c3 ♘c7 22 ♖ac1 ♘e6 23 ♗xd5 ½-½

Summary

As with 4...♗b4+ I'm a fan of blocking the check with ♘b1-d2 and not worrying too much about pawns. On the other hand, it seems that the big boys prefer 6 ♗d2 with some high-level discussions taking place around 6...a5. As this is relatively uncharted territory we can probably expect further interesting developments.

Chapter Ten

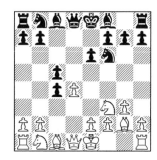

Open Catalan with 5...c5

1 d4 ♘f6 2 c4 e6 3 g3 d5 4 ♗g2 dxc4 5 ♘f3 c5

The variation with 4...dxc4 and 5...c5 is one of the most solid and reliable lines Black can play against the Catalan. He immediately sets about eliminating White's d-pawn and will reinforce the pressure against d4 with 6...♘c6.

Unlike other 4...dxc4 lines it can also be used against the 1 d4 ♘f6 2 ♘f3 e6 3 g3 move order, as Black plays 3...d5 4 ♗g2 c5 5 0-0 ♘c6, after which White's best move is 6 c4 allowing 6...dxc4 transposing. This makes it into a good system for Nimzo/Queen's Indian players who therefore don't need to bother about 4...♗e7 lines. It's no accident that it's a favourite of top players such as Michael Adams.

The old main line here was 7 ♕a4, when 7...cxd4 was played in Van Wely-L'Ami (Game 45). Black sacrificed his queen with 10...♕xd1+, but it's not

clear he's doing that badly after 10...♗xc6 either. If White wants something from 7 ♕a4 I think he should go for Gulko's old 10 ♗e3, but even this isn't much fun.

If Black wants some winning chances he should probably opt for 7...♗d7 8 ♕xc4 b5!?, as in Le Quang-Ismagambetov (Game 46), though the drawback is that it also gives him losing chances. White's 10 ♗g5 is worth noting here as a refreshing change from the hackneyed 10 ♘c3; as the game shows it still has some surprise value.

White's frustration with trying to get something against 5...c5 has led him to try out a variety of gambit approaches. 7 ♘e5 ♗d7 8 ♘a3 was the first of these to become popular, but Eljanov-Adams (Game 47) shows that its terrors have been more or less shorn. Gelfand-Adams (Game 48) featured the fresher 8 ♘xc4, with Gelfand playing the interesting new move, 13 b4. White should also take a look at 7 ♘a3 (Fridman-Inkiov, Game 49) if he wants to pose a few awkward questions. The fun may not last forever, so now's the time to get on board these variations.

The other approach I like for White is illustrated in Gleizerov-Adly (Game 50), which is to transpose into an endgame with 7 dxc5. White's pawns get split with 9...c3, but his position nonetheless seems somewhat preferable.

Game 45
L.Van Wely-E.L'Ami
London 2008

1 d4 ♘f6 2 c4 e6 3 ♘f3 d5 4 g3 dxc4 5 ♗g2 c5 6 0-0 ♘c6 7 ♕a4

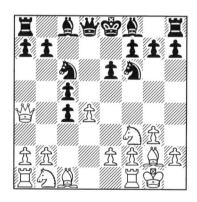

7...cxd4

Black has a major alternative in 7...♗d7 which features in the next game. Frankly I don't think that 7 ♕a4 offers White very much, which is why I've simplified the mass of theory on it.
8 ♘xd4 ♕xd4 9 ♗xc6+ ♗d7 10 ♖d1

White has also tried to eke out a little something with 10 ♗e3, though after 10...♗xc6! (10...♕xb2?! 11 ♗xd7+ ♘xd7 12 ♖d1 b5 13 ♕a6 ♕xa1 14 ♗d4 is good for White) 11 ♕xc6+ ♕d7! 12 ♕xc4 a6 (12...♗e7 13 ♘c3 0-0 14 ♖fd1 ♕c8 15 ♕b5!? a6 16 ♕b6 ♗d8?! 17 ♕b4 was better for White in B.Gulko-Zsu.Polgar, Biel 1987) 13 ♘c3 b5 14 ♕b3 ♗e7 15 ♖fd1 ♕b7 it wasn't much for White in W.Schlemermeyer-J.Stanke, German League 2004.

Another possibility is 10 ♗xd7+ ♕xd7 11 ♕xc4, but after 11...♗e7 12 ♕b3 0-0 13 ♖d1 ♕c6 14 ♗e3 the position was equal and a draw was agreed in A.Stefanova-T.Luther, Recklinghausen 1998.

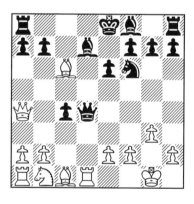

10...♕xd1+

This positional queen sacrifice has proven very difficult for White to break down. In this game Black shows great precision in his handling of the line.

Instead, 10...♗xc6 11 ♕xc6+ bxc6 12 ♖xd4 is supposed to be better for White because of Black's split pawns, but Black nevertheless equalized with 12...c5 13 ♖xc4 ♗e7 14 ♗g5 ♘d7! 15

♗xe7 ♔xe7 16 ♘d2 ♖hb8 17 ♖c2 a5 18 ♖d1 a4 in the game T.Markowski-S.Mamedyarov, European Team Ch., Plovdiv 2003.

11 ♕xd1 ♗xc6 12 ♘d2 b5 13 a4 ♗e7 14 axb5 ♗xb5 15 ♘xc4 0-0 16 b3 ♖fd8

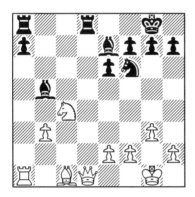

After 16...♖fc8 17 ♗a3 ♗xa3 18 ♘xa3 ♗a6 19 ♘c2 Black had to fight for the draw in J.Hjartarson-H.Olafsson, Reykjavik 1986.

17 ♕c2 ♖dc8 18 ♗a3 ♗xa3 19 ♖xa3 ♖c7 20 ♕a2 ♗xc4 21 bxc4 ½-½

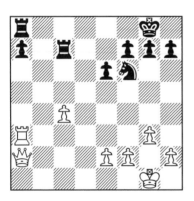

It's going to be impossible for White to do anything here, despite his supposed material advantage. The c- and a-pawns are likely to come off and he won't be able to win on the kingside alone.

Game 46
L.Le Quang-A.Ismagambetov
Macau 2007

---

1 d4 ♘f6 2 c4 e6 3 ♘f3 d5 4 g3 dxc4 5 ♗g2 c5 6 0-0 ♘c6 7 ♕a4 ♗d7 8 ♕xc4

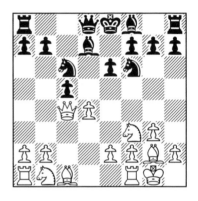

8...b5

There are interesting alternatives here, for example 8...cxd4 9 ♘xd4 ♖c8 10 ♘xc6 ♗xc6 11 ♗xc6+ ♖xc6 12 ♕b5 ♕c8 left Black without much to worry about in I.Hera-D.Pavasovic, European Club Cup, Kallithea 2008; and 8...♕b6!? 9 dxc5 ♕xc5 10 ♘a3 ♗e7 11 ♖d1 0-0 12 ♗f4 ♕b6 13 ♕b5 ♗xa3 14 ♕xb6 axb6 15 bxa3 ♖fc8 gave Black a solid game in B.Avrukh-A.Graf, Spanish Team Ch. 2008.

9 ♕d3 ♖c8

I don't particularly like 9...c4, although ambitious players may want to play this way, as it gives Black a queenside pawn majority. After 10 ♕c2 ♖c8 11 ♘c3 ♗e7 12 ♗g5 0-0 13 ♗xf6

♗xf6 14 ♘xb5 ♕b6 15 ♘d6 ♖c7 16 ♘xc4 ♘xd4 17 ♘xb6 ♘xc2 18 ♘xd7 ♖xd7 19 ♖ac1 Black had inadequate compensation in E.Postny-C.Marcelin, French Team Ch. 2008.

10 ♗g5

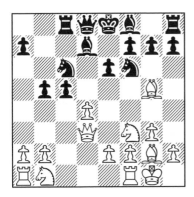

This hasn't been played too much so it still offers some surprise value. In this game Black goes wrong immediately.

The most popular move has been 10 ♘c3, but 10...cxd4 11 ♘xd4 ♘e5!? 12 ♕d1 b4 13 ♘e4 ♘d5 14 ♘g5 ♗e7 15 ♗xd5 exd5 16 ♘gf3 ♘c4 gave Black excellent counterplay in V.Korchnoi-V.Ivanchuk, Istanbul Olympiad 2000.

10...♗e7?!

This isn't good because of White's reply, so instead Black should consider the alternatives:

a) 10...cxd4!? 11 ♘xd4 ♘xd4 (11...♘e5 12 ♕b3 ♕b6 13 ♘f3 ♘xf3+ 14 ♗xf3 ♗e7 15 ♖d1 h6 16 ♗e3 ♗c5 17 ♗xc5 ♕xc5 18 ♘c3 0-0 19 ♖d2 was a bit better for White at this stage in P.Nikolic-S.Pedersen, German League 2005) 12 ♕xd4 ♗c5 13 ♕h4 ♗e7 14 ♘c3 b4 15 ♘e4 ♘xe4 16 ♗xe7 ♕xe7 17 ♕xe4

♕c5 was rather equal in M.Hoffmann-M.Willsch, Solingen 2005.

b) 10...c4 is not a concept that I'm hugely fond of, though it is probably better here than on the previous move. R.Hübner-M.Müller, German League 1997, continued 11 ♕d1 (11 ♕c2 ♗e7 12 e4 h6! 13 ♗d2 0-0 14 a3 ♕b6 15 ♗e3 ♘g4 16 ♗f4 ♘xd4! 17 ♘xd4 e5! was good for Black in B.Gulko-S.Smagin, Moscow 1983) 11...♗e7 12 ♘c3 b4 (12...a6 13 e4 b4 14 ♗xf6 ♗xf6 was comfortable for Black in V.Filippov-J.Piket, European Team Ch., Batumi 1999) 13 ♗xf6 gxf6 14 ♘e4 ♕a5 15 ♕d2 f5 16 ♘c5 ♗xc5 17 dxc5 ♕xc5 18 ♖fd1 and White had compensation for the pawn.

11 dxc5

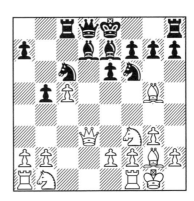

With Black having used a tempo putting his bishop on e7, he doesn't really want to use another one to recapture the pawn. As a result 11 dxc5 is quite awkward.

11...♘b4 12 ♕d2 ♗xc5 13 ♘c3 ♗c6 14 ♕xd8+ ♖xd8 15 ♖ac1

15 a3! looks even stronger, for example 15...♘a6 (or 15...♘bd5 16 ♘e5) 16 ♘e5 ♗xg2 17 ♔xg2 b4 18 axb4 ♘xb4

19 ♖fd1 is unpleasant.

15...♗b6 16 a3 ♘a6 17 ♘e5 ♗xg2 18 ♔xg2 b4 19 ♘b5 bxa3 20 bxa3 0-0 21 ♘c6 ♖d7 22 ♖fd1

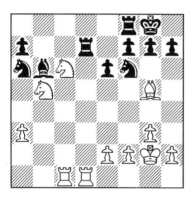

This kind of endgame is typical of the Catalan. White is first to the d- and c-files, and because of this has the initiative.

22...♖b7 23 ♗f4 h6 24 ♗d6 ♖a8 25 a4 ♔h7 26 ♖c4 ♘e8 27 ♗a3 ♖c8 28 ♖dc1 ♘b8 29 ♘e5 ♖xc4 30 ♖xc4 f6 31 ♘d3

31 ♖c8 was worth considering.

31...a6 32 ♘d6 ♘xd6 33 ♗xd6 ♘d7 34 ♘f4 e5 35 ♘d5 ♗a5 36 ♖c6 ♘b6 37 e4 ♔g8

And not 37...♘xa4? because of 38 ♖xa6 ♖b5 39 ♖a7, suddenly turning his attention to Black's kingside and the g7-pawn.

38 ♗c7 ♘xd5 39 ♗xa5 ♘b4 40 ♖d6 ♔f7 41 ♔f3 h5 42 ♗b6 ♘c2 43 a5 ♖e7 44 ♔e2 ♖b7?

This could be the losing move. Having defended himself very solidly, Black seems to have rejected his initial intention of 44...♖e6 for some reason. Now White gets to bring his king in.

45 ♔d3 ♘a3 46 ♖d8 ♘b5 47 ♔c4 ♔e7

48 ♖g8 ♔d6 49 ♖a8 ♘c7 50 ♖d8+ ♔e7 51 ♖c8 ♘e8 52 ♔d5 ♖d7+ 53 ♔c6 ♘d6 54 ♖g8 1-0

I'm not sure if this was on time or due to general depression about Black's prospects. Certainly his position is very difficult, if not lost, but he might have continued for a few more moves.

Game 47
P.Eljanov-M.Adams
Wijk aan Zee 2008

---

1 d4 ♘f6 2 c4 e6 3 g3 d5 4 ♗g2 dxc4 5 ♘f3 c5 6 0-0 ♘c6 7 ♘e5

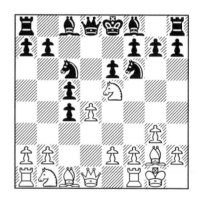

7...♗d7

This seems to be Black's best. Note that 7...♘xd4? is bad because of 8 e3 ♘b5 9 ♕xd8+ ♔xd8 10 ♘xf7+ etc.

White also has the initiative after 7...♘xe5, for example 8 dxe5 ♘d7 (8...♕xd1 9 ♖xd1 ♘d7 10 f4 ♖b8 11 a4 ♗e7 12 ♘a3 0-0 13 ♘xc4 ♖d8 14 ♗e3 gave White strong pressure in the game A.Stefanova-J.Krivec, European Women's Ch., Warsaw 2001; while

8...♘d5!? 9 ♘a3 ♗d7! 10 ♘xc4 ♗c6 was T.V.Petrosian-O.Panno, Palma 1969, and now Petrosian suggested 11 ♘d6+ ♗xd6 12 exd6, rather than his 11 a3) 9 f4 ♗e7 (9...♕c7 10 ♘a3 ♘b6 11 ♘b5 ♕b8 12 ♗e3 ♗d7 13 ♘d6+ ♗xd6 14 exd6 ♕c8 15 ♗f2 ♗c6 was M.Vukic-I.Hausner, Banja Luka 1981, when 16 e4 0-0 17 ♖c1 looks good for White to me) 10 ♘a3 0-0 11 ♘xc4 ♕c7 12 ♗e3 ♘b6 13 ♘d6 ♖d8 was N.Alexandria-N.Ioseliani, 6th matchgame, Tbilisi 1981, and now Ubilava's recommendation of 14 ♕c2 ♗xd6 15 exd6 ♖xd6 16 ♗xc5 looks strong.

8 ♘a3

There is a major alternative in 8 ♘xc4!?, which is covered in the next game.

8...cxd4 9 ♘axc4 ♗c5

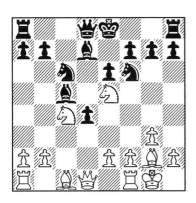

This natural move looks comfortable for Black, though there are some alternatives here too. For example:

a) 9...♖c8 10 ♕b3 ♘xe5 11 ♘xe5 ♕b6! 12 ♕xb6 axb6 13 ♗xb7 ♖c2 14 ♘xd7 ♘xd7 15 ♖d1 ½-½ was B.Avrukh-Z.Azmaiparashvili, European Cup, Chalkidiki 2002.

b) 9...♘xe5 10 ♘xe5 ♕b6 11 b4!? ♖d8 12 a3 ♗e7 13 ♗b2 ♕a6 14 ♗xd4 0-0 15 e3 ♗b5 16 ♖e1 was a bit better for White at this stage in M.Brodsky-M.Ulibin, Bydgoszcz 2001.

10 ♕b3

White has also tried 10 a3, but this doesn't seem to help too much after 10...a5 (or 10...♖c8 11 b4 ♗e7 12 ♗b2 0-0 13 ♘xd7 ♕xd7 14 b5 ♘b8 15 ♕b3 ♕c7 16 ♖ac1 ♗c5 17 ♕f3 ♘d5 as in V.Ivanchuk-A.Sokolov, Minsk 1986) 11 ♗f4 (11 ♘xc6 ♗xc6 12 ♗xc6+ bxc6 13 ♕a4 0-0 14 ♕xc6 ♕d5 15 ♕xd5 ♘xd5 was very comfortable for Black in R.Vera-J.Vilela, Manzanillo 1987) 11...0-0 12 ♖c1 ♖c8 13 ♘d3 ♗e7 14 ♘d6 ♗xd6 15 ♗xd6 ♖e8 16 ♘e5 ♕b6 17 ♗c5 ♕a6, when it was difficult for White to prove anything in I.Ivanisevic-M.Stojanovic, Bosnian Team Ch. 2007.

Another possibility is 10 ♗f4, but after 10...0-0 11 ♕b3 just transposes into the note to White's 11th move below.

10...0-0

Black has also played 10...♘xe5 and 10...♕c8, but the text seems like the most natural.

11 ♕xb7

Here 11 ♗f4 is a major alternative, but Black has a good antidote in 11...♕c8 12 ♘d3 ♗e7 13 ♖fc1 ♘d5, for example 14 ♘ce5!? (14 ♗xd5 exd5 15 ♘ce5 ♖d8 16 ♕xd5 ♗e8 17 ♕b3 ♔f8! 18 ♘xc6 bxc6 19 ♕c4 ♕f5 was fine for Black in V.Ivanchuk-Y.Dokhoian, Irkutsk 1986) 14...♘xf4 15 gxf4 ♖b8 16 ♖c4 ♗f6 17 ♘xc6 ♗xc6 18 ♗xc6 bxc6 19 ♕c2 ♕e8 20 ♖c5 ♔h8 21 ♖c1 ♖g8 22

⤎xc6 e5 23 fxe5 ♗xe5 24 ♕c5 f6 25 ♘xe5 was equal and agreed drawn at this point in V.Tkachiev-A.Sokolov, European Ch., Ohrid 2001.

11...♘xe5 12 ♘xe5 ⤎b8 13 ♕f3 ♗d6 14 ♘c6

Instead, 14 ♘xd7 ♕xd7 15 ♗g5 ♗e5! 16 ⤎ab1 h6 17 ♗f4 ♗xf4 18 ♕xf4 ⤎fe8! 19 ⤎fc1 e5 20 ♕d2 ⤎ec8 was at least equal for Black in R.Vaganian-G.Serper, World Team Ch., Lucerne 1993; while 14 ♗f4 ♘d5! and 14 ♘c4 ♗b5! don't give White anything either.

14...♗xc6 15 ♕xc6 ♕e7!

This looks like an equalizer. 15...e5 is worse after 16 ⤎b1! ⤎b6?! (16...♕d7 is only slightly better for White) 17 ♕a4 ♕b8 18 ♗g5! ♗e7 19 b4! ♗xb4 20 ♗xf6 gxf6 21 ♕d7! and White was clearly better in G.Kasparov-Comp Deep Blue, 2nd matchgame, Philadelphia 1996.

16 ⤎b1

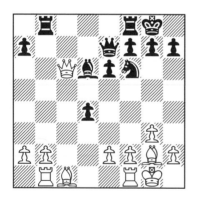

In V.Laznicka-J.Werle, European Ch., Liverpool 2008, White tried to improve with 16 ♕a4, but found himself much worse after 16...e5 17 ⤎b1 h6 18 ♗d2 ♗b4 19 ♗xb4 ⤎xb4 20 ♕a3 e4 etc.

16...h6 17 e3 ♗c5 18 exd4 ♗xd4 19

♕c4 ⤎fd8 20 b3 ½-½

The vulnerability of f2 compensates for White's pair of bishops.

1 d4 ♘f6 2 c4 e6 3 g3 d5 4 ♗g2 dxc4 5 ♘f3 c5 6 0-0 ♘c6 7 ♘e5 ♗d7 8 ♘xc4!?

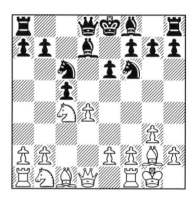

An interesting line, trying to exploit the negative side of Black's last move by probing d6.

8...cxd4

The critical reply. Both 8...b5 9 ♘e5 ⤎c8 10 ♘xd7 and 8...♘xd4 9 ♗xb7 ⤎b8 10 ♗g2 favour White.

9 ♗f4 ♗e7

Black's main alternative is 9...♘d5, for example 10 ♘d6+ ♗xd6 11 ♗xd6 ♘de7 (11...h5 12 h4 g5 13 ♘d2 gxh4 14 ♗a3 b5 15 ♗c5 hxg3 16 ♘e4 gxf2+ 17 ⤎xf2 gave White a huge attack in J.Houska-T.Kett, European Ch., Liverpool 2008; while 11...♕b6 should be met by 12 ♘d2 with a possible sequel of 12...♕xb2 13 ⤎b1 ♕xa2 14 ⤎a1 ♕b2

15 ♗a3 ♕b5 16 ♘e4) 12 ♘d2 (this is more accurate than 12 ♕b3, as apart from 12...0-0 13 ♘d2 transposing, Black has a good alternative in 12...♘a5!, when 13 ♕b4 ♘f5! 14 ♗c5 b6 15 ♗xd4 ♘c6 16 ♗xc6 ♗xc6 17 ♗c3 was equal at best for White in M.Krasenkow-Z.Sturua, USSR 1987) 12...0-0

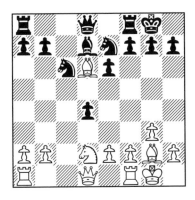

13 ♕b3 (White can also try 13 ♘f3, for example 13...♖e8 14 ♘xd4 ♘xd4 15 ♕xd4 ♘f5 16 ♕b4 ♘xd6 17 ♕xd6 ♗c6 18 ♕xd8 ♖exd8 19 ♗xc6 bxc6 20 ♖fd1 with a nominal advantage in a drawish endgame) 13...b6 (if 13...♗c8 14 ♗a3!? ♖e8 15 ♖ac1 ♘f5 16 ♘e4 e5 17 ♘c5 ♘d6 18 ♗d5 ♔h8 19 ♘xb7 ♘xb7 20 ♗xc6 ♘a5 21 ♕xf7 ♘xc6 22 ♖xc6 ♕d7 23 ♕xd7 ♗xd7 24 ♖c5 with a clear advantage to White in O.Romanishin-S.Smagin, Essen 2001) 14 ♘c4 ♖e8!? (14...♖c8 15 ♖fd1 was M.Krasenkow-S.Shestakov, USSR 1987, when 15...♖e8 would have been best with a double-edged game arising after 16 e3 ♘f5 17 e4 ♘fe7 18 e5) 15 ♗a3 ♘f5 16 ♖ad1 ♖b8 17 e4! b5! (17...♘fe7 18 ♘d6 ♖f8 was B.Gelfand-L.Stratil, Oakham 1988, and now 19 e5! ♘xe5 20 ♖xd4 ♗c6 21 ♘b5!

♗d5 22 ♗xd5 exd5 23 ♘xa7 would have given White a clear advantage according to Gelfand and Kapengut) 18 exf5 (18 ♘d6!? ♘xd6 19 ♗xd6 ♖c8! 20 e5 is also possible) 18...bxc4 19 ♕xc4 e5! was a game G.Orlov-V.Nasybullin, USSR 1988, and now I like the idea of 20 f4!?, for example 20...♘e7 21 fxe5!? ♗b5 22 ♕c2 ♗xf1 23 ♗xf1 gives White two powerful bishops and a dangerous kingside pawn majority for the sacrificed exchange.

Note that stopping the check on d6 with 9...♗c8 is not good. L.Alburt-B.Chesney, Somerset 1986, continued 10 ♘e5 ♘xe5 11 ♗xe5 ♗c5 12 ♕c1! ♗b6 13 ♕g5 0-0 14 ♖d1 h6 15 ♕h4 ♘h7 16 ♘a3 ♕xh4 17 gxh4 ♖d8 18 ♘c4 with more than enough compensation for the pawn.

10 ♘d6+ ♔f8

10...♗xd6 11 ♗xd6 would make it very difficult for Black to develop.

11 ♘xb7 ♕b6 12 ♘d6 ♕c5!

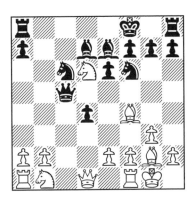

This looks like Black's best, as the alternatives leave White with a powerful initiative:

a) 12...g5? is bad, due to simply 13

♗xg5 ♗xd6 14 ♗xf6 etc.

b) 12...e5? is answered by 13 ♘c4 ♕c5 14 ♘xe5! when the knight on c6 is pinned against the rook on a8.

c) 12...♘d5 13 ♘c4 ♕a6 (13...♕c5 14 ♘e5 ♖d8 15 ♘d3 ♕b5 16 a4 ♕a6 was I.Rogers-E.Varnusz, Balatonbereny 1983, and now according to Rogers he should have played 17 ♗xd5! exd5 18 b4! with a strong initiative) 14 ♘e5 ♗e8 15 ♗xd5! exd5 16 ♘xc6 ♗xc6 17 ♕xd4 ♕xe2?! 18 ♘d2! ♕e6 19 ♖fe1 ♕d7 20 ♖ac1 ♖c8 21 ♘b3! threatening 22 ♘a5 was tremendous for White in I.Rogers-B.Toth, Reggio Emilia 1983/84. Black misses the use of his king's rook here.

d) 12...♕xb2 13 ♘d2 would leave White with more than enough for the pawn; the position is opening up and Black's rook on h8 will be out of play for quite a few moves.

13 b4!?

An interesting new try that makes it far from easy for Black to defend. He has an easier life after other moves:

a) 13 ♕c1 ♗xd6 14 ♕xc5 ♗xc5 15 ♖c1 ♗b6 16 ♗xc6 ♖c8 brings about an endgame in which Black is at least equal.

b) 13 ♕b3 ♗xd6 14 ♖c1 ♕b4 15 ♕xb4 ♗xb4 leaves White with nothing better than 16 ♗xc6 ♖c8 17 ♗xd7 ♖xc1+ 18 ♗xc1 ♘xd7 19 ♗d2 and equality.

c) 13 ♘d2 can be answered by 13...e5, for example 14 ♘6e4 ♘xe4 15 ♘xe4 ♕b6 16 ♗d2 f5 17 ♘g5 h6 with White getting driven back.

d) 13 ♘e4 ♘xe4 14 ♗xe4 g5 15 ♗c1 (15 ♗d2 ♖b8 16 ♘a3 ♖xb2 17 ♖c1 ♕xa3 18 ♗xc6 ♕xa2 19 ♗xg5 ♗xg5 20 ♕xd4

♗xc1 21 ♕xh8+ ♔e7 22 ♗xd7 ♔xd7 23 ♖xc1 ♖b1 fizzled out to a draw in V.Loginov-D.Yevseev, St Petersburg 2004; while 15 b4?! ♕xb4 16 ♗e5 f6 17 a3 ♕b2 18 ♗xc6 ♗xc6! 19 ♗xd4 ♕b7 is rather good for Black who is now defending comfortably and still has his extra pawn) 15...f5 16 ♗g2 ♖c8 17 e3 ♗f6 18 ♘c3 (improving on 18 exd4 ♘xd4 19 ♗e3 ♗b5 20 ♖e1 f4 21 gxf4 gxf4 22 ♗xf4 ♖g8 23 ♗g3 ♘e2+ 24 ♔h1 ♖d8 which was pretty good for Black in V.Loginov-P.Anisimov, St Petersburg 2006) 18...♖d8 19 exd4 ♘xd4 20 ♗e3 ♗c6 21 ♗xd4 ♖xd4 22 ♕e2 ♗xg2 23 ♔xg2 ♕c6+ 24 ♔g1 was approximately even in V.Loginov-M.Zacurdajev, St Petersburg 2007.

13...♕xb4 14 a3 ♕c5 15 ♘d2 e5

15...♗xd6 is strongly met by 16 ♘b3 ♕b6 17 ♗xd6+ with more than enough for the pawn.

16 ♘2e4 ♘xe4 17 ♘xe4 ♕b6 18 ♖b1 ♕c7 19 ♗d2 f5 20 ♘g5 h6 21 ♘f3 ♔f7

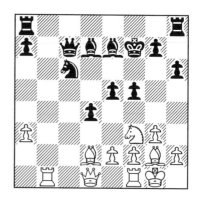

Black's last few moves have connected his rooks, but his king is still quite weak.

22 e3

White has an interesting option in 22 e4!?, for example 22...fxe4 23 ♘h4 ♗xh4 (23...♖he8 24 ♗xe4 ♗xh4 25 ♕h5+ ♔g8 26 ♕xh4 gives him more than enough for the pawn) 24 ♕h5+ ♔g8 25 ♗xe4 ♗e7 26 ♗d5+ ♔h7 27 ♕f7 ♖hf8 28 ♗e4+ ♔h8 29 ♕g6 and Black has to give up the exchange on f5, because 29...♔g8 30 ♗xh6 would be a disaster.

22...e4 23 ♘xd4 ♘xd4 24 exd4 ♖ab8 25 ♖xb8 ♕xb8 26 f3 e3 27 ♗xe3 ♗xa3 28 d5

28 ♕d3 was also playable, and there too I'd prefer White.

28...♖e8 29 ♗d4 ♗b2 30 ♗c5 ♕c7 31 ♗f2 ♗a3 32 ♕b3 ♗d6 33 ♖a1 a5

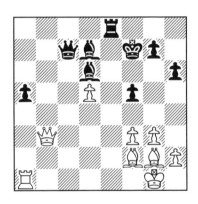

Now Black's king is safe and his a-pawn is starting to look dangerous. White has certainly missed his chance and he's even a bit lucky to draw.

34 f4 a4 35 ♕d3 ♖b8 36 ♗f3 ♖b3 37 ♕d1 ♖c3 38 ♗d4 ♖c4 39 ♔g2 a3 40 ♕d3 ♖c2+ 41 ♔h3 ♖c1 42 ♖xa3 ♗xa3 ½-½

I'm not sure if this was why the players agreed to a draw here, but there does seem to be a perpetual check

after 42...♗xa3 43 ♕xa3 ♗b5 44 d6 ♗f1+ 45 ♔h4 ♕d8+ 46 ♔h5 g6+ 47 ♔xh6 ♕f8+ 48 ♔g5 ♕d8+ 49 ♔h6.

Game 49
D.Fridman-V.Inkiov
Belgian Team
Championship 2008

---

1 d4 ♘f6 2 c4 e6 3 ♘f3 d5 4 g3 dxc4 5 ♗g2 c5 6 0-0 ♘c6 7 ♘a3!?

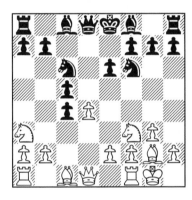

This is another interesting gambit line, and even less well explored than 7 ♘e5 ♗d7 8 ♘xc4 in the previous game.

7...cxd4 8 ♘xc4 ♗e7

The most popular choice in a little explored position. Other games have gone as follows:

a) 8...♗d7 9 ♗f4 ♘d5 10 ♘d6+ ♗xd6 11 ♗xd6 ♕b6 12 ♕d2 was very good for White in S.Bezgodova-E.Semenova, Kazan 2008, Black being unable to castle.

b) 8...♗c5 9 a3 a5 10 ♗f4 0-0 11 ♖c1 ♗d7 (11...♕e7 was played in U.Bönsch-A.Chernin, Austrian Team Ch. 2002, and now White seems to keep a slight edge with 12 ♘ce5 ♘xe5 13 ♗xe5 ♖d8 14 ♕c2 ♖d5 15 ♖fd1 ♗d7 16 ♗xd4 etc; another possibility is 11...♘d5 when 12 ♘ce5 ♗b6 13 ♗d2 gives White ongoing compensation) 12 ♘d6 ♕b6 13 ♘xb7! ♗e7 14 ♘e5 ♘xe5 15 ♗xe5 ♘d5 16 ♗xd5 exd5 17 ♖c7 and White was better in B.Avrukh-A.Mikhalchishin, European Team Ch., Gothenburg 2005.

9 b3!?

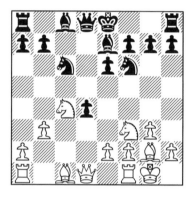

A very interesting novelty from Fridman, simply aiming to recapture the d4-pawn with ♗b2 and ♘xd4.

In previous games White had tried 9 ♗f4, for example 9...♘d5 (9...0-0 10 ♕b3 ♘d5 11 ♖fd1 ♘xf4 12 gxf4 ♗c5 13 ♖ac1 ♕e7 14 ♘g5 gave White sufficient compensation for the pawn in A.Kosten-S.Kozhuharov, Metz 2007) 10 ♘xd4! (10 ♘fe5?! f6 11 ♘xc6 bxc6 12 ♕a4 ♕d7 13 ♖ac1 c5 left White struggling to find enough play in S.Iskusnyh-O.Biriukov, St Petersburg 2005) 10...♘xf4 11 ♘xc6 ♕xd1 12 ♖fxd1 ♘xg2 13 ♘xe7 ♔xe7 14 ♖ac1! ♖d8 15 ♖xd8 ♔xd8 16 ♘d6 f6 17 ♔xg2 ♖b8 will lead to equality according to my analysis.

9...d3

Trying to return the pawn on his own terms, with White getting an isolated d-pawn. Understandably White rejects this possibility.

10 e3 0-0 11 ♗b2 ♘e4 12 ♘fe5 ♘xe5 13 ♘xe5 ♘c5

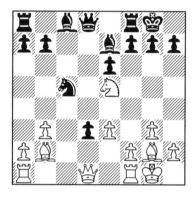

14 b4

There was another possibility in 14 ♗d4, which also looks like an edge for White after, say, 14...♕a5 15 ♘xd3 ♘xd3 16 ♕xd3 ♖d8 17 ♖fd1 ♗f6 18 ♕c2 ♗xd4 19 ♖xd4 ♖xd4 20 exd4. Black's lagging development is a problem in this line.

14...♘d7

After 14...f6 White should probably play just 15 ♘c4 ♘a6 16 a3, when sooner or later the d3-pawn must fall.

15 ♘xd3 a5 16 a3 ♗f6 17 ♖b1 axb4 18 axb4 ♕b6 19 ♕b3 h5?!

This looks rather dodgy to me; in the worse position it's usually advisable to avoid further weaknesses. But Inkiov is an aggressive player and probably wasn't too happy just sitting there without counterplay.

20 ♖fd1 h4 21 ♗xf6 ♘xf6 22 ♘e5 ♕b5 23 ♕b2 hxg3 24 hxg3 ♖a4 25 ♕d4 ♘d5

26 ♗f1 ♕e8 27 e4

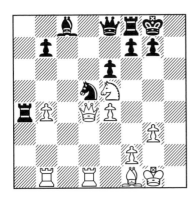

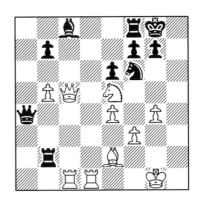

This looks like the end of the counterplay, with Black's position having been further damaged by it. For example, there might be the possibility of an attack down the h-file for White.

27...♘f6 28 f3 ♖a3 29 g4 ♕a4?!

29...♘h7 seems like a better try.

30 ♖bc1 ♖b3 31 ♗c4

Not bad, but 31 g5! looks even stronger. After 31...♘h5 32 ♖c7 ♖xb4 (if 32...♕xb4 33 ♕xb4 ♖xb4 34 ♖dc1 f6 35 gxf6 gxf6 36 ♘g6 wins a piece) 33 ♕d6 ♖d8 34 g6! White has a winning attack.

31...♖a3 32 ♗e2 ♖b3 33 b5

And here 33 ♖c7! is the best way, for example 33...♖xb4 (or 33...♕xb4 34 ♕xb4 ♖xb4 35 ♖dc1 ♘xe4 36 ♖xc8) 34 ♕c3 ♖b3 35 ♕c5 ♕e8 36 g5 ♘h5 37 ♗c4 ♖c3 38 ♕b4 ♖c2 39 ♗e7 etc.

33...♖b4!?

Black was evidently unimpressed with his endgame prospects after the continuation 33...♕xd4+ 34 ♖xd4, and who can blame him. The text gives White more chances to go wrong, and he soon does.

34 ♕c5 ♖b2

35 ♔f1?

The correct line was 35 g5! ♘h7 (if 35...♖xe2 36 gxf6 gxf6 37 ♔h1! is deadly) 36 g6 fxg6 37 ♔f1 when Black is like a squirrel in the headlamps.

35...♘xe4! 36 fxe4 ♕xe4 37 ♖e1

37 ♗f3 was better, but still just a mess now.

37...b6

37...f6! was simpler, for example 38 ♘d3 ♖xe2 39 ♖xe2 ♕xd3 40 ♕e3 ♕d5.

38 ♕xf8+

No doubt shaken by the sudden turn of events White forces a draw. He is probably still better after 38 ♗c4, but with his king in the open the position is not for those of a nervous disposition.

38...♔xf8 39 ♖xc8+ ♔e7 40 ♗f3 ♕h7 41 ♖c7+ ♔d8 42 ♖d1+ ♔c7 43 ♖d7+ ♔b8 44 ♖d8+ ♔c7 45 ♖d7+ ½-½

Game 50
E.Gleizerov-A.Adly
Dubai 2008

---

1 d4 d5 2 c4 e6 3 ♘f3 ♘f6 4 g3 dxc4 5 ♗g2 c5 6 0-0 ♘c6 7 dxc5

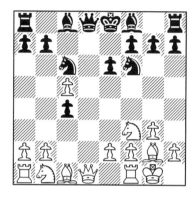

Although this is not the most thrilling alternative, it does give White some chances of an edge without having to know a lot of intricate theory. This is why it's often been my own preference.

7...♕xd1

Black can also play 7...♗xc5, for example 8 ♕xd8+ (or White can avoid the exchange of queens with 8 ♕a4 ♗d7 9 ♕xc4 ♕e7 10 ♗g5 ♗b6 11 ♘c3 h6 12 ♗xf6 ♕xf6 13 ♖fd1 ♕e7 14 ♘a4! 0-0 15 ♘xb6 axb6 16 ♕b3 ♖a6 17 ♘d4! with an edge in J.Speelman-A.Sokolov, Brussels 1988; another way is 8 ♘bd2!?, but then 8...c3! 9 bxc3 e5 10 ♕c2 0-0 11 ♗g5 h6 12 ♘ge4 ♘xe4 13 ♘xe4 ♗e7 14 ♗b2 ♗e6 was very comfortable for Black in D.Kosic-D.Feletar, Bizovac 2004) 8...♘xd8! (8...♔xd8 9 ♘bd2 ♔e7 10 ♘xc4 ♘d5 11 a3 b5 12 ♘ce5 ♘xe5 13 ♘xe5 ♗b7 14 ♘d3 ♖hc8 15 ♗d2 ♗d4 16 ♖fc1 ♖xc1+ 17 ♖xc1 ♖c8 18 ♖xc8 ♗xc8 19 e3 ♗b6 20 e4 was very slightly better for White in A.Miles-A.Sokolov, Crans Montana 2001) 9 ♘e5 ♗d7! 10 ♘d2! c3 (10...♖c8 11 ♘dxc4 ♗b5 12 b3 would also be a bit better for White) 11 ♘xd7 ♘xd7 12 ♘e4 ♖c8 13 bxc3 ♗e7 14 ♖d1

♘b6 15 ♗e3 ♘d5 16 ♗xa7 f5 17 c4 ♖xc4 18 ♘d2 ♖a4 19 ♗xd5 exd5 20 ♗b6 ♗f6 21 ♖ab1 0-0 22 ♘f3 ♖xa2 23 e3 ♘c6 24 ♖xd5 gave White a small edge in S.Atalik-S.Smagin, Yugoslavia 1992, though this wasn't enough to stop Black getting a draw.

8 ♖xd1 ♗xc5 9 ♘bd2 c3

Damaging White's pawn structure but giving him the possibility of play along the b-file.

In one of my own games, N.Davies-A.Chernin, Moscow 1988, Black tried 9...♘a5?!, when 10 ♘e5 c3 11 bxc3 ♘d7 12 ♘ec4 ♘xc4 13 ♘xc4 f6 14 ♘d6+ ♗xd6 15 ♖xd6 put him under serious pressure.

Another possibility is 9...♗e7?!, but after 10 ♘xc4 ♖d8 11 ♖xd8 ♘xd8 12 ♘fe5 ♘d5 13 ♘d3 Black was again under strong pressure in M.Sorokin-F.Benko, Buenos Aires 1997.

10 bxc3 0-0 11 ♘b3 ♗e7 12 ♘fd4 ♗d7

D.King-M.Quinn, Dublin 1993, varied with 12...♖d8 13 ♗f4 ♘d5 14 ♘xc6 bxc6 15 ♘a5 ♗a6 16 ♘xc6 ♖e8, and now 17 ♘xe7+ ♖xe7 18 e3 would have left Black with an uphill struggle.

13 ♗g5

The only move that seems to trouble Black. The alternatives seem to be rather equal, for example:

a) 13 ♗e3 ♖fc8 14 ♘b5 ♘d8 15 ♘d6 ♗xd6 16 ♖xd6 ♗c6 was fine T.Markowski-G.Kaidanov, Moscow 2002.

b) 13 ♘xc6 ♗xc6 14 ♗xc6 bxc6 15 c4 a5?! (15...♘e4 seems better) 16 ♗d2 a4 17 ♘a5 ♖fc8 18 ♖ab1 ♔f8 19 f3 ♖a7 20 ♗c3 and White was pressing in A.Yermolinsky-B.Gelfand, Sverdlovsk 1987.

13...罝fc8

Black has tried other moves here:

a) 13...罝fd8 14 盦xf6 (14 ⬠b5 ⬠d5 15 盦xe7 ⬠cxe7 16 c4 盦xb5 17 cxb5 was marginally more comfortable for White in K.Urban-A.Fernandes, Yerevan Olympiad 1996) 14...盦xf6 15 ⬠c5 ⬠xd4 (15...罝ab8? 16 ⬠xd7! 罝xd7 17 盦xc6 bxc6 18 ⬠xc6 罝xd1+ 19 罝xd1 left Black struggling in M.Ulibin-A.Belozerov, Tomsk 1997) 16 cxd4 盦c6 17 盦xc6!? bxc6 18 e3 罝ab8 19 ⬠d3 罝b5 20 罝ac1 and White had a small edge in K.Miton-G.Papp, World Junior Ch. 2001.

b) 13...罝ac8 14 盦xf6 (14 ⬠b5!? looks like the acid test of 13...罝ac8 as now the a-pawn isn't protected; a game between two amateur players, E.Lomer-B.Schramm, Eckernfoerde 2007, continued 14...罝fd8, when White should have tried 15 ⬠d6) 14...盦xf6 15 ⬠c5 ⬠xd4 16 cxd4 盦b5 17 e3 b6 18 ⬠e4 盦e7 19 a4 盦e2 20 罝d2 盦c4 21 罝b2 subsequently led to a draw in J.Speelman-P.Van der Sterren, Yerevan Olympiad 1996.

14 盦xf6

14 罝ab1!? was played in L.Aronian-R.Vaganian, German League 2006, with White having the chances after 14...⬠d8 (or if 14...⬠d5 15 c4!? is interesting, as 15...⬠c3 is answered by 16 盦xc6) 15 ⬠a5 盦a4 16 罝d3 e5 17 ⬠f5 盦f8 18 罝b2 罝ab8 19 ⬠h6+ gxh6 20 盦xf6 ⬠c6 21 盦xc6 bxc6 22 罝xb8 罝xb8 23 罝d7, though the game later ended in a draw.

14...盦xf6 15 ⬠c5 ⬠xd4 16 cxd4 盦c6

Not 16...盦b5 because of 17 盦xb7.

17 ⬠xb7 盦xg2 18 ⬠xg2 罝ab8 19 ⬠c5

盦xd4 20 罝xd4 罝xc5 21 罝b1

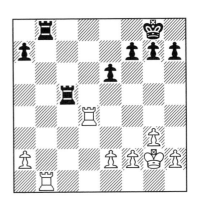

So White gets the slightest of initiatives by taking the open files for his rooks. But as the old expression says, 'all rook endgames are drawn'.

21...罝f8 22 罝b7 罝a5 23 a4 g5 24 h4 h6 25 h5 ⬠g7 26 g4 ⬠f6 27 ⬠g3 a6 28 罝a7 罝b8 29 e3 罝b1 30 f4 罝b3 31 ⬠f3 罝a3 32 罝dd7 gxf4 33 罝xf7+ ⬠g5 34 罝xf4 罝e5

And not 34...罝3xa4? because of 35 ⬠g3 罝xf4 36 exf4+ ⬠f6 37 罝h7 etc.

35 罝g7+ ⬠h4 36 罝e4 罝xe4 37 ⬠xe4 罝xa4+ 38 ⬠f3 a5 39 罝g6 e5 40 罝xh6 罝xg4 41 罝a6 e4+ 42 ⬠f2 ⬠xh5 43 罝xa5+ ½-½

Summary

The Open Catalan with 5...c5 is a solid line for Black and far from easy for White to deal with. For players who like the keg of dynamite approach, 7 ⬠e5 盦d7 8 ⬠xc4 and 7 ⬠a3 are worth examining; those who prefer slow torture are advised to look at 7 dxc5 for their fun.

Chapter Eleven

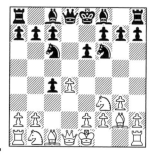

Open Catalan with 5...♘c6

1 d4 ♘f6 2 c4 e6 3 g3 d5 4 ♗g2 dxc4 5 ♘f3 ♘c6

Many strong players have adopted 5...♘c6 as their defence against the Catalan and it's not an easy nut to crack. There are several ideas: pressure on d4, counterattack with ...e6-e5, and defence of the c4-pawn with 6...♖b8 and ...b7-b5.

I recommend 6 ♕a4, pinning the knight and aiming to regain the c4-pawn. In Davies-Nickoloff (Game 51) I ended up a pawn down anyway after 6...♗b4+ 7 ♗d2 ♘d5 8 ♕b5, but White gets pretty good compensation here. If he really doesn't want to be behind there is 8 ♗xb4 or, failing that, a move order which doesn't allow 4...dxc4 at all.

For Black, there's a major alternative to 6...♗b4+ in 6...♘d7, which transposes into an endgame after 7 ♕xc4 ♘b6 8 ♕d3 e5 9 ♘xe5 ♘b4 10 ♕c3 ♕xd4 (see Game 53, Damljanovic-Pavasovic). White doesn't seem to have much here, which is why Kramnik's

wrinkle of 8 ♕b5 (Kramnik-Naiditsch, Game 52) is so fascinating. He wants to get the same endgame but with Black having weakened his queenside with 8...a6, and in the game White could have maintained a healthy edge with Tkachiev's simple 11 0-0.

I'm not a big fan of the nonchalant 6 0-0 because of 6...♖b8, but correspondence chess Catalan guru Mikhail Umansky disagrees. Miton-Charbonneau (Game 54) was interesting because of the natural but little-played 10 ♗f4. White managed to win from a dubious position, but he could also improve his early middlegame play. Note that 6...a6 can transpose into the next chapter.

Game 51
N.Davies-B.Nickoloff
Toronto 1998

---

1 d4 ♘f6 2 ♘f3 d5 3 c4 e6 4 g3 dxc4 5

♗g2 ♘c6 6 ♕a4

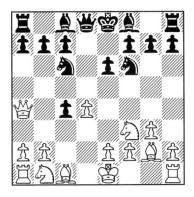

White can also sacrifice a pawn with 6 0-0, after which 6...♖b8 intending 7...b5 is very messy (see Game 54 for coverage of this). If White doesn't like being a pawn down, then 5 ♕a4+ is the cowardly alternative.

6...♗b4+ 7 ♗d2 ♘d5

White can meet 7...♗d6 with 8 ♘e5, when 8...♗xe5 9 ♗xc6+ bxc6 10 dxe5 ♕d5 11 f3 ♘d7 12 ♘c3 ♕c5 13 f4 ♗b7 14 0-0-0 ♘b6 15 ♕c2 gave him the better game in B.Damljanovic-C.Marcelin, French Team Ch. 2008.

8 ♕b5!?

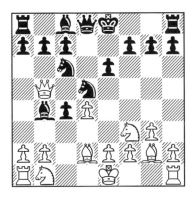

This makes an interesting gambit

out of it, with White getting positional compensation.

There's another possibility in 8 ♗xb4, though it doesn't seem to trouble Black unduly, for example 8...♘dxb4 9 0-0 (9 a3? b5! 10 ♕xb5 ♘c2+ 11 ♔d2 ♗d7 12 ♔xc2 ♘xd4+ 13 ♘xd4 ♗xb5 14 ♘xb5 ♖b8 was good for Black in D.Khismatullin-P.Smirnov, Zvenigorod 2008) 9...♖b8 10 ♘a3 (10 ♘c3 a6 11 ♘e5 0-0 12 ♗xc6 ♘xc6 13 ♘xc6 bxc6 14 ♕xc4 ♕d6 15 ♘e4 ♕d5 16 ♕c2 ♕xd4 was fine for Black at this stage in E.Gleizerov-R.Miedema, Bucharest 2008) 10...0-0 (10...a6 11 ♘e5 0-0 12 ♘xc6 ♘xc6 13 ♕xc4 ♕xd4 14 ♗xc6 ♕xc4 15 ♘xc4 bxc6 16 ♖ac1 ♖d8 17 ♖fd1 ♗d7 18 f4 ♗e8 led to a draw in Wang Yue-E.Ghaem Maghami, Asian Team Ch., Visakhpatnam 2008) 11 ♕b5 b6 12 ♕xc4 ♗a6 13 ♘b5 ♕d5 14 ♕xd5 ♘xd5 (14...exd5 15 a4 ♘a5 seems fine for Black too) 15 a4 ♘a5 16 ♘e5 ♖bd8 17 ♗xd5 ♗xb5 was equal and later drawn in A.Grischuk-B.Gelfand, FIDE Grand Prix, Sochi 2008.

8...♗xd2+ 9 ♘bxd2 c3 10 bxc3 ♘xc3 11 ♕d3 ♘d5 12 0-0 0-0

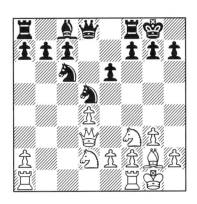

It's easy for Black to assume that he's just a pawn up with no weaknesses. I think that this led to my opponent's claim during the post mortem that 12...0-0 'loses' and that 12...b6 would be better for Black, because he would be able to develop his queen's bishop. Personally speaking, I think this assessment is rather too definitive and feel that White would not be without compensation for his pawn.

13 ♖fc1

In V.Tkachiev-M.Palac, Pula 2000, White varied with 13 ♖fe1, but after 13...♕e7 14 e4 ♘f6 15 ♖ac1 ♖d8 16 ♕e3 h6 17 ♘b3 ♗d7 18 ♖c3 a5 19 ♘c5 b6 20 ♘xd7 ♕xd7 21 ♖d1 ♘e7 agreed a draw. Interestingly, Tkachiev seems to have come round to my way of thinking after this game, playing 13 ♖fc1 against Inkiov (see the next note).

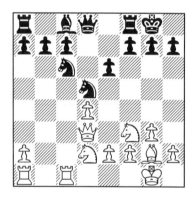

13...♘ce7

V.Tkachiev-V.Inkiov, Aubervilliers (rapid) 2003, went 13...h6 14 ♖ab1 ♘b6 15 e4 ♕e7 16 ♘b3 ♖d8 17 ♕e3 a5 18 ♘c5 a4 19 ♗f1 ♖a5 20 ♕c3 ♖a8 21 ♖d1 a3 22 ♗b5 ♘a7 23 ♗d3 when White had very strong pressure and later

won. This line certainly seems to be a highly unpleasant one for Black in practice, as White has a lot of pressure for the pawn.

14 ♖ab1 h6

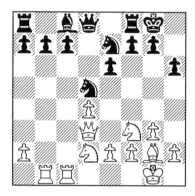

Safeguarding his position against the possibility of ♘f3-g5. When Black played this move I was considering whether or not I could take advantage of an immediate 14...b6. Something like 15 ♘g5 ♘g6 16 h4 is interesting but could hardly masquerade as a refutation.

15 ♕c4 c6 16 ♘e5 f6

After this I was really licking my lips, because of the weakness it creates on e6. Before this Black's position was definitely uncomfortable, but there was no obvious attacking plan available to White.

17 ♘d3 b6 18 ♘f3 g5

There's an interesting parallel here with how an athlete might have a niggling ankle strain but then does something far more serious in an attempt to compensate for it. In a way this is a consequence of 16...f6: Black wants to prevent the possibility of a later ♘d3-

f4, but in doing so weakens his king-side even further.

19 h4 ♔g7 20 hxg5 hxg5 21 e4 ♕e8?

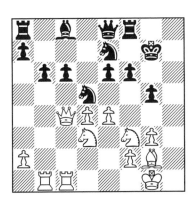

This quite astonishing move is explained by the fact that Nickoloff is a player who likes to exercise control in his games. I was expecting 21...♘c7, which I intended to meet with 22 e5, effectively demolishing Black's kingside pawn structure. After the text there is surely not enough for the piece if White plays with sufficient energy.

22 exd5 exd5 23 ♕b4 ♗f5 24 ♖e1 ♖f7 25 ♖e3 ♕d7

This allows White a decisive breakthrough. 25...♗e4 26 ♘d2 ♗xg2 27 ♔xg2 ♕d7 was a better chance.

26 ♘fe5! fxe5 27 ♘xe5 ♕c7 28 ♘xf7 ♔xf7

After 28...♗xb1 there is 29 ♖xe7 etc.

29 ♖be1 ♘g6?! 30 ♖f3 1-0

Game 52
V.Kramnik-A.Naiditsch
Dortmund 2006

---

1 d4 ♘f6 2 c4 e6 3 g3 d5 4 ♗g2 dxc4 5 ♘f3 ♘c6 6 ♕a4 ♘d7 7 ♕xc4 ♘b6 8 ♕b5!?

This strange-looking move attempts to make it difficult for Black to play ...e6-e5, though it's clear that White will have to lose more time with the queen. For the traditional 8 ♕d3 see the next game, Damljanovic-Pavasovic.

8...♗d7

'Shadowing' the queen but reducing the pressure on the d4-pawn.

The main alternative is 8...a6, when after 9 ♕d3 e5 10 ♘xe5 ♘b4 11 ♕c3 ♕xd4, White should probably try 12 0-0 (12 ♕xc7 is very risky, for example 12...♗e7 13 0-0 ♘6d5 14 ♗xd5 ♘xd5 15 e3 ♕e4 16 ♘d2 ♕f5 left White very weak on the light squares in D.Yevseev-V.Orlov, St Petersburg 2005; however, 12 ♕xd4 is quite interesting, for example 12...♘c2+ 13 ♔d1 ♘xd4 14 ♗e3 ♘f5 15 ♗xb6 cxb6 16 e3 b5 17 ♘c3 ♗d6 18 ♘d3 left White with a nice edge in I.Rausis-A.Gavrilov, Tallinn 2008, because of the central squares available to his minor pieces) 12...♕xc3 13 ♘xc3 ♗d6 14 ♘f3. The fact that Black has played his a-pawn forward one square gives White more prospects than in Damljanovic-Pavasovic; for example 14...0-0 15 ♖d1 ♖b8 16 ♘d4 ♗d7 17 a3 ♘c6 18 ♘xc6 ♗xc6 19 ♗xc6 bxc6 was A.Khalifman-K.Landa, Russian Team Ch. 2007, when the quiet 20 ♖b1 would have kept a little something.

9 ♕b3 ♘a5

With ...e6-e5 having been rendered difficult, Black tries to get in ...c7-c5.

10 ♕d3

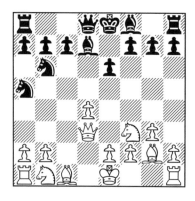

An interesting move which was new at the time. Naiditsch had previously had 10 ♕c2 played against him in two games, B.Avrukh-A.Naiditsch, European Cup, Saint Vincent 2005, and P.H.Nielsen-A.Naiditsch, Dortmund 2005. In both of these he got a very comfortable game with just 10...♖c8 followed by ...c7-c5.

10...c5

The most logical move, though not without risk. With White's queen on d3, 10...♖c8 could be answered with 11 0-0 c5 12 ♘c3, when White's lead in development gives him the initiative.

11 dxc5!?

This represents an attempt to refute

Black's last move. In a later game, V.Tkachiev-F.Libiszewski, French Ch., Besancon 2006, White played just 11 0-0 and, after 11...♗c6 12 ♖d1 cxd4 13 ♘xd4 ♗xg2 14 ♔xg2 ♕d5+ 15 e4, had the better of it thanks to his space and lead in development.

11...♗xc5 12 ♕c3 ♖c8!?

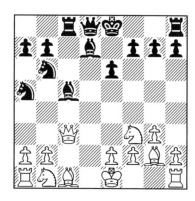

Preparing to give up a lot of material for a dangerous attack. Whether or not it's correct, it certainly manages to make Mr. Kramnik nervous.

13 ♕xg7

On 13 ♕xa5 Black has 13...♗b4+ 14 ♕xb4 ♖xc1+ 15 ♔d2 ♖c4 with a strong initiative for the sacrificed piece. For example, 16 ♕d6 can be met by 16...♖c2+! 17 ♔d1 ♖xe2!, threatening ♗a4+, and meanwhile marauding White's second rank. Kramnik understandably refrains from this.

13...♗f8 14 ♕g5

Bailing out into an endgame. The critical line is 14 ♕xh8!?, which looks very scary but doesn't seem to leave Black with a clear solution. In fact White keeps a large part of his material advantage after 14...♖xc1+ 15 ♔d2

♖xh1 16 ♗xh1 ♗a4+ 17 ♕d4 ♘bc4+ 18 ♔e1.

14...♕xg5 15 ♗xg5 ♗g7 16 ♘bd2 h6 17 ♗f4 ♗xb2 18 ♖b1 ♘d5 19 ♗d6 ♗g7

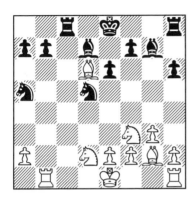

White has the superior pawn structure, Black the more active pieces. The chances are about even.

20 ♘e5 ♘c3 21 ♖c1 ♘xa2 22 ♖xc8+ ♗xc8 23 0-0 ♘c3 24 ♖a1 ♘b5 25 ♖xa5 ♘xd6 26 ♘ec4 ♔e7 27 ♖xa7 ♗d4 28 ♖a8 ♘xc4 29 ♘xc4 b5 30 e3 ♗d7 31 exd4 ♖xa8 32 ♗xa8 bxc4

Black actually has the chances here, but Kramnik steers the game safely to a draw.

33 ♔f1 ♔d6 34 ♔e2 ♗c6 35 ♗xc6 ♔xc6

36 ♔d2 ♔d5 37 ♔c3 ♔e4 38 ♔xc4 ♔f3 39 d5 exd5+ 40 ♔xd5 ♔xf2 41 ♔e5 ♔g2 42 ♔f6 ♔xh2 43 ♔xf7 ♔xg3 44 ♔g6 ½-½

Game 53
B.Damljanovic-D.Pavasovic
Valjevo 2007

1 c4 e6 2 ♘f3 d5 3 d4 ♘f6 4 g3 dxc4 5 ♗g2 ♘c6 6 ♕a4 ♘d7 7 ♕xc4 ♘b6 8 ♕d3 e5

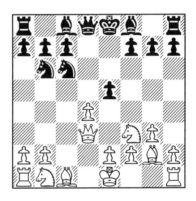

9 ♘xe5

White has experimented with some other moves here, but none of them seem particularly testing:

a) 9 dxe5 ♕xd3 10 exd3 ♘b4 11 ♘a3 ♘xd3+ 12 ♔e2 ♘xc1+ 13 ♖axc1 c6 is fine for Black, whose bishop pair compensate for White's active pieces.

b) 9 ♗e3 can be neutralized by 9...♗b4+, when G.Flear-B.Lalic, Hastings 1996/97, went 10 ♘c3 exd4 11 ♘xd4 ♘xd4 12 ♕xd4 ♕xd4 13 ♗xd4 0-0 14 a3 ♗e7 15 ♘b5 c5 16 ♗c3 ♗d7 with equality.

c) 9 ♗g5 ♗e7 10 ♗xe7 ♕xe7 11

♘xe5 ♘xe5 12 dxe5 ♕xe5 13 ♘c3 0-0 14 0-0 c6 15 ♖fd1 ♗e6 16 ♕d4 ♕c7 17 b4 ♖fd8 was soon drawn in A.Poluljahov-M.Brodsky, Krasnodar 1999.

9...♘b4 10 ♕c3

This leads to an almost equal endgame in which most strong players may slightly prefer White. Attempts to extract more from this position are risky, for example:

a) 10 ♕d1 ♕xd4 11 ♕xd4 ♘c2+ 12 ♔d1 hopes that White's centralized king will be useful, but it can also become a target. B.Gelfand-V.Ivanchuk, Sochi 1986, continued 12...♘xd4 13 e3 ♘e6 14 ♘c3 f6! 15 ♘d3 ♘c5 16 ♘xc5 ♗xc5 17 ♔c2 ♗f5+! 18 e4 ♗e6 19 f4 0-0-0 20 b3 h5 21 h3 f5 and Black had his full share of the play.

b) 10 ♕b3 ♗e6 11 ♕d1 ♕xd4 12 ♕xd4 ♘c2+ 13 ♔d1 ♘xd4 14 ♗xb7 ♖d8 15 ♘d2 f6 16 ♘c6 ♘xc6 17 ♗xc6+ ♔f7 18 ♔c2 ♗c5 and Black had excellent play for the pawn in G.Kaidanov-A.Shariyazdanov, Elista Olympiad 1998.

10...♕xd4 11 0-0

Grabbing the c7-pawn with 11 ♕xc7!? is not for the squeamish: 11...♗e6 (11...♗e7 also seems playable, for example 12 ♘f3 ♕c4 13 ♕xc4 ♘xc4 14 ♘d4 ♗f6 15 a3 was P.Haba-J.Klovans, Leinfelden 2001, and now 15...♗xd4 16 axb4 ♘xb2 17 ♖a2 ♘c4 looks more or less equal) 12 ♗xb7 (12 ♘f3?! ♕c4! 13 ♕xc4 ♘xc4 14 ♘d4 0-0-0 15 a3 ♖xd4 16 axb4 ♗xb4+ 17 ♘c3 a6 gave Black the better endgame in E.Vladimirov-Li Wenliang, Asian Ch., Calcutta 2001) 12...♖d8! 13 ♗c6+ (13

0-0? ♗d6 14 ♗c6+ ♔d7 15 ♗xd7+ ♖xd7 wins material) 13...♘d7! 14 ♗xd7+ ♗xd7 15 ♘xd7?! (of the alternatives 15 ♘f3?? ♕d1+! 16 ♔xd1 ♗a4+ leads to mate; 15 0-0?! ♗d6 16 ♘f3 ♗xc7 17 ♘xd4 ♗h3 wins the exchange; while 15 ♘d2 gives Black a vitriolic initiative after 15...♗d6 16 ♘ef3 ♕d5 17 ♕c3 ♖c8 18 ♕xg7 ♘c2+ 19 ♔d1 ♖f8) 15...♗d6! 16 ♕c3?! (16 ♕b7 ♘c2+ 17 ♔f1 ♘xa1 would be better for Black, but not as good as the game) 16...♗xc3+ 17 bxc3 ♘c2+ 18 ♔d1 ♘xa1 19 ♗b2 ♖xd7 and White didn't have enough for the exchange because of Black's active pieces in A.Flumbort-A.Gavrilov, Novi Sad 2002.

11...♕xc3

11...♗c5 doesn't improve Black's chances after 12 ♘f3 ♕xc3 13 ♘xc3 0-0 14 ♖d1.

12 ♘xc3

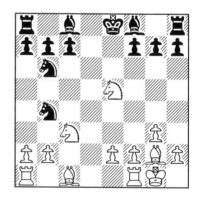

This endgame isn't as promising for White as the equivalent one after 8 ♕b5 a6 9 ♕d3, (see the notes to the previous game). Even so it's playable, and with patience and a strong cup of coffee might even be winnable.

12...♗d6

Black has tried a number of other moves:

a) 12...g6?! 13 ♘b5 ♘a6 14 ♗f4 c6?! (14...♗g7 15 ♘d3 c6 16 ♘d6+ ♔e7 17 e4 would give White an edge without any fireworks) 15 ♘xc6! bxc6 16 ♗xc6+ ♗d7 17 ♗xa8 ♗xb5 (17...♘xa8 18 ♗e5! would be good for White, as Black must misplace his rook) 18 ♗e5! ♖g8 19 ♖fc1! ♗e7? (19...♔d7! 20 ♗f3 ♗e7 21 b3 ♗a3 22 ♖c2 would still have been good for White, but not as clear as in the game) 20 a4! ♗d7 21 ♗f3 ♘xa4 22 ♖xa4 ♗xa4 23 ♖c8+ ♗d8 24 ♗f6 ♔d7 25 ♗g4+ ♔d6 26 ♖xd8+ left White a good pawn up in V.Tukmakov-B.Gelfand, Sverdlovsk 1987.

b) 12...f6 13 ♘f3 c6 (13...♗d7 14 ♖d1 ♗d6 15 ♗f4 ♗xf4 16 gxf4 was slightly better for White in A.Mikhalchishin-G.Kaidanov, USSR 1988) 14 ♗d2!? ♗g4 (14...♘c4!? 15 ♗f4 ♘xb2 16 ♘d2 g5 17 ♗c7 ♗e6 18 ♖ab1 ♘c4 19 ♘xc4 ♗xc4 20 a3 ♘d5 21 ♖xb7! is an interesting line given by Dokhoian) 15 h3 ♗d7 16 ♖fc1! ♔f7 17 a3 ♘4d5 18 ♘e4 ♖e8 19 ♘d4! ♗c8 (19...♗xh3!? 20 ♘xf6! ♔xf6 21 ♗xh3 c5 22 ♘b5 ♖xe2 23 ♖d1 would give White a strong initiative) 20 b4 a6 21 ♘c5 ♗d6 22 ♖ab1! and White had pressure in I.Smirin-S.Kishnev, USSR 1989.

13 ♘f3 c6

In Y.Razuvaev-R.Dautov, Reggio Emilia 1995/96, Black played 13...♗d7, but had the worst of it after 14 a3 ♘4d5 15 ♘xd5 ♘xd5 16 ♘d4 c6 17 ♖d1 ♖d8 18 ♗xd5 cxd5 19 ♗f4 ♗xf4 20 gxf4. The isolated d-pawn is a more significant weakness than White's kingside pawns.

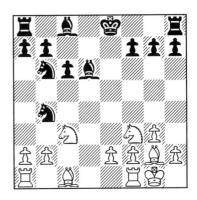

14 ♘e4

Another possibility is 14 ♖d1, for example 14...♗e7 15 ♘d4 0-0 (15...♗d7 16 a3 ♘a6 17 b4 ♘c7 18 ♗f4 0-0-0 19 ♘e4 gave White some pressure in R.Markus-A.Istratescu, European Team Ch., Gothenburg 2005) 16 a3 ♘4d5 17 ♘xd5 ♘xd5 18 e4 (18 ♗d2?! ♖d8 19 ♗a5 ♘b6 20 ♖d3 ♗f6 was very comfortable for Black in A.Beliavsky-M.Adams, Madrid 1998; while 18 ♗xd5 cxd5 19 ♗f4 ♗d7 20 ♖ac1 ♖fc8 isn't going to be much for White either while the dark-squared bishops are still on the board) 18...♘b6 19 b3 ½-½ was possibly a tiny bit better for White in the final position in A.Khalifman-M.Adams, German League 2001.

14...♗e7 15 ♗f4 0-0 16 ♖fc1

This looks like a new move, though it isn't particularly stunning. In K.Sakaev-O.Korneev, Russian Team Ch. 2007, White played 16 ♘d6, but after 16...♘4d5 17 ♘xc8 ♖axc8 18 ♗g5 ♖fe8 19 ♗xe7 ♖xe7 he was no better.

16...♘4d5 17 ♗d2 ♖e8 18 ♘d4 ♘f6 19

♘c5 ♗xc5 20 ♖xc5 ♘e4 21 ♖c2 ♘xd2 22 ♖xd2 ♖d8 23 ♖dd1

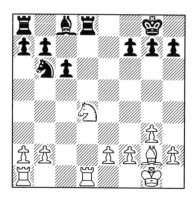

23...♗e6

Rather than allow the weakening of his pawn structure that follows ♘xe6, I think Black should have considered 23...♗d7. It's true that White's position is more comfortable here too, but it's by no means easy to win.

24 f4 ♘c4 25 ♘xe6 fxe6 26 ♔f2 ♔f7 27 b3 ♘b6 28 e4 ♔e7 29 ♔e3 a5 30 ♗f1 ♖d7 31 ♗e2 ♖ad8 32 ♖xd7+ ♘xd7 33 ♖c1 ♖a8 34 h4 h6 35 h5 ♖d8 36 ♖c4 ♖a8 37 ♖c1 ♖d8 38 ♖d1 ♖a8 39 ♖b1

White is in no hurry. He can try out different squares for his pieces while playing on Black's nerves.

39...♖a7 40 a3 ♖a8 41 ♗f3 ♘b6 42 ♖c1 ♘d7 43 e5 ♘b6 44 g4 ♖d8 45 ♖c5 ♖a8 46 ♖c1 ♖d8 47 ♗e4 ♘d5+ 48 ♗xd5 ♖xd5

The best recapture, and probably enough to draw with continued accurate defence. After 48...exd5 49 ♔d4 Black would be under serious pressure, while 48...cxd5 49 ♖c7+ ♖d7 50 ♖xd7+ ♔xd7 51 b4 would give White a winning pawn endgame.

49 a4 ♔d7 50 ♖g1 ♔e7 51 ♖b1 b5?

I think this is wrong as it allows the white rook to get active. Instead he should have played 51...c5! 52 ♖c1 b6, and after 53 ♖c3 ♖d4 54 ♖d3 ♖b4 I don't see how White can make any progress.

52 ♖c1 ♔d7 53 ♖c3 bxa4 54 bxa4 c5 55 ♖b3 ♔c6 56 ♖b8 ♖d7 57 ♖c8+ ♔d5

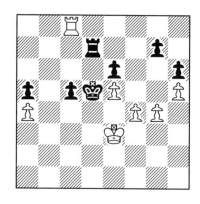

58 ♖a8?!

Time pressure might have been playing its part at this stage. 58 ♔d3 looks like the right move, for example 58...♖f7 59 ♖d8+ ♔c6 60 f5 exf5 61 e6 is winning for White.

58...♔c4 59 f5 ♖d3+?

Giving White another bite at the cherry. Black can draw with 59...♖d5 60 ♖e8 ♖xe5+ 61 ♔f4 ♖e1 62 ♖xe6 ♖f1+ 63 ♔e5 ♔b3 etc.

60 ♔f2 ♖d2+ 61 ♔g3 ♖d3+ 62 ♔h4 exf5 63 e6 ♖e3 64 gxf5 ♔b4

Or 64...♔b3 65 ♖a7 c4 66 ♖xg7 c3 67 ♖b7+ etc.

65 ♖g8 c4 66 ♖xg7 c3 67 ♖c7

Not 67 ♖b7+ because of 67...♔c5!, when Black can attack the passed pawns.

**67...♔b3 68 e7 c2 69 f6 ♔b2 70 ♖xc2+!
♔xc2 71 f7 ♖xe7 72 f8♕ ♖e4+ 73 ♔g3
♖xa4 74 ♕xh6 1-0**

Game 54
K.Miton-P.Charbonneau
Montreal 2007

**1 d4 ♘f6 2 c4 e6 3 g3 d5 4 ♗g2 dxc4 5
♘f3 ♘c6 6 0-0**

A nonchalant approach. But will Black's next move allow him to hold the pawn?

6...♖b8

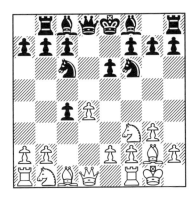

6...a6 produces the same position as 5...a6 6 0-0 ♘c6 which is examined in the next chapter.

7 ♘c3 b5

Here, too, 7...a6 transposes into lines covered in the next chapter.

Another possibility is 7...♗b4. I.Ivanisevic-H.Mas, Biel 2008, continued in entertaining style with 8 a3 ♗xc3 9 bxc3 0-0 10 ♗g5 h6 11 ♗h4!? g5 12 ♘xg5 hxg5 13 ♗xg5 ♔g7 14 e4 ♘e7 15 f4 ♘h7 16 ♕h5 ♘xg5 17 fxg5 e5 18 ♖f6 ♘g8 19 ♖af1, when White had a

winning attack.

8 ♘e5

The great correspondence champion and Catalan expert Mikhail Umansky once played 8 e4 in this position, which is exactly the same treatment as he uses after 5...a6 6 0-0 ♘c6. Evidently he was not worried that Black has saved half a tempo compared with that line. Anyway, M.Umansky-A.Gavrilov, Internet (blitz) 2003, continued 8...♗e7 9 d5 exd5 10 exd5 ♘b4 11 ♘e5 ♗d6 12 f4 ♗b7 13 a3 ♘bxd5 14 ♘xd5 ♗xd5 15 ♘c6 ♗c5+ 16 ♔h1 ♗xg2+ 17 ♔xg2 ♕xd1 18 ♖xd1 ♖c8 19 ♖e1+ ♔f8 20 a4 b4 21 ♗d2 g6 with the game ending in a draw.

8...♘xe5 9 dxe5 ♘d7 10 ♗f4

This move attracts my interest because it is so natural yet has been relatively little played. White has tried several other possibilities here:

a) Another Umansky game, M.Umansky-C.Singer, Fuerth 1999, varied with 10 a4, but after 10...b4 11 ♘b5 ♗c5 12 ♗f4 g5 13 ♗e3 ♗xe3 14 fxe3 a6 15 ♘a7 ♘xe5 it became clear that White didn't have enough.

Umansky's creativity doesn't always work out so well in over-the-board encounters with so little time available.

b) 10 ♗c6 a6 11 ♕d4 ♗b7 12 ♗xb7 ♖xb7 13 ♖d1 is neutralized by 13...c5! 14 ♕g4 ♕c7 15 ♗f4 ♕c6! 16 f3! f5! 17 exf6 ♘xf6 18 ♕g5 ♗e7 (I played 18...♔f7 in P.Taboada-N.Davies, correspondence 2003, with a draw resulting after 19 ♗e5 ♗e7 20 ♘e4 ♖d7 21 ♘xf6 ♗xf6 22 ♗xf6 gxf6 23 ♕h5+ ♔g7 24 ♕g4+ ♔f7 25 ♕h5+ etc) 19 ♕xg7 ♖g8 20 ♕h6 ♖g6 21 ♕h3 b4 was E.Gleizerov-J.Werle, Hoogeveen 2000, and now 22 ♘e4 (rather than 22 ♘b1?! in the game) 22...♘xe4 23 ♕xh7 e5 24 ♕h8+ ♔f7 25 ♕h7+ ♖g7 26 ♕h5+ ♔g8 27 ♗xe5 looks very messy.

c) 10 ♕d4 c5 11 ♕f4 ♕c7 (11...♗e7 12 a4 b4 13 ♘b5 ♗b7 14 ♖d1 0-0 15 ♘xa7 ♗xg2 16 ♔xg2 ♕c7 17 ♘b5 ♕c6+ 18 f3 ♘b6 gave both sides chances in A.Raetsky-A.Groszpeter, Geneva 2003) 12 a4 a6 13 axb5 axb5 14 ♖d1 was D.Antic-V.Savicevic, Leposavic 2003, and now 14...♗e7 was probably best, when 15 ♕g4 ♔f8 16 f4 b4 17 ♘e4 would have been far from clear.

10...♗b7

In M.Ulibin-K.Kulaots, Berlin 1996, Black played 10...♗e7, which White might have exploited with 11 a4 (rather than 11 ♕c2, when 11...♗b7 12 ♗xb7 ♖xb7 13 a4 can be answered with 13...c6!) 11...a6 (11...b4 12 ♘b5 ♗b7 13 ♘xa7 is better for White) 12 axb5 axb5 13 ♕c2 ♗b7 14 ♗xb7 ♖xb7 15 ♖fd1 with strong pressure.

11 ♗xb7 ♖xb7 12 ♕c2

12 a4 is less effective here because

of 12...c6, for example 13 ♕c2 (13 ♘e4 ♘c5 14 ♕c2 ♗e7 15 axb5 cxb5 16 ♗g5 ♘xe4 17 ♕xe4 ♕d5 was at least equal for Black in M.Ivanov-Cu.Hansen, Aars 1995) 13...♗e7 14 ♖fd1 0-0 15 ♘e4 and a draw was agreed in this unclear position in E.Gleizerov-H.Olafsson, Osterskars 1995.

12...♗e7 13 ♖fd1 c6

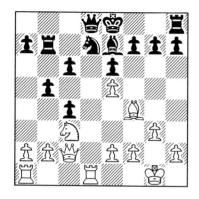

Another Miton game, K.Miton-E.Berg, World Junior Ch. 2001, went 13...♕c8 14 a4 (14 ♕e4 c6 15 ♕f3, as in E.Gleizerov-A.Rustemov, Bydgoszcz 2000, doesn't seem very convincing after 15...f5 16 exf6 ♘xf6) 14...a6 (14...c6 could be an improvement, with White having long-term compensation for his pawn after 15 ♘e4 0-0 16 ♖d2) 15 axb5 axb5 16 ♖a5 c6 17 ♘e4 0-0 18 ♘d6 ♗xd6 19 exd6 e5 20 ♗e3 ♘f6 21 ♗c5 ♖d8 22 ♔g2 and White had enough compensation, but maybe not more than that.

14 ♘e4 ♕c7 15 ♖d2

White should probably take this opportunity to play 15 ♘d6+ ♗xd6 16 exd6, gaining a tempo on Black's queen, and then following up with a2-

a4. In the game he also has 'compensation', but this looked distinctly iffy until Black erred later on.

15...♘xe5 16 ♕c3 f6 17 ♘g5 b4 18 ♕e3 ♕b6 19 ♕e4

19 ♘xe6? ♕xe3 20 fxe3 ♔f7 is just good for Black.

19...♘g4 20 ♘h3 e5

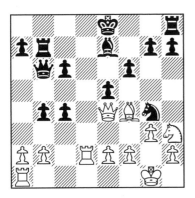

21 ♕f5?

White should go for 21 ♕xc4!? exf4 22 ♕e6, when 22...fxg3 23 hxg3 ♘e5 24 ♕c8+ ♗d8 25 ♖xd8+ ♕xd8 26 ♕xb7 0-0 27 ♕xb4 looks surprisingly equal.

21...♘xf2

Here 21...c3! looks very strong, for example 22 bxc3 bxc3 23 ♖d3 ♕b2 etc.

22 ♘xf2 0-0 23 ♗h6

This is just about the most damage White can do while he gives up the bishop. But he really doesn't have enough for the lost pawns here, at least not yet.

23...gxh6 24 ♔g2 c3 25 bxc3 bxc3 26 ♖c2 ♕e3?!

26...c5 looks good for Black.

27 ♖d1 ♖d8

And here 27...♔h8 is better. Now

White has enough for a draw.

28 ♖xd8+ ♗xd8 29 ♕c8 ♕b6 30 ♖xc3 ♕c7 31 ♕g4+ ♔h8 32 ♖d3 ♗e7 33 ♕e6 c5 34 ♘g4 ♖b6?

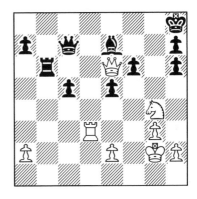

34...♔g7 is the right move, when 35 ♘e3 ♖b6 36 ♘f5+ ♔f8 37 ♕d7 ♖b7 38 ♕e6 ♖b6 was a possible draw by repetition.

35 ♕f7! ♕c6+??

Losing on the spot. 35...♖b8 was the only way to stay on the board, though the position has turned against Black big time.

36 ♔h3 h5 37 ♖d8+! 1-0

A messy game which raises more questions than it answers.

Summary

For once I find myself in agreement with the big boys in preferring 6 ♕a4 to 6 0-0, and think that Kramnik's 8 ♕b5 is a really cool idea. Having said that, there's little doubt in my mind that Umansky will continue to use 6 0-0 and then blast away with the broad pawn centre. Horses for courses.

Chapter Twelve

Open Catalan with 5...a6

1 d4 ♘f6 2 c4 e6 3 g3 d5 4 ♗g2 dxc4 5 ♘f3 a6

As I mentioned in the previous chapter, Black can transpose into 5...a6 lines with 5...♘c6 6 0-0 a6. The problem with that is in persuading White to meet 5...♘c6 with 6 0-0 rather than 6 ♕a4, so if Black wants to do it this way he should play 5...a6 immediately.

After 5...a6 6 0-0 ♘c6 7 ♘c3 ♖b8 8 e4 b5 (Game 55, Umansky-Weber) Black gets to hold on to the c4-pawn, but at a high risk to his king. This is a classic performance by Umansky and makes 8...b5 look like picking up pennies in front of a steamroller. A better approach for Black is 8...♗e7 as in Gelfand-Drozdovskij (Game 56); it's still very dangerous for Black, but at least he isn't staring into the face of those two centre pawns.

If White wants to keep his centre pawns there's a decent alternative in 7 e3 (Kramnik-Carlsen, Game 57), the drawback being that it will lose a tempo if White subsequently advances the e-pawn again. I've played this way myself, though with 8 ♕e2 rather than Kramnik's 8 ♘c3. In either case White has compensation for the pawn.

Besides following up with 6...♘c6, Black has also played 6...c5 as in Beliavsky-Mammadov (Game 58). This approach may appeal to players who are comfortable defending slightly inferior endgames, but it proved to be risky against Big Al. Note that Black can also reach this line via 5...c5 6 0-0 a6, thus avoiding White's alternative to castling, (5...a6) 6 ♘e5, as seen in Kramnik-Morozevich (Game 59).

Game 55
M.Umansky-D.Weber
Correspondence 2003

---

1 c4 ♘f6 2 d4 e6 3 ♘f3 d5 4 g3 dxc4 5

♗g2 a6 6 0-0 ♘c6 7 ♘c3

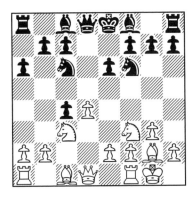

7...♖b8

The critical line, getting ready to hold the c4-pawn with ...b7-b5.

Another possibility is 7...♘d5 8 e4 ♘xc3 9 bxc3 ♗e7, as in M.Umansky-C.Singer, Fürth 1999. White should now play 10 ♕e2 (rather than the 10 ♘d2 of the game) 10...♘a5 11 ♖d1, which would have given him excellent compensation for the sacrificed pawn, one of Black's main problems being his lack of effective pawn levers.

8 e4 b5

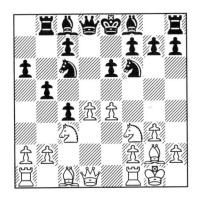

For 8...♗e7 see the next game.

9 d5 ♘b4

9...♘a5 is strongly met by 10 ♗d2, for example 10...b4 (10...exd5 11 ♘xd5 ♘xd5 12 exd5 ♘b7 13 ♘e5 allows White a great game without any material investment) 11 ♕a4+ c6 12 ♖ad1 bxc3 13 ♗xc3 ♕b6 14 dxe6 ♗b4 15 exf7+ ♔xf7 16 ♘e5+, followed by 17 ♗d4, gives White a strong attack.

10 b3

Undermining the c4-pawn so as to stop Black's knight being irritating on d3. Other moves don't do the trick:

a) 10 ♘e5 ♗d6 11 f4 exd5 12 a3 ♘d3 13 ♘xd3 cxd3 14 exd5 ♗c5+ 15 ♔h1 ♗f5! was good for Black in M.Vukic-S.Marjanovic, Yugoslav Ch., Skender Vakuf 1980.

b) 10 ♗g5 ♗e7 11 ♘e5 ♘d7 12 ♗xe7 ♕xe7 13 ♘xd7 ½-½ V.Inkiov-M.Brancaleoni, Montecatini Terme 2001, was a good tactical draw offer by a GM against his sub-2200 opponent. White doesn't stand too well here.

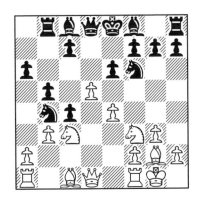

10...cxb3

After 10...exd5?! 11 exd5 cxb3 (or if 11...♘fxd5 12 ♘xd5 ♕xd5 13 ♘d4, with ideas of ♖e1+ and/or ♗a3, is very strong) 12 ♕xb3 ♘d3 13 ♗g5 ♗e7 14

♘d4 ♗d7 15 ♖ad1 ♘c5 16 ♕c2 White had a nice game in S.Gorelov-S.Abramov, USSR 1991.

11 ♕xb3

White can also try 11 ♘d4!?, when 11...c5 (if 11...e5 12 ♘xb3 threatening 13 a3 is awkward; so maybe Black should go the whole hog with 11...bxa2) 12 dxc6 e5 13 ♘d5! ♗d6 14 c7 ♗xc7 15 ♘xb4 ♕xd4 16 ♕xd4 exd4 17 axb3 was better for White in O.Cvitan-T.Luther, German League 1998.

11...c5 12 dxc6 ♘xc6 13 ♗f4

Another possibility is 13 ♖d1, for example 13...♕b6 (13...♕c7 14 ♗f4 e5 15 ♘d5 ♘xd5 16 exd5 exf4 17 ♕c3 seems pretty good for White) 14 ♗f4 ♖b7 15 e5 ♘d7 (15...♘g4 16 ♘e4 is strong) 16 ♘e4 ♘c5 17 ♕e3! ♘xe4 18 ♕xe4 was V.Tukmakov-K.Hulak, Croatian Team Ch. 1999, when 18...♗c5 would have been Black's best with about even play.

13...♖b7 14 ♖ad1

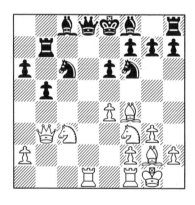

Umansky finds what's probably the strongest move for White. Over the board players have done less well here:

a) 14 e5 ♘d7 15 ♘e4 ♘a5 16 ♕c3 ♕c7 17 ♕d4 ♕b6 18 ♖fc1 ♖b8 saw Black hold on in P.H.Nielsen-L.Van Wely, Dortmund 2005.

b) 14 ♖ac1 ♘a5! 15 ♕c2 ♗a3 16 ♖cd1 ♘d7 17 ♗g5 ♕c7 18 ♗f4 ♕d8 19 ♗g5 f6!? 20 ♘d4 ♖b6 was unclear in R.Bator-Se.Ivanov, Stockholm 2000.

c) 14 ♖fd1 should be met by 14...♖d7, when 15 e5 ♘a5 16 ♕c2 ♘h5!? isn't clear either.

14...♘d7 15 ♕c2

In P.Haba-A.Morozevich, European Club Cup, Kemer 2007, White prepared the knight sacrifice on d5 with 15 ♖fe1, but after 15...♗e7 16 ♘d5 Black simply sidestepped it with 16...♗c5. There followed 17 e5 ♘a5 18 ♕c2 ♘c4 19 ♘g5 ♖a7 20 ♘xh7 ♕a5 21 ♘g5 ♘db6 with very complex play.

15...♘a5 16 ♘d5!?

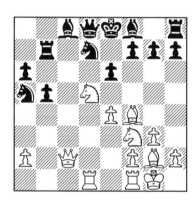

A brilliant sacrifice from Umansky, which I believe was at least partly intuitive. It's fascinating that someone can successfully play this way in a form of chess that's dominated by computers.

16...exd5 17 exd5 ♗e7

There's a critical alternative in 17...♗c5, but White seems to have more than enough. A sample line is 18 ♘g5 ♗b4 19 ♕e4+ ♕e7 20 ♕d4 ♘c4 (if 20...0-0 21 d6) 21 ♕xg7 ♖f8 (or 21...♕f6 22 ♖fe1+) 22 d6 ♕f6 23 ♖fe1+ ♗xe1 24 ♖xe1+ ♔d8 25 ♘e6+ fxe6 26 ♗g5 ♘xd6 27 ♖xe6 etc.

18 ♘d4 0-0 19 ♘c6 ♘xc6 20 dxc6 ♖a7

20...♗c7 is powerfully answered by 21 ♗e4, threatening ♗xc7 and c6xd7.

21 c7! ♕e8 22 ♖fe1 ♘c5 23 ♗d6 ♗xd6 24 ♖xe8 ♖xe8 25 ♗c6! ♖f8 26 ♖xd6

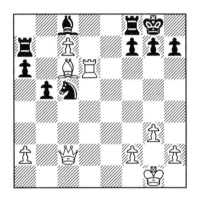

The smoke has cleared to leave White with a material advantage. Umansky solves the technical problems very convincingly.

26...♘e6 27 f4 ♖xc7 28 ♕d2 g6 29 g4 ♘g7 30 ♕a5 ♘e8 31 ♗xe8 ♖c1+ 32 ♔f2 ♖xe8 33 ♖d8 ♖xd8

Black probably considered 33...♗c2+, but after 34 ♔g3 ♖xd8 35 ♕xd8+ ♔g7 36 ♕d4+ ♔g8 37 f5 gxf5 38 ♕d8+ ♔g7 39 ♕g5+ ♔f8 40 gxf5 White is threatening 41 f6.

34 ♕xd8+ ♔g7 35 f5 ♖c6 36 ♕d4+ ♔f8

Or 36...f6 37 ♕a7+ ♔f8 38 ♕xh7 etc.

37 ♕h8+ ♔e7 38 ♕xh7 gxf5 39 g5 ♖c2+ 40 ♔e3 ♖g2 41 h4 ♗e6 42 ♕h8 a5?

42...♖xa2 would have put up more

of a fight.

43 ♕f6+ ♔d7 44 h5 ♖xa2 45 h6 ♖h2 46 ♕g7 ♔d6 47 h7 ♖h3+ 48 ♔f4 ♖h4+ 49 ♔g3 ♖xh7 50 ♕xh7 b4 51 ♕h8 ♔d5 52 ♕a8+ ♔c4 53 g6 fxg6 54 ♕c6+ ♔d4 55 ♕xe6 ♔c5 56 ♔f4 ♔d4 57 ♕d6+ ♔c3 58 ♔e3 1-0

Game 56
B.Gelfand-Y.Drozdovskij
Odessa 2008

---

1 c4 ♘f6 2 d4 e6 3 ♘f3 d5 4 g3 dxc4 5 ♗g2 a6 6 0-0 ♘c6 7 ♘c3 ♖b8 8 e4 ♗e7 9 ♕e2

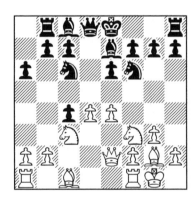

Offering the d-pawn as a gambit. There's also a case for playing 9 d5 ♘b4 10 ♘e5, for example 10...exd5 11 exd5 ♘d3 (if 11...♗f5 12 ♘xc4!? ♗d3 13 ♘e3 ♗xf1 14 ♕xf1 a5 15 a3 ♘a6 16 ♕b5+ ♕d7 17 ♘f5! gives White a strong initiative for the sacrificed exchange) 12 ♘xd3 cxd3 13 ♕xd3 0-0 14 h3 ♗d7 15 ♖d1 ♘e8 16 ♗e3 ♘d6 17 ♖ac1, when White's position was preferable due to his space in B.Lalic-L.Trent, British Ch., Liverpool 2008.

9...②xd4

Black is well advised to take d4 before White defends it. E.L'Ami-S.Sulskis, European Ch., Liverpool 2008, featured 9...b5 10 罝d1 0-0 11 d5 exd5 12 e5 d4 (12...②d7 13 ②xd5 is just good for White) 13 exf6 ②xf6 14 豐e4 ②b4 15 ②xd4 ②b7 16 ②c6! 豐c8 (16...②xc6 17 罝xd8 ②xe4 18 罝xb8 罝xb8 19 ②xe4 leaves Black with inadequate compensation) 17 ②e7+ ②xe7 18 豐xe7 ②xg2 19 ③xg2, when Black didn't have enough for the piece.

10 ②xd4 豐xd4 11 罝d1 豐c5

In A.Zontakh-S.Slugin, Lipetsk 2008, Black played 11...豐a7, after which 12 e5 ②d7 13 豐g4 ③f8 14 ②e3 b6 15 ②g5 left Black's queen totally out of the game, while he had to face horrible threats on the kingside.

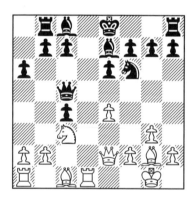

12 e5

There's a noteworthy alternative in 12 ②e3!?, for example 12...豐a5 13 ②d2 (13 豐xc4 e5 14 ②d5 ②xd5 15 罝xd5 ②e6 16 罝xa5 ②xc4 17 罝xe5 f6 18 罝xe7+ ③xe7 19 罝c1 ②xa2 20 罝xc7+ ③f8 gave White just about enough for the exchange in A.Riazantsev-V.Milov, Ve-

naco rapid 2005) 13...豐c5 14 e5 ②d7 15 ②e4 豐b5 (15...豐xe5 16 ②c3 豐f5 17 豐xc4 0-0 18 豐xc7 also left Black in trouble in V.Mikhalevski-I.Krush, Ashdod 2006) 16 a4 豐xb2 17 豐xc4 0-0 18 ②c3 豐b6 19 罝ab1 豐a7 20 ②f6+! ②xf6 21 exf6 罝e8 22 罝xd7 ②xd7 23 豐g4 g6 24 豐g5 ③h8 25 罝b4 豐b6 26 豐h6 1-0 was the brilliant game E.Gleizerov-B.Itkis, Predeal 2007. After 26...罝g8 27 豐xh7+ Black gets mated.

All these lines are highly complex so it's difficult to know what the 'absolute truth' is, at least without further tests. Personally I wouldn't like to face White's powerful initiative after either 12 e5 or 12 ②e3.

12...②d5

Or 12...②d7 13 ②e4 (13 ②f4, as played in E.Bareev-A.Timofeev, Serpukhov 2007, probably isn't necessary, as after 13 ②e4 Black is ill advised to take the e5-pawn) 13...豐b4 (after 13...豐xe5 a sample line is 14 ②f4 豐a5 15 豐xc4 e5 16 ②g5 ②f6 17 b4 豐b6 18 ②e3 ②e6 19 ②xb6 ②xc4 20 ②xc7 with much the better endgame) 14 豐g4 ②f8 (on 14...③f8 White can consider opening more lines with 15 b3!?) 15 a3 豐b3 16 ②d2 豐xb2 17 ②c3 豐b6?! (17...豐b3 is better) 18 罝ab1 豐a7 19 ②d4 c5 20 ②d6+ ②xd6 21 exd6 cxd4 22 豐xg7 罝f8 23 罝e1 1-0 T.Thaler-ChessWorld.net, correspondence 2004, as Black is defenceless against the threat of 24 罝xe6+.

13 ②e4

Playing for the attack rather than the recovery of material. In an earlier game, B.Gelfand-E.Vallejo Pons, Monte Carlo (blindfold rapid) 2006, Boris opted for 13 ♘xd5!? exd5 14 ♗xd5, but after 14...0-0 15 ♗e3 ♕a5 16 ♗a7 ♖a8 17 e6 ♗xe6 18 ♗xe6 ♖xa7 19 ♖d7 ♗d6 20 ♖xf7 ♖xf7 21 ♕f3 ♔h8 22 ♗xf7 ♕b4 23 ♕e4 ♖a8 found himself in an equal and drawish position.

K.Miton-M.Perunovic, Vrsac 2008, varied with 13 ♗xd5 exd5 14 ♘xd5, but after 14...♗d8 (14...♗e6 15 ♗e3 ♕c6 16 ♘xe7 ♔xe7 also looks okay for Black) 15 ♗e3 ♕c6 16 ♘b4 (16 ♖ac1 0-0 17 ♖xc4 ♕e6 18 ♗c5 ♖e8 19 ♖cd4 b6 20 ♘f4 ♕c6 21 ♖xd8 ♗b7 22 ♖8d5 bxc5 wasn't clear in A.Huzman-M.Venkatesh, Montreal 2008) 16...♕b5 17 ♖xd8+ ♔xd8 18 ♖d1+ ♔e8, White had nothing better than 19 ♘d5 ♕c6 20 ♘b4 ♕b5 21 ♘d5 with a draw by repetition.

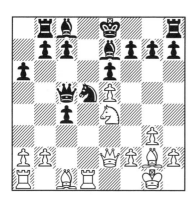

13...♕b5 14 ♕g4 ♔f8 15 ♗g5 ♗xg5 16 ♕xg5 ♗d7 17 a4?!

This may be asking too much, but after 17 ♘c3 ♕xb2 18 ♗xd5 ♕xc3 19 ♗xb7 h6 it would fizzle out to a draw.

17...♕b4

17...♕xb2 is the critical line, for example 18 ♘c5 ♗c6 and does White have enough for the pawns? If so, I don't see it.

18 ♘c3 h6 19 ♕h4

After 19 ♘xd5 exd5 20 ♕f4, Black can defend via 20...♗e6 21 ♗xd5 ♕e7 22 ♕xc4 ♗xd5 23 ♕xd5 h5, intending ...h4 and/or ...♖h6.

19...c6 20 ♕d4 ♔e7

Black probably took fright at the prospect of 20...♕xb2 21 ♕c5+ ♔g8 22 ♘xd5 exd5 23 ♕d6 ♖d8 24 ♖ab1, but he is still defending here with 24...♕c2 25 ♖dc1 ♕f5.

21 ♘e4 ♖hd8 22 ♘d6 c3 23 ♕xb4 ♘xb4 24 bxc3 ♘d5 25 c4 ♘b4 26 a5 c5 27 ♘xb7

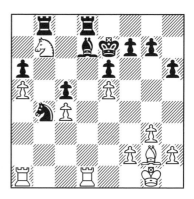

White has emerged with an edge, but Black holds a draw.

27...♖dc8 28 ♘d6 ♖c7 29 ♖ab1 ♗c6 30 ♗xc6 ♘xc6 31 ♖xb8 ♘xb8 32 f4 ♘c6 33 ♖b1 f6 34 ♖b6 fxe5 35 fxe5 ♘xe5 36 ♖xa6 ♖d7 37 ♘e4 ♖c7 38 ♘d6 ♖d7 39 ♘c8+ ♔f6 40 ♘d6 ♔e7 ½-½

Game 57
V.Kramnik-M.Carlsen
Wijk aan Zee 2007

1 ♘f3 ♘f6 2 c4 e6 3 g3 d5 4 d4 dxc4 5

♗g2 a6 6 0-0 ♘c6 7 e3

This is less direct than 7 ♘c3 but has similar aims: White wants to build a broad pawn centre with e2-e4, but keeps his d-pawn defended while preparing ♕e2 and ♖d1.

7...♗d7

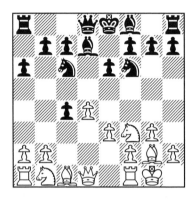

After 7...♖b8 White recovers his pawn with 8 ♘fd2, while 7...b5 is answered by 8 ♘e5.

8 ♘c3

White has a major alternative here in 8 ♕e2 b5 9 ♖d1 (9 ♘e5!? ♘xe5! 10 ♗xa8 ♕xa8 11 dxe5 ♘e4 gave Black more than enough for the exchange in R.Janssen-J.Piket, Dutch Ch., Rotterdam 1999; but both 9 a4 ♖b8 10 axb5 axb5 11 b3 cxb3 12 ♘bd2 ♗d6 13 ♗b2 0-0 14 ♘xb3 as in Kir.Georgiev-P.Leko, Dubai (rapid) 2002, and 9 e4 ♗e7 10 b3! cxb3 11 axb3 0-0 12 ♖d1 ♘b4 13 ♘e5 ♗c8 14 ♘c3 ♗b7 15 ♗a3 ♖e8 16 ♖ac1 ♕b8 17 g4! as in Z.Ilincic-O.Cvitan, Bosnian Team Ch. 2004, can be considered) 9...♗e7 (another possibility is 9...♗d6 when, after 10 e4 e5 11 dxe5 ♗xe5 12 ♘c3 0-0 13 ♗g5 ♗xc3 14 bxc3 ♕e8, White's best may be 15 h3!? ac-

cording to Acs and Hazai) 10 ♘c3 ♖b8 (10...0-0 11 ♘e5 ♕e8 12 b3 ♘d5 13 ♗xd5 exd5 14 ♘xd5 ♘xe5 15 dxe5 ♖a7 16 bxc4 c6 17 ♘f4 ♕c8 18 ♗b2 g5 19 e4 gxf4 20 gxf4 gave White a strong attack for the sacrificed piece in L.Aronian-M.Carlsen, Morelia/Linares 2007, though Black held a draw with accurate defence; while 10...♘b4 11 e4 ♘d3 12 ♘e5! ♘xc1 13 ♖axc1 0-0 14 g4!? gave White the initiative for his pawn in P.Haba-L.Gorin, Pardubice 1999) 11 e4 0-0 12 ♗f4 ♖e8 13 ♘e5 h6 14 ♘xf7 ♔xf7 15 e5 ♔g8 16 exf6 ♗xf6 was N.Davies-M.Chandler, British League 1999, and now the quiet 17 ♗e3 might have been best with ongoing compensation for the pawn.

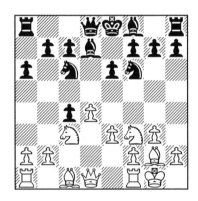

8...♘d5

Not the only move by any means. The alternatives are as follows:

a) 8...♗d6 9 ♕e2 0-0 (on 9...b5 White can play 10 e4, when 10...e5 11 dxe5 ♘xe5 12 ♘xe5 ♗xe5 13 f4 ♗d4+ 14 ♗e3 c5 15 h3 looks promising) 10 ♕xc4 b5 11 ♕e2 b4 12 ♘b1 ♘a5 13 ♖d1 ♗b5 14 ♕e1 ♕e8 15 b3 ♖c8 16 ♗b2 c5 17 dxc5 ♗xc5 18 ♘bd2 was better for White in

A.Beliavsky-L.Portisch, Paks 2004, because of the weakness of Black's queenside pawns and White's harmonious development.

b) 8...♖b8 9 ♘e5 ♘a5 can be answered by 10 e4! b5 11 g4! b4 12 g5 bxc3 13 bxc3! as in G.Sosonko-J.Piket, Dutch Ch., Rotterdam 1997, when 13...♘g8? (13...♖b5 14 gxf6 gxf6 15 ♘xd7 ♕xd7 16 ♕f3 ♖g8 17 ♔h1 was quite promising for White in the game; as is 13...♘c6 14 ♘xc6 ♗xc6 15 gxf6 ♕xf6 16 ♕e2) 14 ♕f3 f6? (14...♕e7 would lose immediately to 15 ♗a3; so the only way to hang on would be with 14...♘f6) 15 ♕h5+ g6 16 ♘xg6 hxg6 17 ♕xg6+ ♔e7 18 ♗a3+ leads to mate.

c) White can take advantage of 8...b5 with the immediate 9 ♘e5!, when 9...♘xe5 10 dxe5 ♘d5 11 ♘xd5 exd5 12 ♕xd5 c6 13 ♕d4 c5 14 ♕d5 ♖b8 15 a4 bxa4 16 ♖d1 ♗b5 17 ♗d2 was better for White in B.Gelfand-L.Van Wely, Monte Carlo (rapid) 2001.

c) 8...♗b4 9 ♘e5 (on 9 ♕e2 Black can try 9...♘d5!?) 9...♘xe5 10 dxe5 ♗xc3 11 bxc3 ♘d5 12 ♗a3! ♕g5 13 ♕d4 0-0-0 14 ♕a7 ♗c6 15 ♖fd1 ♕xe5 16 ♖d4 b6 17 ♕xa6+ ♗b7 18 ♕xc4 c5! 19 ♖b1 offered complex play and chances for both sides in B.Gelfand-M.Adams, Enghien les Bains 2003.

9 ♘d2

Again there is 9 ♕e2, but after 9...b5 (9...♘xc3 10 bxc3 ♗d6 11 ♖d1 b5 12 ♘e5! ♗xe5 13 dxe5 ♘xe5 14 ♕h5! ♘d3 15 ♗a3 ♖b8! 16 ♗e4 b4! 17 ♗xb4 was A.Khalifman-A.Petrosian, Moscow 1987, and now 17...♖b5! 18 ♕g4 ♕g5 would have been best, when 19 ♕xg5

♖xg5 20 ♗xd3 cxd3 21 c4! ♗c6 22 f4! is just slightly better for White) 10 ♘xd5 exd5 11 e4 ♗d6 (11...♕e7?! 12 a4 b4 13 ♖e1 0-0-0 14 ♕f1 dxe4 15 ♕xc4 ♔b7 16 ♘g5 gave White a powerful attack in A.Beliavsky-E.Van den Doel, European Ch., Dresden 2007) 12 exd5+ ♘e7 13 b3 cxb3 14 axb3 0-0 15 ♘e5 ♗c8 16 ♗b2 a5 17 ♖fc1 a4 18 bxa4 bxa4 19 ♘c4 ♗b7 20 ♘xd6 cxd6 Black had completely equalized in D.Yevseev-D.Jakovenko, St Petersburg-Moscow match 2003.

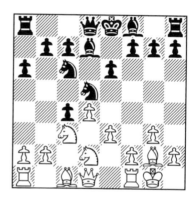

9...♘b6

In view of the possibility of 12 ♗d2 below, maybe Black should prefer 9...♘xc3 10 bxc3 b5 here, for example 11 a4 ♗e7! (11...♖b8 12 axb5 axb5 13 ♕g4 g6 14 ♕e2! ♗d6! 15 ♘e4 0-0 16 ♗a3! ♕e7 17 ♕f3! was good for White in F.Berkes-L.Aronian, World Junior Ch. 2002, the point being that 17...♗xa3 18 ♖xa3! ♕xa3 19 ♘f6+ ♔g7 20 ♘xd7 ♘a5 21 ♕f6+ ♔g8 22 h4!, followed by h4-h5, gives White a strong attack) 12 ♗a3 ♖b8 (12...♗xa3 13 ♖xa3 0-0 14 ♘e4 gave White more than enough for the pawn in V.Filippov-K.Sakaev, Moscow 2004, due to his control of c5) 13 axb5 axb5 14 ♘e4 0-0 15 ♕e2 ♗xa3 16 ♖xa3 e5 17 d5 ♘e7 18 ♘c5 ♗h3! 19 e4 ♗xg2 20 ♔xg2 c6 21 ♖a7 ♕b6 22 ♖xe7 ♕xc5 23 ♖xe5 fizzled out to equality in F.Berkes-P.Leko, Budapest 2003.

10 ♕e2 ♘a5 11 ♘de4

11 e4 ♗b4 (or 11...♗e7 12 ♘f3 0-0 13 ♗e3 ♖c8 14 ♖ad1 ♘a4 15 ♘e5 ♘xc3 16 bxc3 ♗a4 17 ♖d2 c5! 18 d5 ♕c7 19 ♘g4 exd5 20 ♗f4 ♕b6 21 exd5 was A.Lastin-Kir.Georgiev, Serbian Team Ch. 2004, when 21...♖ce8! would have produced a complex position with chances for both sides) 12 ♕g4 ♕f6 13 ♘f3 h5 14 ♕f4 ♕xf4 15 ♗xf4 0-0-0 16 ♖ac1 gave White only nebulous compensation for the pawn in T.Radjabov-M.Adams, FIDE World Ch., Tripoli 2004.

11...♗e7

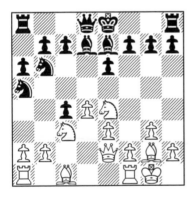

12 ♘c5

In M.Sebenik-V.Vehi Bach, European Ch., Plovdiv 2008, White tried to improve on Kramnik's play with 12 ♗d2, shadowing the knight on a5. In fact he stood better after 12...0-0 13 ♖fd1 ♕e8 (if 13...♗c6 14 ♘b1 forces Black to play 14...♗xe4 15 ♗xe4 ♘c6 in order to save the knight on a5) 14 ♘c5

♖b8 15 ♘xd7 ♕xd7 16 d5 e5 17 ♘e4 c3 (17...♕b5 is strongly met by 18 b3) 18 ♗xc3 ♘ac4 19 a4 threatening 20 a5, which was very unpleasant for Black.

12...♗c6 13 ♗xc6+ ♘xc6 14 ♘xb7 ♕c8 15 ♘c5 0-0 16 ♘5a4 ♘b4 17 ♗d2 ♖d8 18 a3 ♘c6 19 ♖ac1 ♖b8 20 ♖fd1 e5 21 ♘xb6 cxb6

21...♖xb6? would run into 22 ♕xc4 exd4 23 ♘d5.

22 ♕xc4 exd4 23 ♘e4 dxe3 24 ♗xe3 ♖xd1+ 25 ♖xd1 ♕b7

Carlsen's accurate defence gradually steers the game towards equality.

26 ♖c1 ♘e5 27 ♕c7 f6 28 ♕xb7 ½-½

Game 58
A.Beliavsky-A.Mammadov
Baku 2008

---

1 d4 d5 2 c4 e6 3 ♘f3 ♘f6 4 g3 dxc4 5 ♗g2 a6 6 0-0 c5

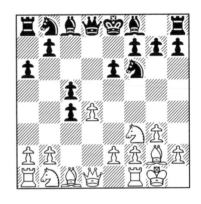

An unusual line, which attempts to equalize by exchanging off White's d-pawn. But it seems that such simple methods will not really work, given White's Catalan bishop bearing down on Black's queenside from g2. Note that it can also be reached via a 5...c5 6 0-0 a6 move order.

7 dxc5 ♕xd1 8 ♖xd1 ♘c6

In Y.Razuvaev-E.Geller, USSR 1988, Black tried 8...♗xc5, but lost in dramatic fashion after 9 ♘e5 ♘bd7 10 ♘xc4 ♖a7 (or 10...0-0 11 ♘c3 ♖a7 12 ♘a4 with strong pressure) 11 ♘c3 b5 12 ♘d6+ ♔e7? (12...♗xd6 is mandatory, though unpleasant because of White's bishop pair) 13 ♘ce4 ♘xe4 14 ♘xe4 ♖c7 15 ♗d2! 1-0. Black has suddenly found himself without a decent move, for example if 15...♗b6 16 ♗b4+, or 15...f5 16 ♘xc5 ♘xc5 17 ♗a5 ♖d7 18 ♗b4, or 15...♗b7 16 ♗a5 ♖cc8 17 ♖xd7+ ♔xd7 18 ♘xc5+ ♖xc5 19 ♗xb7 b4 20 ♖d1+ wins.

9 ♘fd2!

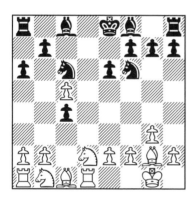

Unveiling the mighty Catalan bishop, while routing his knight to the queenside. In A.Lastin-A.Schupaleev, Vladimir 2004, White played 9 ♘bd2, but after 9...♗xc5 10 ♘xc4 ♘d5 11 e4 ♘b6 12 ♘d6+ ♗xd6 13 ♖xd6 ♔e7 he had only a slight advantage.

9....♗d7

After 9...♗xc5 White has a pleasant choice between, say, 10 ♘xc4 ♘d5 11 ♘c3 ♘xc3 12 bxc3, with strong piece play coming on the queenside, and mangling Black's pawns with 10 ♗xc6+.

10 ♘xc4 ♗xc5 11 ♘c3 0-0 12 ♗f4 ♖ad8 13 ♗c7 ♖c8 14 ♗d6 ♗xd6 15 ♘xd6 ♖c7 16 ♖ac1

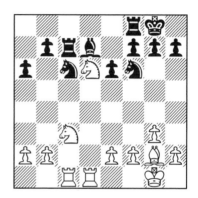

This position is deeply unpleasant for Black. He can hope for a draw at best and is unlikely to get even that.

16...♘e8 17 ♘ce4 ♘xd6 18 ♘xd6 ♖b8 19 b4 b5 20 a3 ♔f8 21 ♘e4 ♗e8 22 ♘d6 ♗d7 23 f4

The repetition of moves is a Capablancan technique to clarify the position in your mind while increasing the psychological pressure.

23...♔e7 24 e4 ♖a7 25 e5 ♘d8 26 ♗e4 h6 27 ♖c5 f6

Understandably trying to free himself. Unfortunately it creates weak pawns that Big Al can set about attacking.

28 exf6+ ♔xf6 29 ♗f3 ♘f7 30 ♘e4+ ♔e7 31 ♖c2 ♖b6 32 ♘c5 ♖d6 33 ♖e1 ♖c7 34 ♖ce2 ♘d8 35 f5

The pressure on e6 is mounting.

35...♔f7 36 ♗h5+ ♔g8?

It seems that Black has been tortured enough and takes the chance to end it all. 36...♔e7 was mandatory.

37 fxe6 1-0

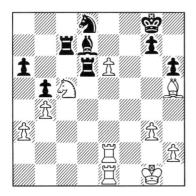

Black loses a piece when he recaptures on e6, and otherwise the pawn goes on to e7.

Game 59
V.Kramnik-A.Morozevich
World Championship,
Mexico City 2007

---

1 ♘f3 ♘f6 2 c4 e6 3 g3 d5 4 d4 dxc4 5 ♗g2 a6 6 ♘e5

This is thought to be a safer move than 6 0-0, aiming for the immediate recovery of the pawn. Black is supposed to be able to equalize with 6...c5, but with Kramnik inviting this and Morozevich avoiding it, the likelihood is that it's not so simple.

6...♗b4+

On 6...c5 White has tried several different moves:

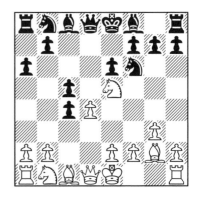

a) 7 e3 cxd4 8 exd4 ♘bd7 9 ♘xc4 ♘b6 10 ♘e5 ♗e7 11 0-0 0-0 12 ♘c3 ♘bd5 was fine for Black in A.Lukin-Y.Balashov, USSR 1967, as White's bishop is not appropriately placed on g2 in this isolated queen's pawn position.

b) 7 ♗e3 ♘d5 was thought to be good for Black, because both 8 dxc5 and 8 0-0 are well met by 8...♘d7!, but White has an interesting and little tried alternative in 8 ♘c3!?. C.Bauer-Al.David, Cannes 2006, continued 8...♘xe3 9 fxe3 ♗e7 10 ♕a4+ ♘d7 11 dxc5 0-0 12 0-0-0!? ♘xe5 13 ♖xd8 ♗xd8 14 ♖d1 ♗g5 15 ♘e4 ♗xe3+ 16 ♔b1 and Black had inadequate compensation for the queen.

c) 7 ♘a3 is the current favourite, for example 7...cxd4 (7...♖a7?! 8 dxc5! ♕xd1+ 9 ♔xd1 ♗xc5 10 ♘axc4 b5 11 ♘d3! ♖d7 12 ♘ce5 ♖d8 13 ♗d2 ♗b6 14 a4 was better for White at this stage in Y.Razuvaev-A.Beliavsky, Baku 1977; while 7...♕xd4 8 ♕xd4 cxd4 9 ♘axc4 ♘bd7 10 0-0! ♘xe5 11 ♘xe5 ♗d6 12 ♘c4 ♗c7 13 ♗f4 ♗xf4 14 gxf4 ♖b8 15 ♖fd1 ♔e7 16 ♖xd4 ♗d7 17 ♘d6! gave

White an edge in A.Karpov-L.Van Wely, Monte Carlo blindfold 2001) 8 ♘axc4 ♗c5 (8...♖a7 9 ♗d2 b6 10 0-0 ♗b7 11 ♗xb7 ♖xb7 12 ♖c1 ♗c5 13 b4 ♗e7 14 ♗e3! 0-0 15 ♗xd4 ♘fd7 16 ♕b3 ♘xe5 17 ♗xe5 was uncomfortable for Black in A.Huzman-I.Novikov, Montreal 2004; and 8...♗e7?! 9 ♗d2 a5!? was played in I.Almasi-L.Vadasz, Budapest 1997, when 10 ♕a4+ would have given White some pressure) 9 ♗d2 (9 0-0 0-0 10 ♘d3 ♗e7 11 ♗d2 ♘c6 12 ♖c1 ♘d5 13 ♕b3 b5 left White with less than convincing compensation in I.Ivanisevic-D.Blagojevic, Niksic rapid 2008) 9...♘d5 10 ♖c1 0-0 11 0-0 ♘d7 12 ♘d3 b6 (12...♖a7 13 ♗a5 ♕e7 was B.Gulko-Y.Shulman, US Ch., Tulsa 2008, when 14 ♗xd5 exd5 15 ♗b4 ♕f6 16 ♘d6 seems to give White pressure) 13 ♘a5! ♖e8 14 ♘c6 ♕f6 15 b4 ♗b7 was P.Kiss-A.Beliavsky, Hungarian Team Ch. 1999, and now White should play 16 ♘xc5 bxc5 (or 16...♘xc5 17 bxc5 ♗xc6 18 cxb6) 17 ♘a5 with a clear advantage.

7 ♘c3 ♘d5 8 0-0!?

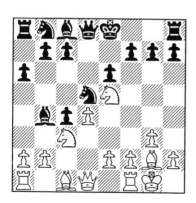

An excellent new move by Kramnik, simply ignoring Black's threat to

capture on c3.

White had previously played 8 ♗d2, but then 8...b5 9 0-0 ♗xc3 (9...♗b7!?) 10 bxc3 0-0 11 e4 (11 a4 f6 12 ♘g4 ♗b7 13 e4 ♘b6 14 ♕b1?! was I.Ivanisevic-D.Pavasovic, Valjevo 2007, when 14...f5!? would have given Black a good chance to blockade on the light squares) 11...♘b6 12 f4 ♗b7 13 f5 exf5 14 ♖xf5 ♘8d7 15 ♘g4 ♕e7 16 ♕c2 ♖ae8 17 ♖e1 f6 saw Black regroup nicely in J.Nogueiras-V.Ivanchuk, Havana 2006.

8...0-0

After 8...♘xc3 9 bxc3 ♗xc3 White should probably play 10 ♖b1 (10 ♗a3?! seems wrong because of 10...♕xd4), when 10...♗xd4 (10...♕xd4 11 ♕a4+ b5 12 ♕a3 ♕xe5 13 ♗f4 would see White recover most of his material and keep a strong initiative) 11 ♘xc4 0-0 12 ♗a3 ♖e8 13 ♘a5 ♖a7 14 ♘xb7 ♗xb7 15 ♗xb7 c5 16 e3 leaves him with a powerful initiative for his pawn.

9 ♕c2 b5 10 ♘xd5 exd5 11 b3 c6 12 e4

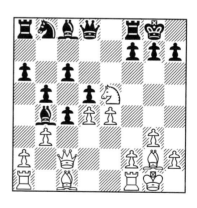

Ambitious play by Kramnik, pouring gasoline onto the flames. There was a safe option in 12 bxc4, but after 12...dxc4 13 ♘xc6 ♘xc6 14 ♗xc6 ♗h3

Black would stand well, so White should probably just protect his d4-pawn with 13 ♖d1.

12...f6!?

12...♗e6 has been suggested as a possible improvement, but it seems that White is better after 13 bxc4 dxc4 (or 13...bxc4 14 ♖b1) 14 d5.

13 exd5!?

A brilliantly creative piece sacrifice from Kramnik. Is it sound? Who knows. Certainly it gives White a most dangerous initiative.

13...fxe5 14 bxc4 exd4 15 dxc6 ♗e6 16 cxb5!

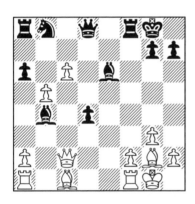

Of course Kramnik never intended to win the rook on a8 via 16 c7 ♕xc7 17 ♗xa8, as this would surrender the initiative, and Black would have more than enough for the exchange after 17...♕xc4.

16...d3?!

After this the position clarifies in White's favour. Kramnik might have had a more difficult task after 16...♖a7, when 17 ♖b1 can be answered by 17...d3 18 ♕d1 ♗c5 with pressure against f2. The position is still very

complicated, but this definitely seems like an improvement for Black.

17 c7

There was another possibility in 17 ♕a4!?, when 17...♕a5 18 ♕xa5 ♗xa5 19 a4 d2 20 ♗a3 ♖e8 21 c7 ♘d7 is again difficult to assess.

17...♕d4?

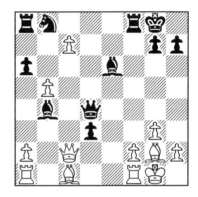

This might be the losing move. Black would also be in big trouble after 17...dxc2 18 cxd8♕ ♖xd8 19 ♗xa8 axb5 20 ♗g5 ♖c8 21 a4, but 17...♕d6!? was an interesting alternative: for example, 18 ♕a4 d2 19 ♗xd2 ♗xd2 20 ♗xa8 ♕xc7 21 bxa6 ♕a7 22 ♗b7 ♗h3 23 ♕e4 ♗xf1 24 ♖xf1 gives White three pawns for the piece, though the a-pawns are doubled.

18 ♕a4

Kramnik probably rejected 18 ♗e3 because of 18...dxc2 19 ♗xd4 ♘d7 20 ♗xa8 ♖xa8, which still looks very messy.

18...♘d7 19 ♗e3 ♕d6 20 ♗xa8 ♖xa8 21 ♗f4?!

This slip could have had serious consequences. White had a very convincing move in 21 ♖ac1!, after which

21...♖c8 22 ♖c6 ♕d5 23 ♕xb4 ♗h3 24 ♕b3 would leave him with a winning endgame.

21...♕f8??

Missing his chance to complicate matters with 21...♕d5!, and if 22 ♕xb4? ♕f3 threatens ...♗d5 and ...♗h3.

22 b6!

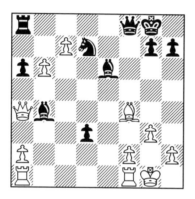

A bone-crusher from Kramnik, the point being that 22...♘xb6 loses a piece to 23 ♕c6. Morozevich tries desperately to counterattack, but it's too late. **22...♘e5 23 ♗xe5 ♕f3 24 ♕d1 ♕e4 25 b7! ♖f8 26 c8♕ ♗d5 27 f3 1-0**

Summary

White gets pretty good compensation for a pawn after either 6 0-0 ♘c6 7 ♘c3 and 8 e4, or 7 e3, the latter being more likely to appeal to players who make it up as they go along. Endgame specialists will probably want to avoid all this with 6 ♘e5, but they must still know about 5...a6 6 0-0 c5 (as in Game 58), because it can also be reached via 5...c5 6 0-0 a6.

Chapter Thirteen

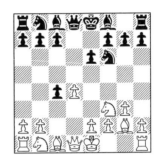

Open Catalan with 5...b5 And Others

1 d4 ♘f6 2 c4 e6 3 g3 d5 4 ♗g2 dxc4 5 ♘f3

The 5...b5 variation is appropriately placed in Chapter 13, because someone is likely to get unlucky. The position gets completely randomized, as you will see in Game 60 (Balashov-Beliavsky). I couldn't find many recent examples of this line and the reason may be that nobody wants to roll the dice. On the other hand, I think this is the best White can do; there are other lines which try to get compensation but they are rather nebulous by comparison.

In Ulibin-Kharlov (Game 61) Black avoided the mayhem with 9...f6 and went on to win, but White certainly had his chances here. 13 ♖e1 looks like one of many possible improvements for White, and 10 ♘g4 another. To me it looks like promising compensation.

After 5...c6 6 a4 Black can play 6...b5 and transpose into the 5...b5 variation.

In Pashikian-Meier (Game 62) he chose to play 6...c5, attempting to show that 6 a4 actually damages White's position. I don't think it does, but he should try to improve on Pashikian's play. 11 ♘g5 looks like one way to do this.

My own game against Lukacs (Game 63) features the move 5...♗d7, which had a brief period of popularity before disappearing into the sunset. One of the curious things about this game is that I had anticipated 8...♗e7 before the tournament while being ensconced in a caravan in North Wales. It seems I was a very serious player in those days.

Game 60
Y.Balashov-A.Beliavsky
USSR Championship, Kiev 1986

---

1 d4 d5 2 c4 e6 3 ♘f3 ♘f6 4 g3 dxc4 5 ♗g2 b5 6 a4 c6

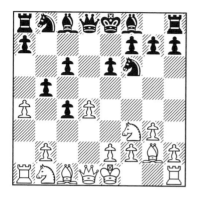

7 axb5

White has tried various other moves in this line, many of which offer him compensation. But I won't be looking at them because I think the text is the best and I don't want to spread my coverage too thin.

7...cxb5 8 ♘e5 ♘d5 9 ♘c3 ♗b4

9...f6!? is featured in the next game.

10 0-0 ♗xc3 11 e4!

Upping the ante! 11 bxc3 ♘xc3 12 ♕d2 ♘d5 would also give White compensation, but it's not clear how much.

11...♗xb2

The critical line. After other moves White is doing very nicely:

a) 11...♘e7 12 bxc3 f6 (12...0-0 13 ♗a3 f6 14 ♘xc4! bxc4 15 e5 ♘bc6 16 ♗xe7 ♕xe7 17 ♗xc6 recovers the material and leaves White with a positional advantage) 13 ♕h5+! g6 14 ♘xg6 ♘xg6 15 e5 ♘c6 16 ♗xc6+ ♗d7 17 ♗xa8 ♕xa8 18 ♗h6 ♔f7 19 exf6 a5 20 ♗g7 won quickly for White in B.Gulko-A.Mikhalchishin, Volgodonsk 1981.

b) 11...♗xd4 was tried in Frunko-J.Matousek, correspondence 1982, but it seems to be very good for White after

12 ♕xd4! ♕b6 13 ♘f3! ♕xd4 14 ♘xd4 ♘e7 15 e5 ♘d5 16 ♘xb5.

c) 11...♘f4 also seems very good for White after Oll's 12 ♗xf4!, for example 12...♗xb2 (or 12...♗xd4 13 ♘xc4 bxc4 14 e5) 13 ♖b1 ♗xd4 14 ♘xc4! bxc4 15 e5 etc.

12 exd5

White can also consider 12 ♗xb2, for example 12...♘e7 (12...♘f6 13 ♗a3 would leave Black unable to castle) 13 d5! 0-0 14 ♗a3 (14 d6?! is worse due to 14...♘ec6 15 ♕h5 a6 16 ♘g4 f6 as in Y.Dokhoian-L.Oll, USSR 1984) 14...♘d7?! (Oll's recommendation of 14...f6!? may be best met by 15 ♘f3 intending 16 ♘d4) 15 ♘xf7! ♔xf7 (if 15...♖xf7 16 dxe6 ♖f8 17 exd7 ♗xd7 18 e5 is strong) 16 dxe6+ ♔xe6 17 ♕h5 g6 18 ♕xh7 ♘e5 19 ♖ad1 ♘d3 20 ♗h3+ gave White a winning attack in I.Polovodin-V.Zhelnin, Moscow 1983.

12...♗xa1 13 ♗a3

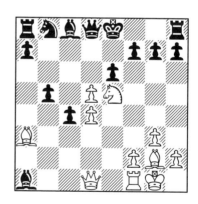

13...a5

Black has a couple of other moves he can try:

a) 13...exd5 14 ♕h5! g6 (14...♗e6 is strongly met by 15 ♘xf7! g6 16 ♕f3) 15

♕f3! (15 ♘xg6 hxg6 16 ♕xh8+ ♔d7 lets Black's king get away) 15...f6 (15...f5 16 ♖e1 ♗e6 17 ♘xg6 hxg6 18 ♖xe6+ ♔f7 19 ♖d6 was good for White in A.Vikulov-O.Mitlashevsky, Moscow 2003) 16 ♖e1! ♗e6 17 ♘xc4 (17 ♗h3) 17...bxc4 (or 17...dxc4 18 ♖xe6+ ♔f7 19 ♕e3) 18 ♖xe6+ ♔f7 19 ♕xd5 and Black is defenceless.

b) *Fritz 11* pointed out the amazing 13...♗b2!? which is far from easy to deal with. Together with my German friend I analysed the lines 14 ♗xb2 (14 ♕h5 g6 15 ♕f3 f5 16 ♗xb2 ♗b7 is good for Black) 14...exd5 15 ♗a3 (another possibility is 15 ♘xf7!?, for example 15...♔xf7 16 ♕h5+ g6 17 ♗xd5+ ♔g7 18 ♕e5+ ♕f6 19 ♕c7+ ♗d7 20 ♗xa8 ♖c8 21 ♕a5 ♘c6 22 ♗xc6 ♗xc6 23 ♖e1 with a messy and double-edged position) 15...♗e6 16 f4 g6 (16...♕a5 17 f5 ♕xa3 18 fxe6 fxe6 19 ♕g4 ♕e7 20 ♗xd5 exd5 21 ♕c8+ ♔d8 22 ♕e6+ ♕e7 23 ♕xd5 is good for White) 17 ♖e1 (17 g4 is answered by 17...♕a5) 17...♕a5 18 f5 gxf5 19 ♗xd5 ♕xa3 20 ♘xf7 ♔xf7 (on 20...0-0 White plays 21 ♖xe6) 21 ♕h5+ ♔e7 22 ♕g5+ ♔d6 23 ♖xe6+ ♔xd5 24 ♕xf5+ ♔xd4 25 ♕f4+ ♔c3 26 ♖e3+ ♔b2 27 ♕f2+ ♔b1 28 ♖xa3 and White wins.

14 ♕g4

There is a major alternative in 14 dxe6 ♗xe6 15 ♗xa8, when E.Kengis-Y.Meister, Togliatti 1985, continued 15...♗xd4? (Black has several better moves, for example 15...b4 16 ♕a1 0-0! 17 ♗b2 c3 18 ♗xc3 bxc3 19 ♕xc3 is only a bit better for White; while 15...♗c3!? 16 ♗c5 ♗b4 17 ♘c6 ♕d5 18 ♘xb4 ♕xa8 19 d5 ♘d7 20 ♕d4 ♘xc5 21 ♕xc5 axb4

22 ♕xb5+ ♗d7 23 ♖e1+ ♔d8 24 ♕b6+ ♔c8 25 ♕c5+ leads to a draw by perpetual check; and 15...♕xd4 16 ♕xa1 ♕xa1 17 ♖xa1 b4 18 ♗c1 0-0 19 ♖xa5 ♖d8! gives Black adequate compensation for the piece) 16 ♘c6 ♗xf2+ 17 ♔xf2 ♕c7 (if 17...♕b6+ 18 ♔g2 ♘xc6 19 ♕d6 ♗d7 20 ♖d1 wins), and now 18 ♘xb8 (rather than 18 ♗d6 ♕b6+ 19 ♕d4 as in the game, when 19...♘d7 would have been a tough nut to crack) 18...♕a7+ (or 18...b4 19 ♕a4+ ♔f8 20 ♗c1) 19 ♔e2 ♕xa8 20 ♕d6 is winning for White.

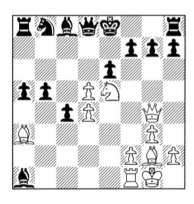

14...b4

Here, too, there are other moves:

a) 14...♕f6 15 ♖xa1 ♖a6 16 ♕e2 (16 ♗c5 has been recommended, but I don't see what White should play after 16...♘d7 17 ♘xd7 ♗xd7) 16...♘d7 17 ♖b1 b4 18 ♕xc4 0-0 19 ♘xd7 ♗xd7 20 ♕xa6 bxa3 21 ♕xa5 ♕xd4 22 ♕xa3 exd5 23 ♕d6 ♕d3 24 ♖b8 ♕d1+ 25 ♗f1 ♖e8 26 ♖xe8+ ♗xe8 27 ♕d8 ♔f8 28 ♕d6+ leads to a draw by repetition.

b) 14...♗xd4!? 15 ♕xg7 ♗xe5 16 ♕xe5 ♖g8 17 dxe6 ♗xe6 18 ♗xa8 b4 19 ♗c1 leaves an enormously complex and difficult position in which Black's king is in grave danger, but he does have three connected passed pawns.

c) 14...g6 15 ♖xa1 ♖a6 16 ♕f4 was unhelpfully agreed drawn at this point in I.Glek-L.Oll, Tallinn 1986. An 'unclear' assessment is probably the safest, for example 16...f6 17 ♘xc4 (17 ♕h6 b4 18 ♘xg6 hxg6 19 ♕xh8+ ♔d7 allows Black's king to get away; while 17 ♘g4 fails to impress after 17...e5 18 dxe5 ♗xg4 19 ♕xg4 fxe5 20 ♖e1 ♘d7) 17...bxc4 (17...b4 is also possible, for example 18 ♕xb8 bxa3 19 dxe6 ♖xe6 20 ♗d5 0-0 21 ♘e3 ♔g7 22 ♗xe6 ♗xe6 23 ♕xd8 ♖xd8 24 ♖xa3 leads to a drawn endgame) 18 ♕xb8 ♖b6 19 ♕a7 ♖b7 20 ♕c5 gives White more than enough for the sacrificed exchange.

15 ♕xg7 ♖f8 16 ♖xa1 ♖a6!?

In A.Chernin-L.Yudasin, Sverdlovsk 1984, Black played 16...bxa3, the game going 17 dxe6 ♗xe6 (17...♖a7 18 exf7+ ♖axf7 19 ♘xf7 ♕e7 20 ♗d5 is good for White) 18 ♗xa8 ♕xd4 19 ♖b1! (19 ♖xa3? ♗h3! 20 ♗f3 ♕b2 wins for Black) 19...♘d7 (if 19...♕d6 20 ♕g5! ♘d7 21 ♘xd7 ♗xd7 22 ♗f3 a2 23 ♖e1+ ♗e6 24 ♕xa5 with a clear advantage) 20 ♗c6 ♕d6? (20...a2! is critical, for example 21 ♗xd7+ ♗xd7 22 ♖b8+ ♔e7 23 ♕xf8+ ♔e6 24 ♕xf7+ ♔xe5 25 ♕e7+ ♗e6 26 ♖b5+ ♔e4 27 ♕xe6+ ♔d3 28 ♕f5+ ♔d2 29 ♕g5+ would lead to a draw by perpetual check) 21 ♗xd7+ ♗xd7 22 ♘xc4 ♕c5 (22...♕c7 23 ♖e1+ ♗e6 24 ♖xe6+ is also winning) 23 ♖b8+ ♗c8 24 ♖xc8+ 1-0.

17 ♗c1 exd5?!

17...c3?! would be strongly met by

18 ♗f1!, but Black has another possibility in 17...f6, for example 18 ♘xc4 (neither 18 ♗h6?! ♕e7 19 ♕xe7+ ♔xe7 20 ♗xf8+ ♔xf8 21 ♘xc4 a4!, nor 18 ♗f3 ♕e7 19 ♗h5+ ♔d8 20 ♘f7+ ♔d7 21 ♗h6 exd5 22 ♕xf8 ♕xf8 23 ♗xf8 b3 gives White convincing compensation) 18...♖f7 19 ♕h6 exd5 20 ♘e3 ♖d6 21 ♗f3 produces a messy and unclear position.

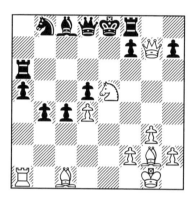

18 ♗h6! ♖xh6?

Had Black foreseen the strength of 20 ♖e1 he might have tried 18...♕e7! 19 ♖e1 ♗e6! (19...f6? 20 ♕xe7+ ♔xe7 21 ♘g6+ ♔f7 22 ♘xf8 is good for White), after which 20 ♕xh7 ♘d7 is very difficult to assess.

Note that 18...♕d6 is inferior due to 19 ♖e1 ♕xh6 20 ♘g4+ (if 20 ♘c6+ ♕e6 21 ♖xe6+ ♗xe6 22 ♘xb8 ♖d6 holds Black's position together) 20...♖e6 21 ♖xe6+ ♕xe6 22 ♘f6+ ♔e7 (or 22...♕xf6 23 ♕xf6 ♗e6 24 ♗xd5 etc) 23 ♘xd5+ ♔d7 24 ♕xf8, when White has recovered most of his material with his attack still in progress.

19 ♕xh6 ♗e6 20 ♖e1!

This key move reignites the flames

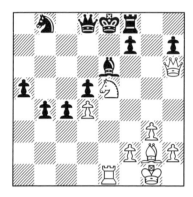

20...♕e7 21 ♘xc4!

Another possibility is 21 ♘xf7 ♕xf7 22 ♖xe6+ ♔d7 23 ♖e5, since 23...♕xf2+ 24 ♔h1 is fine for White.

21...dxc4 22 d5 ♔d7

After 22...♕c5 there follows 23 dxe6 fxe6 24 ♕xe6+ ♔d8 25 ♖d1+ ♔c7 26 ♖d5 ♕c6 27 ♕e5+ ♔b6 28 ♖d6, winning the queen.

23 ♕e3

23 ♕h5 might have been even stronger.

23...♕d6 24 ♕a7+ ♕c7

On 24...♔c8 there would follow 25 dxe6 fxe6 26 ♗b7+ ♔d8 27 ♕xa5+ ♔e7 28 ♕g5+ ♖f6 29 ♗d5 h6 30 ♕g7+ ♖f7 31 ♕d4 ♖f6 32 ♕xc4, reaching material equality but with ongoing problems for Black's king.

25 dxe6+ fxe6 26 ♕d4+ ♔c8?

The losing move. Black had to try 26...♕d6, when 27 ♕g7+! (neither 27 ♕xc4 ♖f5!, nor 27 ♕a7+ ♕c7 28 ♖d1+ ♔c8 does the trick for White) 27...♕e7 28 ♕e5! ♕d6 29 ♕b5+ ♔e7 30 ♕xc4 leaves White for choice, but with Black able to put up staunch resistance.

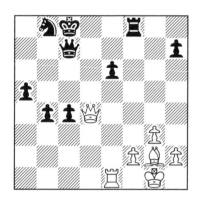

27 ♖xe6 c3

Or 27...♖d8 28 ♕g4 h5 (28...♘d7 can be answered by 29 ♖c6) 29 ♕f5 ♖d1+ 30 ♗f1 ♖d7 31 ♖e8+ ♔b7 32 ♕b5+ ♔a7 33 ♖xb8 ♕xb8 34 ♕xd7+ and White wins.

28 ♗h3 ♔b7

If 28...♘d7 29 ♖a6 ♔b8 30 ♗g2 wins.

29 ♕d5+ ♔a7

29...♘c6 30 ♗g2 is also decisive.

30 ♗g2 ♘a6 31 ♖c6! 1-0

Game 61
M.Ulibin-A.Kharlov
St Petersburg 1993

---

1 d4 d5 2 c4 e6 3 ♘f3 ♘f6 4 g3 c6 5 ♗g2 dxc4 6 ♘e5 b5!? 7 a4 ♘d5 8 axb5 cxb5

Normally this position would be reached via 4...dxc4 5 ♗g2 b5 6 a4 c6 (or 5...c6 6 a4 b5) 7 axb5 cxb5 8 ♘e5 ♘d5.

9 ♘c3 f6!?

An interesting alternative to 9...♗b4 in the previous game, but one with which there is very little practical experience.

10 ♘f3

Other games with 9...f6 have seen White play 10 e4, for example 10...♘xc3 (10...♘b4? allows 11 ♕h5+ g6 12 ♘xg6 hxg6 13 ♕xh8 ♘c2+ 14 ♔e2 ♘xa1 15 ♗h6 ♘d7 16 e5 ♖b8 17 ♘e4 with a winning attack) 11 ♕h5+ g6 12 ♘xg6 hxg6 13 ♕xh8 (13 ♕xg6+ ♔d7 14 bxc3 ♗b7 15 0-0 gave White questionable compensation for the piece in R.Milovanovic-V.Raicevic, Pula 1990) 13...♕xd4 14 ♗h6 ♘d7 15 0-0 was M.Hackel-S.Rausch, German League 1996, and now 15...♘e2+ (rather than 15...f5 16 ♕g8, which was good for White in the game) 16 ♔h1 ♗b7 17 ♖ad1 ♕xb2 18 ♖d2 ♕b4 19 ♖xe2 0-0-0 would give Black more than enough for the exchange.

One other possibility is 10 ♘g4, though this has yet to be tried.

10...♘xc3 11 bxc3 ♗b7 12 0-0 ♗e7

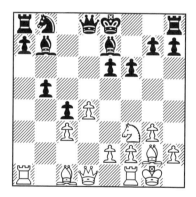

13 ♕c2

White needs to prepare e2-e4 because 13 e4 ♗xe4 14 ♘g5 (or 14 ♘e5 ♗xg2 15 ♕h5+ g6 16 ♘xg6 ♕d5! 17 ♘e5+ ♔d8 18 ♘f7+ ♔d7 19 ♕xd5+ ♗xd5 20 ♘xh8 ♘c6 21 ♘f7 e5 22 ♘h6 exd4

would be very good for Black) 14...♗xg2 15 ♘xe6 ♕d7 (if 15...♕c8 16 ♘xg7+ ♔f7 17 ♕h5+ ♔xg7 18 ♗h6+ ♔g8 19 ♖fe1 ♘c6 20 ♔xg2 threatening d4-d5 is strong) 16 ♖e1 (16 ♘xg7+?! doesn't work after 16...♔f7 17 ♕h5+ ♔xg7 18 ♗h6+ ♔g8 19 ♔xg2 ♗f8) 16...♗d5 17 ♕h5+ g6 18 ♕xd5 ♕xd5 19 ♘c7+ ♔d7 20 ♘xd5 ♗d8 21 ♗f4 ♘c6 leaves White a pawn down in the endgame.

But is 13 ♕c2 the best way, or should 13 ♖e1 have been tried?

13...f5 14 ♘h4

14 ♖d1 is an interesting move, intending to meet 14...0-0 with 15 d5 ♗xd5 16 ♘e5 (or maybe 16 ♘g5 ♗xg5 17 ♗xg5 ♕xg5 18 ♖xd5 exd5 19 ♗xd5+) 16...♗f6 17 ♖xd5 exd5 18 ♕xf5 with a dangerous initiative for the sacrificed exchange.

14...♕c8 15 ♗xb7 ♕xb7 16 ♘g2 0-0 17 ♘f4 ♖f6 18 ♘h5

18 ♖e1 can be answered by 18...♘c6!, intending 19 e4 e5! 20 ♘d5 exd4! 21 ♘xf6+ ♗xf6 etc. The theme of a counter-sacrifice by Black seems very common in this line.

18...♖f7 19 ♘f4 ♕c6 20 e4

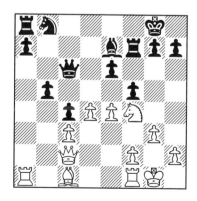

20...♘d7

White would get more play after either 20...♕xe4?! 21 ♕xe4 fxe4 22 ♘xe6 ♘c6 23 ♖e1, or 20...fxe4 21 ♖e1 followed by 22 ♕xe4.

21 exf5?!

After this White's initiative seems to peter out. 21 ♖e1 would have been better, so that after 21...♘b6 22 ♗d2 he could double rooks on the e-file.

21...exf5 22 ♖e1 ♗d6 23 ♘e6 ♘b6 24 ♗g5 ♕d7 25 ♗f4 ♖e8 26 ♘c5

26 ♗xd6 ♖xe6 27 ♖xe6 ♕xe6 28 ♗c5 ♘a4 leaves Black with a lot of light square control.

26...♗xc5 27 dxc5 ♘a4 28 ♗d6 h6 29 ♕d2 ♖xe1+ 30 ♕xe1

30 ♖xe1 ♘xc5! would exploit the pin on White's bishop.

30...f4!

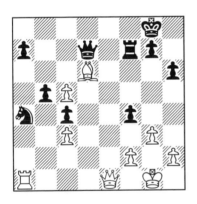

Emerging from defence, Black suddenly takes the initiative.

31 ♖d1

Neither 31 ♗xf4 ♘xc5, nor 31 gxf4 ♕g4+ 32 ♔h1 ♕f3+ 33 ♔g1 ♖f6 would be helpful to White.

31...f3 32 ♗f4 ♖e7! 33 ♕f1 ♕c8 34 ♖e1 ♕xc5 35 ♖xe7 ♕xe7

And the rest, as they say, is a matter of technique.

36 ♕c1 ♕e2 37 h4 ♘b2 38 ♕a1 ♔h7 39 ♗e3 ♘d3 40 ♕b1 a6 41 ♔h2 ♕e1 42 ♕xe1 ♘xe1 43 g4 ♘g2 44 ♗b6 b4 45 cxb4 c3 46 ♗d4 c2 47 ♗b2 ♘xh4 0-1

Game 62
A.Pashikian-G.Meier
Martuni 2008

---

1 d4 ♘f6 2 ♘f3 e6 3 c4 d5 4 g3 dxc4 5 ♗g2 c6

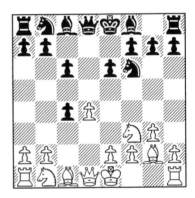

6 a4

This may be the simplest way of answering Black's last move.

After 6 ♘e5 Black has an additional possibility in 6...♗b4+ (on 6...b5 White should transpose into the last two games with 7 a4, rather than play 7 ♘xc6?! ♕b6) 7 ♘c3 (7 ♗d2 ♗e7 8 ♗c3 a5 9 a4 ♖a6 10 ♘a3 ♗xa3 11 bxa3 ♘d5 12 ♕d2 b5 13 ♖b1 ♗d7 led to a complex game in E.L'Ami-P.Negi, Malmo 2007) 7...♘d5 8 0-0 (8 ♗d2 b5 featured in S.Conquest-D.Sengupta, Hastings 2008/09, once again with a very messy position) 8...♘xc3 9 bxc3 ♗xc3 10 ♗a3 ♕xd4 11 ♕xd4 ♗xd4 12 ♘xc4 ♗xa1 13 ♖xa1 f6 14 ♘d6+ ♔d7 15 ♖d1 ♔c7 left White with distinctly dubious compensation in I.Ivanisevic-G.Meier, Mainz (rapid) 2008, though this didn't stop him winning!

6...c5

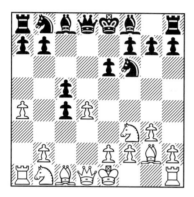

Attempting to reach positions akin to those in Chapter 10, but with White having played his a-pawn forward two squares. Instead, 6...b5 7 axb5 cxb5 8 ♘e5 ♘d5 would lead to lines covered in the last two games.

7 0-0

Another possibility is 7 ♘a3!?, for example H.Melkumyan-G.Meier, Martuni 2008, went 7...♘c6 8 ♘xc4 cxd4 9 0-0 ♗c5 10 ♗f4 ♘d5 11 ♗e5 ♘xe5 12 ♘cxe5 0-0 13 ♘xd4 f6 14 ♘c4 with balanced chances at this stage. But I must admit to liking the simplicity of Pashikian's play, taking the view that a2-a4 will be useful in the queen exchange line.

7...♘c6 8 dxc5 ♗xc5

There's also 8...♕xd1 9 ♖xd1 ♗xc5, when 10 ♘bd2 c3 11 bxc3 ♗d7 12 ♘b3

♗e7 13 ♘fd4 0-0 14 ♗a3 ♗xa3 15 ♖xa3 ♖ac8 16 ♘c5 gave White some pressure in L.Ftacnik-A.Lauber, German League 2008.

9 ♘bd2 c3 10 bxc3 e5 11 a5!?

I'm not very convinced by this a-pawn charge. The immediate 11 ♘g5 looks more promising, just routing the knights into the game via e4.

11...0-0 12 ♕a4 ♕c7 13 ♘g5

White's pieces are getting quite active here, though it's not clear if this is anything more than a temporary thrill.

13...♗d7 14 ♘de4 ♗e7 15 ♘xf6+

15 ♕c2 ♘xe4 16 ♗xe4 can be answered by 16...h6 17 ♗xc6 hxg5, which is an argument for preceding this with 15 a6!? b6 16 ♕c2 ♘xe4 17 ♗xe4, the point being that 17...h6 18 ♗xc6 would now win the exchange.

15...♗xf6 16 a6 b6 17 ♖d1 ♖ac8 18 ♖xd7?!

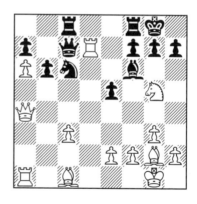

It's not clear that White should have taken advantage of this possibility. 18 ♕e4 ♗xg5 19 ♗xg5 seems better, getting the two bishops at least.

18...♕xd7 19 ♗h3 ♕d5 20 ♗xc8 ♖xc8 21 ♘e4 ♗e7 22 ♗a3?

This could have landed White in deep trouble. 22 ♖b1 is better here.

22...♗xa3??

Missing the reply. Black should play 22...b5!, when 23 ♕c2 ♗xa3 24 ♖xa3 f5 is very good for him.

23 ♘f6+! gxf6 24 ♕g4+ ♔f8 25 ♕xc8+ ♔e7 26 ♖xa3 ♕d1+ 27 ♔g2 ♕d5+ 28 f3 ♕c4 29 ♔f1 h5 30 ♖a1 1-0

Not a particularly good game, but one with some interesting points. For example I'd prefer to play White after 11 ♘g5, which would make sense out of his opening strategy.

Game 63
N.Davies-P.Lukacs
Budapest 1993

1 d4 d5 2 ♘f3 ♘f6 3 c4 e6 4 g3 dxc4 5 ♗g2 ♗d7

This has not been played much in the last few years, but it deserves respect nonetheless.

6 ♘e5

I think this is the most thematic move, though it involves the sacrifice of a pawn.

White's other move is 6 ♕c2, but it's not easy to prove anything after 6...c5 7 0-0 (7 ♘e5 ♘c6 8 ♘xc6 ♗xc6 9 ♗xc6+ bxc6 10 dxc5 ♗xc5 11 0-0 ♕d5 12 ♘c3 ♕h5 13 ♔g2 0-0 14 ♘a4 ♕d5+ 15 f3 ♗e7 16 ♖d1 ♕b5 17 ♖d4 ♘d5 18 ♖xc4 ♖fd8 19 a3 ♖ac8 was equal in R.Vaganian-L.Portisch, 6th matchgame, Saint John 1988; and 7 ♕xc4 ♗c6 8 dxc5 ♘bd7 9 ♗e3 ♗d5 10 ♕b4 a5 11 ♕f4 ♗xc5 12 ♗xc5 ♘xc5 13 ♘c3 0-0 14 ♘xd5 ♘xd5

15 ♕d4 ♕b6 16 0-0 was equally equal in G.Sosonko-A.Karpov, Wijk aan Zee 1988) 7...♗c6 8 ♕xc4 ♘bd7 9 ♗g5 (9 ♘c3 b5! 10 ♕d3 b4 11 ♘b1 cxd4 is fine for Black) 9...♖c8 10 ♗xf6! ♘xf6?! (10...♕xf6! seems better, for example 11 ♘c3 ♗e7 12 e4 0-0 13 d5 ♘b6 14 ♕d3 exd5 15 exd5 ♖fd8 16 ♘d2 c4 17 ♘xc4 ♘xc4 18 ♕xc4 ♗xd5 19 ♘xd5 ♖xc4 20 ♘xf6+ would fizzle out to a draw) 11 dxc5 ♗xf3 12 ♗xf3 ♗xc5 13 ♕b5+ ♕d7 14 ♘c3 ♕xb5 15 ♘xb5 ♗e7 16 b4! and White managed to take the initiative in G.Kasparov-V.Korchnoi, 7th matchgame, London 1983.

6...♗c6

Black has also played 6...♘c6, but after 7 ♘xc4 ♗b4+ 8 ♘c3 ♘d5 9 ♕d3 ♕f6 10 e3 ♕g6 11 ♗e4 ♕h5 12 a3 ♗xc3+ 13 bxc3 ♘f6 14 ♗g2 0-0 15 h3!? ♖ad8 16 g4 ♕b5 17 a4 ♕a6 18 ♕e2 White kept an edge in Y.Razuvaev-J.Klovans, Bern 1993.

7 ♘xc6 ♘xc6 8 0-0

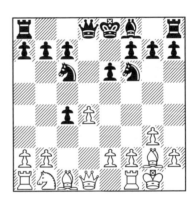

8...♗e7

Interestingly enough, I had half expected this move, even though it had rarely been seen at the time. I had noticed that Lukacs' compatriot, Istvan Farago, had played it and guessed it might have been studied in Hungarian circles.

White also seems to have a promising game after other moves, for example:

a) 8...♘xd4?! is just good for White after 9 ♗xb7 ♖b8 10 ♗g2 ♗c5 11 ♘d2 c3 12 bxc3 ♘b5 13 ♕c2 0-0 14 a4 as in B.Gulko-V.Korchnoi, Amsterdam 1989.

b) 8...♕d7 9 e3 (it's time for White to defend his d4-pawn, since 9 ♘c3 is fine for Black after 9...♘xd4 10 ♗xb7 ♖b8 11 ♗g2 ♗e7 12 e3 ♘b5 13 ♕c2 ♘xc3 14 ♕xc3 ♕b5 15 b3 0-0 16 bxc4 ♕b6 as in A.Yusupov-A.Karpov, Belfort 1988) 9...♖b8 10 ♕e2 b5 11 a4 (11 b3 cxb3 12 axb3 ♗b4 seems okay for Black, for example 13 ♖a6 ♘d5 14 ♗d2 ♗xd2 15 ♘xd2 ♖b6 16 ♖xb6 cxb6 17 ♕xb5 ♘cb4 18 ♕xd7+ ♔xd7 as in L.Janjgava-B.Abramovic, New York Open 1990) 11...a6 12 axb5 axb5 13 b3 cxb3 14 ♘d2 ♗e7 15 ♘xb3 0-0 16 ♗d2! (16 ♗b2 ♘b4 17 ♖fd1 ♖fd8 18 ♖ac1 ♘a2 19 ♖a1 ♘b4 20 ♖ac1 ♘a2 21 ♖a1 ½-½ was A.Yusupov-L.Portisch, Linares 1988) 16...♖fc8 17 ♖fc1 ♘d5 was Kir.Georgiev-V.Anand, Wijk aan Zee 1989, and now 18 h4!, intending h4-h5-h6, would have kept an edge for White according to Anand.

9 e3

9 ♕a4 is less good after 9...0-0 10 ♖d1?! b5!. N.Sulava-I.Farago, Vinkovci 1993, continued 11 ♕xb5 ♘xd4 12 ♕a4 ♘xe2+ 13 ♔f1 ♘d4 and White was already in trouble.

9...0-0

In Zsu.Polgar-A.Maric, Tilburg Candidates 1994, Black tried to improve on this with 9...♕d7, but White was better following 10 ♕a4 ♘b4 11 ♕xd7+ ♘xd7 12 ♘d2 ♘b6 13 ♗xb7 ♖b8 14 ♗f3 thanks to the useful pair of bishops.

10 ♘d2 ♘a5 11 ♕a4 c6

On 11...c5 White's simplest is 12 dxc5 ♗xc5 13 ♘xc4 ♘xc4 14 ♕xc4 with an edge, thanks to the powerful Catalan bishop.

12 b4 c3 13 bxa5 cxd2 14 ♗xd2

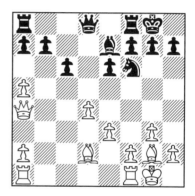

White is clearly better here because of his strong pair of bishops and potential for pressure down the c- and b-files.

14...♘d5 15 ♖ab1 ♕d7 16 ♖fc1 ♖fc8 17 ♕b3 ♖ab8 18 a4 h6 19 h4 ♗d6 20 e4 ♘e7 21 ♕b2

Introducing the possibility of taking aim at g7 via ♗d2-c3, followed by a later d4-d5. So Black makes a bid for freedom.

21...b5 22 axb6 ♖xb6

22...axb6 would keep the pawns together but leave Black very passive.

23 ♕a1 ♖xb1 24 ♖xb1

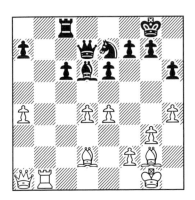

24...f5

Trying to get the d5-square, but creating weaknesses along the e-file. 24...c5 would have been a better move, for example 25 ♗c3 cxd4 26 ♗xd4 f6 and Black is still fighting.

25 ♖e1 ♖d8 26 ♕a2 ♔h8 27 h5 fxe4 28 ♖xe4 ♘d5 29 ♕c4 ♖f8 30 ♕e2 ♘c7 31 ♗h3 ♖f6 32 ♔g2

I was trying to follow Capablanca's advice not to hurry.

32...c5 33 ♗c3 ♖f8?!

It would have been more stubborn to play 33...♘d5, though this is still good for White after 34 ♗b2 c4 35 ♕xc4 ♕b7 36 ♕c2.

34 ♗xe6 ♕c6

35 ♔g1?!

35 ♕g4!, threatening 36 d5, or even 36 ♕xg7+, followed by d4-d5+, would have been immediately decisive.

35...c4?!

Here, too, Black missed a more stubborn defence in 35...♘d5, when White would do well to find the variation 36 ♗xd5 ♕xd5 37 dxc5 ♗xc5 38 ♕g4 ♗xf2+ 39 ♔h2 ♕b7 40 ♕g6 ♔g8 41

♗b4!, threatening both 42 ♗xf8 and 42 ♖e7.

36 ♗xc4 ♕xa4 37 d5

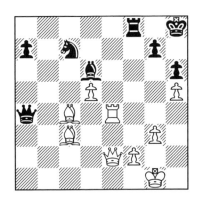

This unveiling of the dark-squared bishop spells the beginning of the end.

37...♕d7 38 ♕e3 ♔g8 39 ♕e2 a6 40 ♖g4 ♖f7 41 ♕e4 ♘b5 42 ♗b2 ♕a7 43 ♕e8+ ♗f8 44 d6! ♕xf2+ 45 ♔h1 1-0

After 45...♕f3+ 46 ♔h2 ♕f2+ 47 ♔h3 Black runs out of checks.

Summary

5...b5 isn't played much right now but, as far as I can see, it's quite a problem for White. The complications of Balashov-Beliavsky (Game 60) are far from being resolved, but I think this is the best that White can do. The other approach is to avoid 4...dxc4 altogether by carefully picking an appropriate move order.

I slightly prefer White after 5...c6, though this is also a tough nut to crack. As for 5...♗d7 I think its best days are behind it; White gets a very pleasant initiative, albeit at the cost of a pawn.

Chapter Fourteen

Open Catalan with 5 ♕a4+

1 d4 ♘f6 2 c4 e6 3 g3 d5 4 ♗g2 dxc4 5 ♕a4+

I've included this section on 5 ♕a4+ largely to serve as a point of reference if the reader comes across any recent games with this move. Frankly I think it is rather innocuous, as compared with the main line (4...♗e7 5 ♘f3 0-0 6 0-0 dxc4 7 ♕c2 a6 8 ♕xc4), Black hasn't had to play ...♗f8-e7. This is significant because he aim for ...c7-c5, when d4xc5 ♗f8xc5 would save a tempo.

After 5...♘bd7 6 ♕xc4 Black gave us a good demonstration of how to equalize in Mecking-Portisch (Game 64). White tried to spice things up a little with 6 ♘f3 and 7 ♘c3 in Karpov-Nisipeanu (Game 65), but the draw came just one move later. In fact White only seems to get chances in this line if Black himself becomes overambitious, and this is what happened in Bacrot-Korchnoi (Game 66). Unfortunately White missed his chance (7 dxc5 seems

to be more of a test) and found himself being ground down by the old warrior.

```
Game 64
H.Mecking-L.Portisch
Bazna 2008
```

1 d4 ♘f6 2 c4 e6 3 ♘f3 d5 4 g3 dxc4 5 ♕a4+ ♘bd7

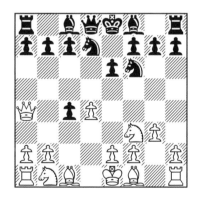

6 ♕xc4

If White wants something from 5

₩a4+ he should probably try 6 ♗g2 a6 7 ♘c3 as in the next game. Here Black equalizes with some ease.

6...a6 7 ₩c2

After 7 ♗g2 c5 (7...b5 is not bad either, for example 8 ₩c2 ♗b7 9 ♗g5 ♖c8 10 0-0 c5 11 ₩d1 ₩b6 12 ♗xf6 ♘xf6 13 dxc5 ♗xc5 14 ♘e5 ♗xg2 15 ♔xg2 0-0 was fine for Black in N.Kelecevic-A.Beliavsky, Sarajevo 1982) 8 0-0 (8 ₩c2 b6 9 dxc5 ♗xc5 10 ♘d4 ♘d5 11 ♘b3 ♗b7 12 0-0 ♗e7 13 ♘c3 ♖c8 was nothing for White in B.Kurajica-A.Kolev, La Laguna 2007) 8...b5 9 ₩c2 ♗b7 10 a4 cxd4 11 ♘xd4 ♗xg2 12 ♔xg2 ♖c8 13 ₩d1 b4 was very comfortable for Black in P.Salzmann-N.Guliev, German League 2008.

7...b6

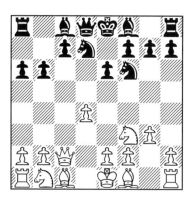

S.Djuric-J.Pinter, Szirak 1985, varied with 7...c5, which proved to be more entertaining after 8 dxc5 ♗xc5 9 ♗g2 b5 10 ♘d4 ♖b8 11 ♘c6 ₩c7 12 ♘xb8 ♗xf2+ 13 ♔d1 ₩xb8. Unfortunately most of the entertainment will fall to Black as, with an extra pawn and the white king on d1, he has more than enough for the exchange.

8 ♗g2 ♗b7 9 0-0 c5 10 ♘c3 cxd4 11 ♘xd4 ♗xg2 12 ♔xg2 ₩c8 13 e4 ♗b4 14 ♘de2

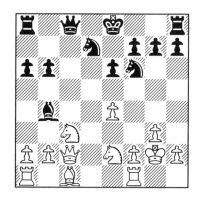

A new move from Mecking, but one which has little impact on the assessment of this line. Two earlier games had gone as follows:

a) 14 f3 ♗xc3 15 bxc3 0-0 16 ♗a3 ♖d8 17 ♗e7 ♖e8 18 ♗d6 ₩c4 19 ♖ab1 b5 20 a4 ♖ec8 21 ♖fc1 ₩xa4 22 ₩xa4 bxa4 was very comfortable for Black in R.Hübner-P.Van der Sterren, Munich 1994.

b) 14 ♗d2 0-0 15 ♖fd1 ₩c4 16 ♗e1 ♖fd8 17 a3 ♗f8 18 f3 ♖ac8 19 ♖ac1 ₩c7 was similarly fine for Black in L.Konietzka-A.Naiditsch, Senden 2000. **14...0-0 15 f3 ₩b7 16 ♗e3 ♖ac8 17 ♖ac1 ♗e7 18 ♘f4 ♘e5 19 ♘d3 ♘xd3 20 ₩xd3 ♖fd8 21 ₩e2 ½-½**

Game 65
A.Karpov-L.D.Nisipeanu
Vitoria Gasteiz 2007

---

1 ♘f3 ♘f6 2 c4 e6 3 g3 d5 4 d4 dxc4 5 ₩a4+ ♘bd7 6 ♗g2 a6 7 ♘c3

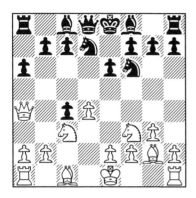

7...♗e7

With this tricky move order (if 7...b5? 8 ♘xb5!) White is trying to get his opponent to waste a tempo on ...♖a8-b8 before recapturing on c4. But even that may not be much, and Black can also try 7...c5. For example:

a) 7...♖b8 8 ♕xc4 b5 9 ♕d3 ♗b7 10 0-0 c5 (10...♗d6 11 ♘g5 ♗xg2 12 ♔xg2 ♗e7 13 ♗f4 ♘h5! 14 ♘ce4 ♘xf4+ 15 gxf4 ♘b6 16 ♖ac1 h6 17 ♘f3 ♘d5 18 e3 ♖b6 19 ♖fd1 g5! was unclear in A.Graf-A.Naiditsch, German Ch., Höckendorf 2004) 11 ♗f4 ♖c8 12 dxc5 ♗xc5 (12...♘xc5 13 ♕xd8+ ♖xd8 14 ♖ac1 b4 15 ♘d1! ♘d5 16 ♘e5 f6 17 ♘c4 was a bit better for White in B.Kurajica-E.Sveshnikov, Sarajevo 1983) 13 ♖ad1 (in B.Kurajica-S.Marjanovic, Yugoslav Ch. 1983, White tried 13 ♘g5, but after 13...♗xg2 14 ♔xg2 ♕b6 15 ♖ad1 h6 16 ♘f3 Black could equalize with just 16...0-0) 13...0-0 (13...b4?! 14 ♘a4 ♗e7 15 ♘e5! ♗xg2 16 ♔xg2 ♕a5 17 ♘xd7 ♕xa4 18 ♘xf6+ ♗xf6 19 b3 ♕c6+ 20 ♕f3 ♕xf3+ 21 ♔xf3 left White better because of Black's queenside pawn weaknesses in U.Andersson-V.Milov,

FIDE World Ch., Groningen 1997) 14 ♘e5 ♗xg2 15 ♔xg2 ♘xe5 16 ♗xe5 ♗e7 (16...♕xd3 17 ♖xd3 ♖fd8 18 ♖xd8+ ♖xd8 19 ♗xf6 gxf6 20 ♖d1 ♖xd1 21 ♘xd1 f5 was also equal in U.Andersson-A.Karpov, Wijk aan Zee 1988) 17 ♕f3 (17 ♕xd8 ♖fxd8 18 ♖xd8+ ♖xd8 19 ♖c1 ♖c8 20 ♗f4 ♔f8 was nothing in U.Andersson-Y.Gonzalez, Havana 2003) 17...♕a5 (17...♕b6 18 ♖d2 b4 19 ♗xf6 ♗xf6 20 ♘e4 gave White some hope of an edge in U.Andersson-V.Inkiov, Rome 1985) 18 ♕b7 ♖fe8 19 a3 b4 20 ♗xf6 gxf6 21 axb4 ♕xb4 22 ♕xb4 ♗xb4 23 ♘e4 ♔g7 24 ♘d6 ½-½ U.Andersson-G.Kasparov, 6th match-game, Belgrade 1985.

b) 7...c5 8 0-0 (8 ♕xc4 b5 9 ♕d3 ♗b7 10 0-0 ♕b6 11 ♗e3 cxd4 12 ♗xd4 ♗c5 13 a4! ♗xd4 14 ♕xd4 b4 15 ♘d1 0-0 16 ♘e3 ♖ac8 17 ♖fd1 ♖fd8 was about equal at this stage in G.Agzamov-I.Novikov, Riga 1985) 8...♗e7 (8...♘d5 9 dxc5 ♘xc3 10 bxc3 ♗xc5 11 ♕xc4 gave White some active piece play in G.Kaidanov-P.Blatny, Chicago 2000) 9 dxc5 ♗xc5

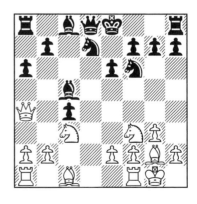

10 ♘d2!? (10 ♕xc4 b5 11 ♕h4 ♗b7

12 ♗g5 0-0 13 ♖ad1 was U.Andersson-I.Radulov, Indonesia 1983, when 13...♕c7! 14 ♖c1 ♕b6 would have been about equal) 10...♖a7!? 11 ♕xc4 b5 12 ♕d3!? ♗b7 13 ♘de4 ♘xe4 14 ♘xe4 ♗xe4 15 ♗xe4 f5!? 16 ♗g2 0-0 17 ♗e3 gave White some chances due to Black's slightly exposed pawns in I.Nikolaidis-S.Skembris, Greek Ch., Agios Nikolaos 2000.

8 ♗f4

Ulf Andersson has made a speciality out of 8 ♘e5, but without wreaking any particular havoc, for example 8...0-0 (8...♖b8 9 ♘xd7 ♕xd7 10 ♕xc4 b5! 11 ♕d3 ♗b7 12 ♗xb7 ♖xb7 13 ♕f3 ♖b6 14 0-0 ♕c6 15 ♕xc6+ ♖xc6 16 ♗g5 ♖c4! 17 e3 c5 18 ♗xf6! gxf6! 19 dxc5 0-0!? 20 ♖ac1 ♖d8 21 ♘b1 ♖xc5 22 ♖xc5 ♗xc5 23 ♖c1 ♗b4! held the balance for Black in U.Andersson-R.Hübner, Tilburg 1981) and now:

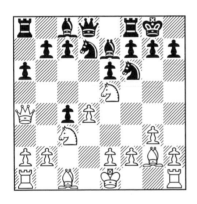

a) 9 ♘xd7 ♗xd7!? (9...♕xd7 10 ♕xc4 b5 11 ♕c6 ♕xc6 12 ♗xc6 ♖b8 13 0-0 ♗b7 14 ♗xb7 ♖xb7 15 ♖d1 c5 was rather equal in U.Andersson-A.Aleksandrov, Polanica Zdroj 1997) 10 ♕xc4 b5 11 ♕b3 b4 12 ♘e4 ♗b5 13

♘xf6+ ♗xf6 14 ♗e3 (14 ♗xa8 ♕xa8 15 f3 ♗xd4 gives Black compensation for the exchange) 14...♖b8 15 ♖d1 c5! 16 dxc5 ♕a5 17 ♖d2 ♗a4 18 ♕c4 ♗c3! 19 0-0! ♗b5 20 ♕b3 was U.Andersson-A.Sokolov, Bar 1997, when Black should have repeated the position with 20...♗a4 21 ♕c4 ♗b5 etc.

b) 9 ♘xc4 c5 (9...♘d5 10 ♕d1 c5 11 dxc5 ♘xc3 12 bxc3 ♗xc5 13 ♗f4 gave White some initiative in B.Kurajica-A.Brkic, Croatian Ch., Split 2008) 10 dxc5 ♗xc5 11 ♗e3 (11 0-0 ♖b8 12 ♕d1 b5 13 ♘d6 ♕e7 14 ♗f4 e5 15 ♘xc8 ♖bxc8 16 ♗g5 h6 17 ♘d5 ♕e6 18 ♗xf6 ♘xf6 19 ♘xf6+ ♕xf6 was very drawish in U.Andersson-M.Tal, Niksic 1983) 11...♗xe3 12 ♘xe3 ♖b8 13 0-0 b5 14 ♕f4 was just a shade better for White in B.Kurajica-V.Malakhatko, Spanish Team Ch. 2007.

Another possibility is 8 ♕xc4, but after 8...b5 9 ♕d3 ♗b7 10 0-0 0-0 11 ♗e3 ♘b6 12 ♗g5 c5!? 13 ♗xf6 gxf6 14 ♖fd1 c4 15 ♕c2 f5 Black was doing quite well in A.Lein-R.Hübner, Chicago 1982.

8...♘d5

9 ♕xc4 ♘xf4 10 gxf4 b5

In R.Vera-A.Antunes, Havana 1990, Black tried to do without this move by playing 10...0-0 11 0-0 ♘b6. Although this is a solid way to play it, it does leave Black rather passive, and after 12 ♕b3 ♘d5 13 e3 c6 14 ♖ac1 ♔h8 15 ♖fd1 f6 16 ♘a4 White's position was preferable.

11 ♕d3 ♗b7 12 ♖d1

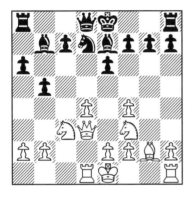

This seems to be a new move from Karpov, aimed at inhibiting ...c7-c5. But it doesn't do that for long and thus does little to affect the assessment of this line.

In earlier games White had played 12 0-0, whereupon 12...c5 (12...0-0 13 ♖fd1 c5 14 d5 exd5 15 ♘xd5 ♘f6 16 ♘e5 ♘xd5 17 ♗xd5 ♕xd5 18 ♕xd5 ♗xd5 19 ♖xd5 ♖fd8 20 ♘c6 ♖e8 21 a4 ♗f8 was also fine for Black in C.Bauer-J.Lautier, Enghien les Bains 1999) 13 ♖ad1 c4 14 ♕c2 ♘f6 15 ♘e5 ♗xg2 16 ♔xg2 0-0 17 e3 ♖c8 18 f5 b4 19 ♘e2 ♕d5+ even gave Black the initiative in I.Hausner-V.Babula, Martin 2003.

12...♘f6 13 0-0 0-0 14 a3 c5 15 dxc5 ♗xc5 16 ♕xd8 ♖fxd8 17 ♘e5 ♗xg2 18 ♔xg2 ♖dc8

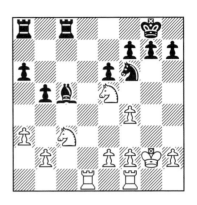

There's nothing much happening in this endgame, even for Karpov.

19 ♖d3 ♗e7 20 ♔f3 ♖c7 21 ♖fd1 ♖ac8 22 e3 g6 ½-½

Game 66
E.Bacrot-V.Korchnoi
Odessa 2007

---

1 ♘f3 e6 2 c4 ♘f6 3 g3 d5 4 d4 dxc4 5 ♕a4+ ♗d7 6 ♕xc4 c5

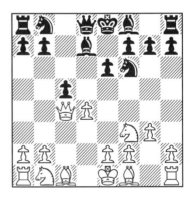

A little played and rather risky move, all of which will make it attractive to an old warrior like Korchnoi.

Another, safer possibility is 6...♗c6,

when White doesn't have anything special, for example 7 ♗g2 (7 ♘c3 ♗xf3 8 exf3 c6 would leave White with a lack of structural dynamism on account of the firmly restrained d4-pawn) 7...♗d5 (7...♘bd7 8 0-0 ♘b6 9 ♕d3 ♕d5 10 ♘c3 ♕h5 11 e4 was better for White in K.Hulak-B.Ivanovic, Yugoslav Ch., Borovo 1981) 8 ♕d3 (8 ♕c2 ♗e4 9 ♕a4+ ♕d7 10 ♕xd7+ ♘bxd7 11 0-0 ♗d6 12 ♘c3 ♗c6 13 ♖d1 was a tiny bit better for White in M.Konopka-S.Cifka, Zdar nad Sazavou 2008) 8...♗e4 9 ♕d1 c5 10 ♘c3 ♗c6 11 0-0 ♘bd7 12 ♕d3! (more testing than 12 ♗g5 h6 13 ♗xf6 ♘xf6 ½-½ as in U.Andersson-M.Krasenkow, Polanica Zdroj 1997; while 12 ♗e3 ♗e7 13 dxc5 ♗xc5 14 ♗xc5 ♘xc5 15 ♕xd8+! ♖xd8 16 ♖ac1 ♔e7 was also rather equal in U.Andersson-M.Illescas Cordoba, Pamplona 1997) 12...cxd4!? 13 ♘xd4 ♗xg2 14 ♔xg2 ♗c5 15 ♘b3 ♗b4 16 ♘e4 0-0 17 ♖d1 ♘e5 18 ♕xd8 ♖fxd8 19 ♖xd8+ ♖xd8 20 ♗g5 ♗e7 21 ♖c1 ♔f8 22 ♘xf6 gxf6 23 ♗e3 led to Black being tortured in the endgame in U.Andersson-C.Lutz, Katrineholm 1999, though to his credit he survived.

7 ♗g2

There's another, and probably superior, possibility in 7 dxc5, after which 7...♗c6 8 ♘c3 ♘bd7 9 ♗e3 ♖c8 10 ♗g2 (10 b4!? is interesting too) 10...♘d5 11 ♘xd5 ♗xd5 12 ♕d4 ♗e7!? 13 ♕xg7 ♗f6 14 ♕g4 ♗xb2 15 0-0 h5 16 ♕b4 ♗xa1 17 ♖xa1 gave White compensation for the exchange in U.Andersson-J.Van der Wiel, Wijk aan Zee 1984.

7...♗c6 8 0-0 ♘bd7 9 ♘c3 ♖c8

Black is developing very efficiently

here, and his opening has been a complete success. This is one of the advantages of surprise in the opening.

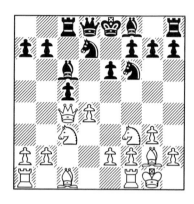

10 ♗g5 cxd4 11 ♕xd4 ♗c5 12 ♕f4 h6 13 ♗xf6 ♕xf6 14 ♖fd1 ♕xf4 15 gxf4 ♗b4 16 ♖ac1 ♔e7 17 a3 ♗xf3

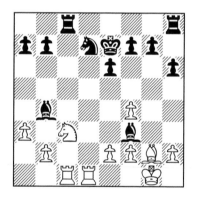

18 ♗xf3

18 axb4 ♗xg2 19 ♔xg2 ♖hd8 would also be better for Black due to White's somewhat tatty pawns.

In the rest of the game Korchnoi presses the young Frenchman all the way, narrowly falling short of converting to a full point.

18...♗xc3 19 ♖xc3 ♖xc3 20 bxc3 ♖c8 21 ♗xb7 ♖xc3 22 ♖a1 ♘c5 23 ♗a8 a5 24

e3 f5 25 ♖a2 ♘d3 26 ♗b7 ♔d6 27 ♗a6
♘c5 28 ♗f1 a4 29 ♗b5 g5 30 fxg5 hxg5
31 ♔g2 ♔c7 32 h3 ♔d6 33 ♖d2+ ♔e7
34 ♖a2 e5

The advance of Black's kingside pawns adds to the pressure.

35 ♖d2 f4 36 exf4 gxf4 37 ♖a2 e4 38 h4
♔f6 39 h5 ♔g5 40 ♗e8

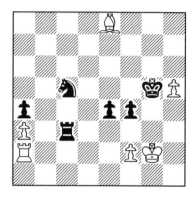

40...♘d3?!

Perhaps this was the point at which Black could have won. 40...f3+ looks very unpleasant after 41 ♔h2 e3 42 fxe3 ♖xe3, threatening both 43...♖e2+ and 43...♘e4.

41 ♗g6 ♖c4

41...e3 looks like the last chance to keep it going. Now White manages to equalize.

**42 ♖d2 f3+ 43 ♔g3 ♘f4 44 ♖b2 ♘xh5+
45 ♗xh5 ♔xh5 46 ♖b5+ ♔g6 47 ♔f4
♖c3 48 ♖b4 ♖xa3 49 ♖xe4 ♔h5 50 ♔g3
♔g5 51 ♖f4 ½-½**

Summary

Given the fact that such friendly Grandmasters as Ulf Andersson and Bojan Kurajica play 5 ♕a4+, I would really have liked to say something better about it. Unfortunately I cannot escape the conclusion that it's as dull as dishwater.

Rather than try to grind away in these positions I think that the simplest way to avoid such lines as 4...dxc4 5 ♘f3 b5 is to adopt a Flank Opening move order, say with 1 ♘f3 d5 2 g3 ♘f6 3 ♗g2 e6 4 c4. If Black then plays 4...dxc4, there is 5 ♕c2 followed by recovering the pawn on c4 with either the queen or one of the knights (♘f3-e5xc4 or ♘b1-a3xc4). There's plenty of play in this position as White hasn't moved his centre pawns.

Index of Variations

1. Main Line with 10 ♗d2

1 d4 ♘f6 2 c4 e6 3 g3 d5 4 ♗g2 ♗e7 5 ♘f3 0-0 6 0-0 dxc4 7 ♕c2 a6 8 ♕xc4 b5 9 ♕c2 ♗b7 10 ♗d2

2. Main Line with 10 ♗f4 and Others

1 d4 ♘f6 2 c4 e6 3 g3 d5 4 ♗g2 ♗e7 5 ♘f3 0-0 6 0-0 dxc4 7 ♕c2 a6 8 ♕xc4 b5 9 ♕c2 ♗b7

3. Main Line with 8 a4

1 d4 ♘f6 2 c4 e6 3 g3 d5 4 ♗g2 ♗e7 5 ♘f3 0-0 6 0-0 dxc4 7 ♕c2 a6 8 a4

4. Main Line with 7 ♘e5 and Others

1 d4 ♘f6 2 c4 e6 3 g3 d5 4 ♗g2 ♗e7 5 ♘f3 0-0 6 0-0 dxc4

5. Main Line with 6 ♕c2 and 6 ♘c3

1 d4 ♘f6 2 c4 e6 3 g3 d5 4 ♗g2 ♗e7 5 ♘f3 0-0
6 ♕c2 c5 (6...dxc4 7 ♘bd2 – *62*; 6...♘a6 – *69*) 7 0-0 – *64*; 7 dxc5 – *66*
6 ♘c3 dxc4 7 ♘e5 (7 0-0 – Chapter 4, *Games 17-18*) 7...♘c6 – *70*; 7...c5 – *72*

6. Closed Catalan with 7 ♕c2

1 d4 ♘f6 2 c4 e6 3 g3 d5 4 ♗g2 ♗e7 5 ♘f3 0-0 6 0-0 ♘bd7 7 ♕c2
7...c6 (7...c5 – *89*) 8 ♘bd2 (8 b3 – *77*; 8 ♖d1 – *81*; 8 ♗f4 – Chapter 8, *Games 34-36*)
8...b6 9 e4 ♗b7 – *85*; 9...♗a6 – *87*

7. Closed Catalan with 7 ♘c3

1 d4 ♘f6 2 c4 e6 3 g3 d5 4 ♗g2 ♗e7 5 ♘f3 0-0 6 0-0 ♘bd7 7 ♘c3
7...dxc4 8 e4 c5 – *91*; 8...c6 – *95*
7...c6 8 ♕d3 b6 – *97*; 8...a6 – *99*

8. Closed Catalan with 4...♗b4+

1 d4 ♘f6 2 c4 e6 3 g3 d5 4 ♗g2 ♗b4+
5 ♗d2 (5 ♘bd2 – *111*) 5...♗e7 6 ♘f3 0-0 7 0-0 c6 8 ♗f4 (8 ♗g5 – *109*) 8...♘bd7 9 ♕c2
b6 – *102*; 9...a5 – *106*; 9...♘h5 – *107*

9. Open Catalan with 5...♗b4+

1 d4 ♘f6 2 c4 e6 3 g3 d5 4 ♗g2 dxc4 5 ♘f3 ♗b4+
6 ♗d2 (6 ♘bd2 ♘c6 – *123*; 6...b5 – *126*; 6 ♘c3 – *128*) 6...a5 (6...♗xd2+ – *121*) 7 0-0 –
115; 7 ♕c2 – *117*

10. Open Catalan with 5...c5

1 d4 ♘f6 2 c4 e6 3 g3 d5 4 ♗g2 dxc4 5 ♘f3 c5 6 0-0 ♘c6 (6...a6 – Chapter 12, *Game 58*)
7 ♘e5 (7 ♕a4 cxd4 – *131*; 7...♗d7 – *132*; 7 ♘a3 – *139*; 7 dxc5 – *142*) 7...♗d7 8 ♘a3 –
134; 8 ♘xc4 – *136*

11. Open Catalan with 5...♘c6

1 d4 ♘f6 2 c4 e6 3 g3 d5 4 ♗g2 dxc4 5 ♘f3 ♘c6

6 ♕a4 (6 0-0 ♖b8 – *153*; 6...a6 – Chapter 12, *Games 55-57*) 6...♘d7 (6...♗b4+ – *145*) 7 ♕xc4 ♘b6 8 ♕b5 – *147*; 8 ♕d3 – *149*

12. Open Catalan with 5...a6

1 d4 ♘f6 2 c4 e6 3 g3 d5 4 ♗g2 dxc4 5 ♘f3 a6
6 0-0 (6 ♘e5 – *166*) 6...♘c6 (6...c5 – *164*) 7 ♘c3 (7 e3 – *162*) 7...♖b8 8 e4 b5 – *156*; 8...♗e7 – *159*

13. Open Catalan with 5...b5 and Others

1 d4 ♘f6 2 c4 e6 3 g3 d5 4 ♗g2 dxc4 5 ♘f3
5...b5 (5...c6 6 a4 c5 – *176*; 5...♗d7 – *178*) 6 a4 c6 7 axb5 cxb5 8 ♘e5 ♘d5 9 ♘c3 ♗b4 – *170*; 9...f6 – *174*

14. Open Catalan with 5 ♕a4+

1 d4 ♘f6 2 c4 e6 3 g3 d5 4 ♗g2 dxc4 5 ♕a4+
5...♘bd7 (5...♗d7 – *185*) 6 ♕xc4 (6 ♘f3 a6 7 ♘c3 – *182*) 6...a6 7 ♕c2 b6 8 ♘f3 – *181*

Index of Complete Games